Advance Prai

T0270548

"Finally! A vital missing piece in the landscape of eating disorder treatment! As a clinician specializing in both couples therapy and eating disorders, I've felt the frustration of treating these complex conditions separately. Dr. Lampson offers a transformative mode of therapy by seamlessly merging the renowned Gottman Method with innovative approaches to eating disorder treatment. Concise and easy-to-read, this groundbreaking resource is an informative must-read not only meant for clinicians. Highly recommended!"

—**Cristina Castagnini, PhD,** psychologist,
Certified Eating Disorder Specialist, and host of
the eating disorder podcast *Behind the Bite*

"Dr. Lampson delightfully weaves metaphor and story as she teaches therapists how to conceptualize and treat eating disordered couples. She offers innovative interventions to use with Gottman method couple therapy and clearly explains why it is so important to include partners in the journey toward recovery. This volume is an essential read for couple therapists."

—**Carrie Cole, PhD,** research director at Gottman, Inc.

"Life is relational. What I love most (and there are many things to love) about Dr. Lampson's book is that she walks us directly into the relational dynamics that eating disorders create in couples. Dr. Lampson's keen insights about complex cases are what makes this book a must-read for everyone who aspires to work with couples . . . or clients with eating disorders . . . or both at once."

—**John Sommers-Flanagan, PhD,** professor of counseling,
University of Montana, and author of *Clinical Interviewing*

"The vast majority of adults with an eating disorder are married or in a committed relationship and report that the presence of a supportive partner is invaluable. Yet most therapists who treat eating disorders are not specifically trained to treat couples. Kim Lampson takes on this monumental task by educating and training clinicians in the highly regarded work of Gottman Method Couples Therapy as it applies to relationships where an eating disorder is present.

In *Therapy for Relationships with Eating Disorders*, clinicians will find what amounts to a college course covering the myriad factors that must be understood, empathized with, and worked through in order to balance the needs of each individual in a couple where an eating disorder is present, working toward helping the relationship become a protective factor.

Cleverly using several case examples to bring the training to life, the book covers competencies, first for the therapist and then for couples, to attain. From assessments to communication and preparing for inevitable turbulence, Lampson describes the details of dealing with issues beyond food, weight, and body image, covering restrictions on social life and struggles with intimacy and future planning which are ever-present in these relationships.

I've treated eating disorders for 45 years, written six books and served in a variety of capacities in the eating disorder field. I can say without reservation that *Therapy for Relationships with Eating Disorders* needs to be added to the library of every eating disorder clinician, whether they plan to do couples work or not. Firstly, because any eating disorder clinician will learn invaluable insights, gain resources, and discover interventions from this book to use with clients, whether they do couples therapy or not. Secondly, because all eating disorder clinicians are dealing in one way or another with how the eating disorder affects their client's relationships, and vice versa."

—Carolyn Costin, MA, MEd, MFT, FAED, CEDS,
director of The Carolyn Costin Institute and author of
8 Keys to Recovery from an Eating Disorder

Therapy for Relationships
with Eating Disorders

Therapy for Relationships *with* Eating Disorders

A CLINICIAN'S GUIDE

TO GOTTMAN-RED

COUPLES THERAPY

KIM LAMPSON

FOREWORD BY JOHN M. GOTTMAN
AND JULIE SCHWARTZ GOTTMAN

Norton Professional Books

An Imprint of W. W. Norton & Company
Independent Publishers Since 1923

Note to Readers: This book is intended as a general information resource for professionals practicing in the field of psychotherapy and mental health. It is not a substitute for appropriate training or clinical supervision. Likewise, any member of the general public who is not a professional practicing in the field of psychotherapy and mental health, should regard the recommendations in this book as suggestions only and any such recommendations should not be seen as a substitute for obtaining professional advice. Standards of clinical practice and protocol vary in different practice settings and change over time. No technique or recommendation is guaranteed to be safe or effective in all circumstances, and neither the publisher nor the author(s) can guarantee the complete accuracy, efficacy, or appropriateness of any particular recommendation in every respect or in all settings or circumstances.

Any URLs displayed in this book link or refer to websites that existed as of press time. The publisher is not responsible for, and should not be deemed to endorse or recommend, any website other than its own or any content that it did not create. The author, also, is not responsible for any third-party material or any content that appears on third-party websites.

Contribution copyright © 2025 by John M. Gottman and Julie Schwartz Gottman
Copyright © 2025 by Kim Lampson

All rights reserved
Printed in the United States of America
First Edition

For information about permission to reproduce selections from this book, write to Permissions, W. W. Norton & Company, Inc., 500 Fifth Avenue, New York, NY 10110

For information about special discounts for bulk purchases, please contact W. W. Norton Special Sales at specialsales@wwnorton.com or 800-233-4830

Manufacturing by Lake Book Manufacturing, Inc.
Production managers: Gwen Cullen/Ramona Wilkes

ISBN: 978-1-324-05297-5

W. W. Norton & Company, Inc., 500 Fifth Avenue, New York, NY 10110
www.wwnorton.com

W. W. Norton & Company Ltd., 15 Carlisle Street, London W1D 3BS

1 2 3 4 5 6 7 8 9 0

To John Gottman and Julie Schwartz Gottman.
Thank you for believing in me, supporting me,
and inspiring me to write this book.

Contents

Foreword

We have dedicated our lives to helping couples and the therapists who work with them. Our research has spanned over 52 years and we have written over 50 books so that we can share what we have learned with people all over the world. We have trained over 100,000 therapists over the years, and every once in a while, a therapist steps forward and catches our attention. Kim Lampson is one of these therapists. We first met her at one of our Seattle trainings when she gave us a copy of her first book about eating disorders, which she coauthored with her husband Dan. We had heard of her work with eating disorders and were excited to know she was enamored with our couples therapy. By this time, we had expanded our trainings to include treating affairs and trauma as well as substance abuse, in the goal of helping as many couples as possible. We realized that couples with comorbidities seemed to have the most challenges to overcome. Julie had always wanted to do something for people with eating disorders, but felt she lacked the clinical experience working with this population that Kim had, so she and Kim met for breakfast at a tiny restaurant in Seattle. It was here, between sips of delicious coffee, that the dream that become Gottman-RED (Relationships with Eating Disorders) couples therapy took flight.

Why this particular population? The answer to this question is simple. Eating disorders frequently have a chronic course and the behaviors that go with them significantly affect one of the most basic ways of socially connecting—sharing a meal. What can be more romantic than a candlelit dinner at a very special restaurant? How often do we celebrate anniversaries and birthdays with a special food? Many of us have childhood memories of holiday traditions or religious celebrations involving sumptuous main courses, delicious desserts, or symbolic food elements. What we eat becomes intertwined with what we remember about significant life events; however, when people suffer from disordered eating, are haunted by weight issues, or are tormented by a distorted body image, the memories that should have been joyous can, in the blink of an eye, take a turn for the worse and become traumatic.

Contrary to the popular belief that most people with eating disorders are single, over 85% of people with an eating disorder have experienced a long-term love relationship. Few will seek any kind of therapy, and even with therapy, coping with their eating disorder may last a lifetime.

The complex interplay between the inability of a partner to fully understand and communicate about the impact of the eating disorder and the trauma caused by the events that preceded the onset of the disorder can profoundly affect the quality of life of both partners. The terrible tragedy for couples unable to collaboratively and empathetically discuss their thoughts and feelings regarding the eating disorder is that both partners are racked with loneliness. The effects of this loneliness can be profound.

We agreed that Kim was the ideal person to write this book. Just like us, she has dedicated her life to helping people. Kim is passionate about providing therapy for couples and people with eating disorders as well as teaching graduate students the skills they need in order to become highly effective therapists. These interests combined with her experience as a university professor, clinician, and Certified Gottman Therapist make her uniquely qualified to develop this approach.

In this valuable book, Kim reviews the enormous impact that an eating disorder typically has on the quality of life for both partners in a love relationship, and she summarizes the methods that have been used to date in helping these relationships, highlighting their strengths as well as their limitations. The potential contributions of Gottman Method couples therapy for couples dealing with an eating disorder are: recognizing the physiological basis for escalating quarrels, understanding the existential meaning basis of many gridlocked conflicts, processing emotional wounds of previous conflicts surrounding the disorder, treating the ubiquitous comorbid traumas of the eating-disordered partner from the past, and linking issues related to friendship, romance, and sexual intimacy—especially surrounding body image—to the couple's world.

The ability of Gottman-RED couples therapy to tackle the multidimensional issues related to the consequences of the eating disorder for the love relationship holds great promise in constructing an integrated approach to the treatment of relationships with eating disorders. In addition, the exercises the couples therapist shares in this therapy finally give a voice to those who may have fallen between the cracks: those who have never been diagnosed with an eating disorder, but who have struggled in silence for their whole lives with their weight, chronic dieting, body hatred, obsessive exercise, purging behaviors, or rigidity around food.

The book is deeply personal. In four widely disparate cases, Lampson guides the reader through a compassionate look at the intricacies of the integrated approach of Gottman-RED couples therapy for handling the nuances of treatment. The stories of these four couples will deeply move the reader as they reveal the pain, struggle, challenges, and courage of people facing a nemesis that overshadows almost every aspect of their relationship, including sexual intimacy, social eating, parenting, and friendship.

Kim Lampson's brilliant book, *Therapy for Relationships with Eating Disorders*, speaks to the art of effective couples therapy and offers content that will benefit all who counsel people in love relationships. For this reason, we believe that this book is a valuable and essential addition to the library of the informed couples therapist. Thank you, Kim, for writing it!

—JOHN M. GOTTMAN AND JULIE SCHWARTZ GOTTMAN
Orcas Island, Washington

Acknowledgments

After finishing my dissertation, then working with my husband on our book about eating disorders, I never thought I would undertake a huge writing project again. However, I made a wise decision when I said "yes" to this writing project as I believe this book will help many people. An undertaking like this one takes a village. I want to think all who made this book possible.

My amazing editors. It has been an honor to collaborate with my editors, Deborah and Jamie. Working together with you has been a pleasure. I am very thankful for your support, wisdom, kindness, patience, and persistent nudges. Consequently, I want to express my gratitude to Carolyn Costin for kindly introducing us. I also want to acknowledge the other members of the team at Norton—especially my copyeditors, Irene and Olivia, for their ability to focus on and correct details. I used to think I was good with commas . . .

My family. Only because of the support and prayers of my family was I able to finish this project. They were my cheering section. I am so grateful to my husband, Dan, for believing in me, encouraging me when I was tired, tolerating my mood swings, and rubbing my back after hours of writing. I extend special appreciation to my daughters, Krisanna and Stevie, and my son-in-law, Nick, for reading sections of the manuscript and offering extremely helpful feedback while communicating consistent confidence in me. I am very appreciative of the much-needed moral support offered by my son, Chris, and son-in-law, Jeremy. In addition, the companionship of our dog, Merlin, and cat, Pogo, kept me going when working for long stretches.

My friends. Thank you to my friend, Sarah, for your encouragement during walks with our dogs and to my lifelong friends, Ronnie and Eiko, for your supportive texts. I am also grateful for my friends at ballet who regularly checked in with me and applauded my efforts.

My faith. I thank God for inspiration, wisdom, words, and strength. I could not have done this without Him.

My associates and students. I appreciate the input and support from my colleagues Sam and Arizona, my doctoral program classmate, Doug, my dean, Matt, and my faculty buddies, Jenny and Nikki. I also want to thank my students who cheered me on and had confidence that I could do this! I particularly want to extend heartfelt appreciation to Caden, Stephanie, and Mandi for the hours they spent working on the pilot study of Gottman-RED couples therapy.

My colleagues. I am indebted to Dave Penner, Julie Gottman, and John Gottman whose vision and encouragement led to the development of this therapy. Thank you! Lastly, I want to extend special thanks to my good friends and colleagues, Carrie and Don Cole, who have supported me and lifted my spirit many times along the way.

Introduction: In Sickness and in Health

"There is something I have been wanting to tell you . . . "

Carmen hesitates, watching Luciano very carefully. He stiffens, then says,

"Please tell me."

"I have an eating disorder." She looks down, not wanting to see the expression on his face. Were she to look, she would see relief in his eyes. He thought she was going to say something much worse. Besides, he has suspected for a long time that she has food issues, but has not known how to bring it up. He says nothing, but holds her hand reassuringly.

She continues, "It started when I was 15 and is a lot better now, but I still have it. It comes and goes." Carmen is now 28 years old. "It seems to be getting worse again, so I think I need to get some help."

Luciano waits, then, measuring his words, replies, "We will do whatever it takes for you to get better. I will help you. Why didn't you tell me before?"

Carmen and Luciano have been dating for 2 years and are engaged to be married.

"I was afraid you wouldn't want to marry me if you knew, but I decided to tell you before our wedding in case you wanted to change your mind."

"Nothing will change my mind. I love you and want to marry you. Would it help if we ate dinner together every night? You can get over it pretty fast with some good therapy, right?"

Carmen squeezes his hand and says nothing. She knows it could take a long, long time.

Carmen and Luciano's conversation is representative of many couples in which one person has an eating disorder: interwoven throughout the conversation is the shame felt by the person with the eating disorder, the trepidation they experience before bringing it up with their partner, the denial of the chronic nature of the problem, the desperate need to downplay its potential impact on the relationship, and the naïveté of both partners regarding the toll it will take on each of them and on the relationship. Most couples have no idea of the full implication of the words "In sickness and in health" when applied to the complexity of eating disorder issues faced by those in long-term relationships.

Luciano waits. Carmen's mind is racing, memories flashing by. She remembers making some progress toward recovery during her first stay at a residential treatment center when she was a teenager, followed by months in intensive outpatient therapy. Then came the relapse and a second less helpful stay in a different residential treatment center. Finally, her family tried Family-Based Treatment, an at-home treatment approach developed by James Lock and Daniel LeGrange (Lock & LeGrange, 2015), and her behaviors quieted. Outwardly, she seemed fine. She replays images of her parents crying—tears made of a strange mixture of helplessness, fear, rage, and then relief when her weight stabilized and she stopped throwing up. Even so, they made her attend intensive therapy groups, followed by more outpatient therapy, until she had had enough and they agreed she could stop. Her behaviors resurfaced in college, then quieted again following graduation, like the eye of the hurricane: a calm, seemingly stable place. She met Luciano and he entered that calm, but now, as she approaches marriage, the winds are blowing again. She can feel them intensifying, and she is scared.

Luciano breaks the silence. "How long will it take?"

Carmen whispers, "I don't know. I don't know if I want to."

"Want to what?" He asks.

Again, a long pause. Carmen measures her words. "Do the

work to get better," she lies. What she really wants to say is, "To get better at all."

She glances up at him to see his reaction. He just smiles at her and says, "Don't worry. I will help you. I just want you to be happy. An eating disorder isn't a big deal, is it? I mean, everyone diets sometimes and worries about how they look if they gain a few pounds. It doesn't matter to me. When you said you had something to tell me, I thought you were going to tell me you had cheated or something." He laughs uncomfortably. "I can deal with an eating disorder."

All Carmen can think is, "He doesn't get it. He just doesn't get it."

"I don't know, Luciano. I think it is a big deal and I am scared. I'm scared for me and scared for us."

For those adults who are fortunate enough to recover from an eating disorder (about 50–60%), the recovery process takes several years at best. If in a committed relationship, the couple will need to learn how to work together during the recovery journey. For those who stay in partial remission or experience a chronic course of illness, the eating disorder will always be part of the relationship. Carmen is considered to be in partial remission; she no longer meets the diagnostic criteria for a severe eating disorder, yet is still consumed with thoughts about weight and food and is afraid of gaining weight. In her case, she likes the low body weight and eating patterns that she has adopted over the years. Although she has not used the behavior since college, she values the reassurance that self-induced vomiting gives her; it is the ace up her sleeve that she could pull out if she ever starts to binge again or gains too much weight. For the most part, the vestiges of her eating disorder have minimal impact on her daily activities, and she is able to keep a demanding work and home schedule.

Luciano cannot stop thinking about the conversation with Carmen. A few days later, he asks, "Remember when you told me about the eating disorder?" Carmen nods, feeling a pit in her stomach at the sound of those words.

"Why did you say you may need to get some help?"

She is just not ready to tell him. She feels too much shame. She has started binge eating again—not often, but enough that she knows it could become a pattern—and, even more unnerving for her, she has thrown up once. She knows it is a slippery slope.

Carmen panics. What can she say? "I don't know. I am just having some thoughts that are bothering me. Like I used to." That is the truth—the partial truth.

"Like what?"

"Like I am fat and ugly."

Luciano laughs. "That is so ridiculous. You are so pretty! I love your body. If anyone in this relationship is fat, it's me!"

Carmen just smiles. She can feel herself withdrawing. He just doesn't get it. Carmen mumbles something about needing to take the dog out and walks away.

Luciano watches her go, shaking his head, wondering, "Did I say something wrong?"

It was while I was attending the Treating Affairs and Trauma training in Seattle, about 8 years ago, that the seeds were planted for Gottman-RED (**R**elationships with **E**ating **D**isorders) couples therapy, a new therapy for couples in which one or both partners have an eating disorder. John and Julie Gottman were the trainers. During one of the breaks, my long-time colleague who was the Gottman Institute clinical director at that time, Dave Penner, approached me and said, "You know, I think I should introduce you to John and Julie. They are looking for someone to develop a way to use Gottman Method couples therapy to help people with eating disorders. Are you interested?"

I was more than interested. I had specialized in treating people with eating disorders for over 20 years and was now developing my couples therapy skills as a certified Gottman Therapist.

Even before Dave suggested that the Gottmans and I have a conversation, I had been pondering the potential benefits of including couples therapy as an integral component in the treatment of people with eating disorders. Aware of the effectiveness of Family-Based Treatment (FBT) for adolescents with anorexia nervosa (Lock & LeGrange, 2015), I wondered if there was a parallel intervention that could help adults with eating disorders. Intuitively, it made sense that couples therapy could fill this void. In FBT for adolescents with anorexia nervosa, weight gain, weight stabilization, and food behavior change are of paramount importance. Would it be the same for couples? Would behavior change be the focus or would it be something else?

My longtime friend and colleague, Wallace Hodges, an internal medicine physician, has treated eating disorder patients for many years. During one of our countless conversations, I asked him, "Do many people die from an eating disorder?" He replied, "For most people, an eating disorder does not take their life. It does something much more insidious—it destroys the quality of their life." And, I might add, often has a deleterious effect on an intimate relationship.

Gottman-RED (**R**elationships with **E**ating **D**isorders) couples therapy, also called Gottman-RED, is built upon a foundation of traditional Gottman Method couples therapy interventions. Gottman-RED couples therapy adds more than ten new interventions designed specifically to help couples address difficult issues related to food, weight, body image, and/or exercise. Gottman-RED couples therapists are *not* treating the eating disorder. The focus of this therapy is on improving the quality of life for both partners by equipping the couple so that their relationship stays strong during the eating disorder journey—whether there is full remission, partial remission, or a chronic course. Although this therapy does not address behavior change directly, it is thought that the stability of the relationship will open a window of opportunity for recovery for those in the latter two categories. These individuals may have given up hope after trying various modes of treatment unsuccessfully on their own, but might be willing to try once again with the aid of a supportive partner who is open to learning about eating disorders and to having the hard conversations necessary to facilitate mutual understanding, support, and ultimately recovery.

In this book, you will be introduced to all of the interventions. Five of them are explained in depth in the text and can be downloaded from https://wwnorton.com/therapyrelationships. The remaining interventions will be available through workshops and trainings.

Five years have passed; Carmen and Luciano have been married for four. The first-year adjustment was rough. Carmen's sister passed away suddenly and then Luciano lost his job. He was offered a lucrative but demanding 60-hour per week position at a technology company and they moved to Seattle, meaning that Carmen left her family and her job back in California. It took longer than she expected to establish her practice as a physical therapist. One bright spot has been the birth of their now 3-year old daughter, Luna. However, tension between them is mounting regarding in-laws, work/life balance, having more children, and sexual intimacy. Carmen and Luciano are constantly fighting.

Carmen has relapsed. Her eating disorder behaviors have intensified. Luciano is aware of the binge eating, but she is still hiding the purging from him, or so she thinks.

"I heard you throwing up. Are you sick?"

"It must be something I ate. My stomach is upset."

"Is it upset every night?"

"Maybe." *Carmen's response is intentionally vague.*

"If you didn't eat so much, maybe this wouldn't happen."

"What do you mean?"

"You know what I mean. Last night, I went to get some ice cream and it was all gone. The night before, the bag of chips had only 3 left and most of the pie I bought to serve to my parents on Friday night was eaten. We are spending way too much on food. How can you eat like that and not gain a lot of weight? Are you throwing up on purpose?" *Luciano's tone is tinged with disgust.*

Carmen gasps. She is not ready to have this conversation.

She lies. "No, there must be something wrong with my stomach. I think I'm allergic to gluten."

"So is that why you don't want to have sex with me?"

Carmen does not understand the abrupt transition from talking about being allergic to gluten to talking about sex, but is not surprised he brought it up . . . again. She hates her body right now and hates it more when it is bloated and full after a binge. She does not want to be touched. When she throws up, she feels awful afterwards and the last thing she wants to do is to be intimate.

"That's all you care about, isn't it? I could be dying of a ter-

rible disease, and you wouldn't even notice as long as we were having sex."

Luciano's blood is boiling, but instead of retorting, he finds himself shutting down; he just switches off. He will stay this way for several days: cold and distant.

"There you go again—shutting me out. We need help, Luciano. I am going to find a marriage counselor for us."

"Good luck!" Luciano walks out, goes downstairs, and turns on the game.

Carmen, standing alone in the kitchen, tears streaming down her face, begins mindlessly eating the chocolate chip cookies on the counter, staring at her phone and searching for a couples counselor, not having any idea what she is looking for or how to know when she has found it. Then she sees something that piques her interest: a couples therapist who offers a couples therapy for relationships with eating disorders.

She feels a little flicker of hope for the first time in years.

Therapy for Relationships
with Eating Disorders

1

Eating Disorders: What Are They?

In this book, we will be following four couples in which one partner has an eating disorder. You have just met Carmen and Luciano. You will soon meet three more: Ezra and Abe, Demarcus and Quisha, and Amy and John. You will learn of their struggles as they attempt to navigate the complexities of a relationship with an eating disorder and will see how couples therapy can help them. Before you meet them, it is important to review the etiology and criteria used to diagnose an eating disorder.

Almost all of us have had some exposure to eating disorder behaviors at some time in our lives; they are ubiquitous—and not as alien as they may appear at first glance. However, very few of us carry these behaviors to the extreme that affects quality of life, damages physical health, hurts our primary relationships, or results in the clinical diagnosis of an eating disorder.

Most people have undergone food restriction or a diet (not necessarily for weight loss) at least once in their lifetime either on their own volition or due to the recommendations of a health care provider. According to the CDC, at any point in time, 17% of Americans are eating a modified diet, with 10% of these following a weight loss plan (Associated Press, 2020; Steirman et al., 2020). In addition to those related to weight management, dietary changes may be required for religious reasons (fasts or modified fasts); in preparation for surgery or procedures like endoscopies or PET scans; to accommodate certain medical conditions; prior to or following dental procedures like extractions or dental implants; or while wearing braces.

The concept of dieting is familiar; however, bulimic behaviors may at first glance appear alien, but they truly are not. Most people have vomited because of illness, pregnancy, motion sickness, a ride at an amusement park, or food poisoning. This type of vomiting differs from bulimic vomiting in that it is rarely self-induced and is typically preceded by nausea, whereas in bulimia, the vomiting is self-induced and there is no nausea. Anyone who has had a colonoscopy has experienced the effects of a laxative. And a preponderance of us have overdone it with exercise on at least one occasion, pushing our bodies beyond their limits for healthy exertion.

Even more relatable than dieting or purging is binge eating. The vast majority of us have binged (felt like we have eaten too much) on one or more occasions, most likely at Thanksgiving or other holiday dinners, experienced feeling way too full, or had a "food hangover" the next day after over-indulging. In a world where many of us are surrounded by easily accessible, highly palatable foods, it easy to overeat or mindlessly consume more than we intended. As Fairburn (2013) aptly stated, "Sometimes a binge is just a binge" (p. 41).

Eating disorders affect up to 24 million people in the United States each year, of every age, race, ethnicity, and gender and have one of the highest mortality rates of all mental disorders. In anorexia nervosa, the mortality rate is 5% per decade, with death caused by medical complications from the disorder or by suicide. In bulimia nervosa, the mortality rate is 2% per decade (American Psychiatric Association (APA), 2022). Despite advances in treatment, less than half of those with anorexia nervosa fully recover and a little more than half of those with bulimia nervosa fully recover when recovery is defined as being symptom free for at least 3 years (Von Holle et al., 2008). It appears that many with anorexia nervosa never achieve full remission, experiencing a chronic course involving multiple hospitalizations without remission that can continue for 20 years or more (Levinson et al., 2020). The average duration of illness prior to engaging in treatment is 6 years, with the probability of recovery decreasing 10 years after onset. The risk of relapse is highest 6–17 months after discharge from treatment (Fairburn, 2013; Von Holle et al., 2008). In sexual and transgender minorities, disordered eating, eating disorders, and body dissatisfaction are frequent occurrences. Among sexual minority adults in the United States, the lifetime prevalence of anorexia nervosa is 1.7%; for bulimia nervosa it is 1.3%; and for binge eating disorder it is 2.2% (5.2% when the eating disorders are combined). These data are higher than the lifetime prevalence among heterosexual cisgender adults (Nagata et al., 2020). The incidence is even higher among transgender people, with 10.5 % of transgender men and 8.1% of transgender women reporting an eating disorder, with body dissatisfaction being a core stressor (Nagata et al., 2020).

Once mistakenly viewed as a problem affecting only wealthy, white people, the reality is that eating disorders touch each and every one of us. In the first nationwide eating disorders screening initiative of 35,000 high school students, 15% of girls and 4% of boys indicated a possible eating disorder. Among girls there were few significant differences between ethnic groups, whereas among boys, African American, American Indian, Asian/Pacific Islander, and Latino boys reported more symptoms than did white boys. Of concern was that most of those had never received treatment. In a different study of 81,000 high school students, 56.5% of females and 30% of males reported disordered eating, (defined as using one or more of the following behaviors to lose or control weight: fasting or skipping meals, diet pills, vomiting, laxatives, smoking cigarettes, or binge-eating) a risk factor for developing an eating disorder, with Hispanic and American Indian youth reporting the highest prevalence of disordered eating across both genders. Extreme thinness was the only difference that significantly increased the likelihood of receiving treatment regardless of gender or ethnicity (Austin et al., 2008; Croll et al., 2002). Given that disordered eating is often the precursor to the development of a diagnosable eating disorder, these trends among high school students are very concerning.

DSM 5-TR Diagnostic Criteria

Anorexia Nervosa (AN)

Diagnostic features of anorexia nervosa include maintenance of weight that is less than minimally normal, intense fear of gaining weight or becoming fat regardless of degree of emaciation, and body image disturbance such that the person is unable to recognize the seriousness of the low body weight. People with anorexia nervosa are further differentiated by type: there is a restricting type that includes weight loss primarily through dieting, fasting, and/or excessive exercise; and a binge eating/purging type that includes binge eating followed by purging using self-induced vomiting or misuse of laxatives, diuretics, or enemas. Partial remission means body weight has returned to normal, but the fear of gaining weight/ becoming fat and/or the body image disturbance continues. Full remission means no diagnostic criteria have been met for a sustained period of time (APA, 2022).

The lifetime prevalence of anorexia nervosa is between 0.3% to 1%, with a 10:1 female-to-male ratio of occurrence. People with anorexia are 57 times more likely to die by suicide than people in the general population. Up to 20% of people meeting diagnostic criteria for anorexia nervosa remain chronically ill, with 30–40% remaining in partial remission and chronically symptomatic (Bulik et al., 2012; Selekman & Beyebach, 2013). About 25% of people with AN have a chronic illness fraught with medical health complications (Murray, 2014). Estimates of the duration of episodes of anorexia nervosa range from 5 years to 10 years (Dobrescu et al., 2020; Treasure et al., 2020). Whether it is 5 or 10 years or somewhere in between, people with anorexia nervosa are suffering for a long time.

While it used to be considered a disorder of young women, anorexia nervosa is now recognized as affecting both men and women of all ages. Unfortunately, clinical trials indicate that treatment results are disappointing, and treatment dropout is very high with many not seeking treatment at all (Bulik et al., 2012: Treasure et al., 2020).

Bulimia Nervosa (BN)

Diagnostic features of bulimia nervosa (more commonly known as bulimia) include recurrent episodes of binge eating followed either by purging (using vomiting, laxatives, enemas, or diuretics) or by restricting (by fasting, severely limiting food intake, or overexercising). A binge is defined as eating an amount of food larger than what most people would eat in a 2-hour period, accompanied by a sense of lack of control over eating during this time. The binge/purge behavior needs to occur at a minimum of once a week over a 3-month period, although in extreme cases there can be an average of 14 or more episodes per week. Partial remission occurs when some but not all of the criteria are met for a sustained period. Full remission occurs when none of the criteria have been met for a sustained period (APA, 2022).

The lifetime prevalence of bulimia nervosa is 1–5%, with a 10:1 female-to-male ratio. It is estimated that 15% remain chronically ill (Selekman & Beyebach, 2013). The shame surrounding bulimic behaviors governs the rate at which people reach out for help. When they are finally able to muster the courage to seek support, they find themselves caught in a terrible double bind in which they are desperate to stop their behaviors yet concomitantly afraid they will gain weight if they do. The irony and tragedy of this disorder is that, contrary to what the person with bulimia believes, bulimic behavior is not a very effective means of weight control due to the rapidity of caloric absorption, the inability to purge all food that is ingested by vomiting, and the fact that laxatives act on the large intestine whereas most absorption takes place in the small intestine (Reiff & Reiff, 1999).

Binge Eating Disorder (BED)

Diagnostic features of binge eating disorder include recurrent episodes of binge eating, marked distress about the binge eating, binge eating at least once a week for 3 months, and no compensatory behaviors immediately following the binge. A binge is defined as eating an amount of food larger than what most people would eat in a 2-hour period, accompanied by a sense of lack of control over eating during this time. The binge eating episodes are associated with three or more of the following criteria: eating much more rapidly than normal, eating until feeling uncomfortably full, eating large amounts of food when not physically hungry, or feeling disgusted with oneself, depressed, or very guilty afterward (APA, 2022).

Unlike bulimia nervosa, dieting typically follows the development of a binge eating pattern, whereas in bulimia, binge eating typically follows a period of restrictive dieting. Partial remission means binge eating occurs less than one episode per week for a sustained period. Full remission means none of the criteria are met for a sustained period (APA, 2022).

Binge eating disorder affects people of all ages. Similar to bulimia nervosa, the behaviors tend to be secretive in nature, with an absence of noticeable impact on functioning (Gorin et al., 2003; Selekman & Beyebach, 2013). The prevalence among females from racial or ethnic minorities is equivalent to the prevalence among white females (APA, 2022). BED is unique in that the proportion of men having BED is higher than any other eating disorder (ratio of females to males is 2:1), most clients are middle-aged, and binge eating is intermittent rather than persistent (Selekman & Beyebach, 2013). Men are more likely to binge eat in response to positive emotions (happiness, joy, socializing, having fun) and women to negative emotions (sadness, anger, powerlessness, loneliness, and exhaustion) (Levine, 2012).

Accustomed to rapid weight loss dieting, people with BED often want quick results from therapy that are not realistic for lasting behavior change. Interestingly enough, 30–50% of overweight adults seeking weight loss treatment are affected by BED (Gorin et al., 2003).

Other Specified Feeding or Eating Disorder (OSFED)

People whose quality of life is significantly negatively impacted by food- or weight-related behaviors but do not meet the full criteria for diagnosis of any of the other eating disorders may fall into the category of other specified feeding or eating disorder (OSFED). Examples include people who meet all of the criteria for anorexia nervosa except for significant weight loss, people who meet all of the criteria for bulimia nervosa or binge eating disorder but their behaviors are low frequency or of limited duration, people who use purging to influence weight or shape but do not binge eat, or people who have night eating syndrome, where they have recurrent episodes of excessive food consumption after the evening meal (APA, 2022). In a recent study by Nadia Micali and colleagues, OSFED was found to be the most common eating disorder of women during midlife (Micali et al., 2017).

Orthorexia Nervosa

Although not recognized in the current edition of the Diagnostic and Statistical Manual of Mental Disorders, *DSM-5-TR*, that lists criteria for health professionals to use when diagnosing mental disorders, orthorexia nervosa is a term for a subclinical form of eating in which a person is obsessed with healthy eating, with associated restrictive eating behaviors. If these behaviors become extreme enough, they have the potential to affect an intimate relationship.

Is Eating Disorder a Transdiagnostic Term?

The *DSM 5-TR* groups what we typically think of as an eating disorder under the umbrella term "Feeding and Eating Disorders." This term covers anorexia nervosa, bulimia nervosa, binge eating disorder, pica, rumination disorder, and avoidant/restrictive food intake disorder, as well as "other specified feeding or eating disorder" and "unspecified feeding or eating disorder." Each eating disorder is differentiated by the diagnostic criteria mentioned previously (APA, 2022). However, even the authors of the *DSM 5-TR* alluded to the blurriness of the distinctions between the disorders when they wrote that crossover from BED to another eating disorder is common; they also noted that 10–15% of those with bulimia nervosa cross over to anorexia nervosa, while others stop purging and cross over to BED (APA, 2022).

Some of the leading researchers in the field are of the opinion that the transdiagnostic term *eating disorder* is preferable to differentiating between the distinct disorders. A key reason is the diagnostic migration that is very common among people with eating disorders. A person may start out meeting the diagnostic criteria for bulimia nervosa, then meet the diagnostic criteria for anorexia nervosa, then the diagnostic criteria for binge eating disorder, then bulimia nervosa again, and finally other specified feeding or eating disorder, moving in and out, back and forth amongst the diagnoses. Does it mean that they had separate eating disorders or recovered from one only to develop a different one? No; it means that their behaviors evolved over time (Fairburn, 2013). Others prefer to think of eating disorders on a continuum, with anorexic behavior on one end and binge eating on the other, with purging anorexia and nonpurging bulimia in the middle. This conceptualization was developed before binge eating disorder was included in the *DSM*, but is noteworthy nonetheless (Selekman & Beyebach, 2013).

In Gottman-RED, the term *eating disorder* is applied loosely, implying a transdiagnostic conceptualization. The interventions are intended to strengthen the relationship and quality of life of the couple seeking treatment through enabling difficult conversations about food-, weight-, body image-, exercise- and recovery-related topics regardless of the eating disorder diagnosis. Thus, the interventions in this approach are not limited by diagnosis and are best thought of as transdiagnostic interventions.

Etiology

> "Of theories there are many, but none adequately explain how starvation and vomiting serve to lessen pain." (Lampson, 1983)

When offering therapy to couples with eating disorders, the clinician and the couple will develop a better working alliance if there is a common understanding of the complex etiology of an eating disorder and of the psychological functions of eating disorder behaviors that go beyond food, exercise, body image, and weight. In the professional literature, there is a lack of consensus regarding the etiology of eating disorders, but most would agree that they are caused by a combination of factors. Early risk factors such as death of a parent, parental separation or divorce, and child sexual abuse, low maternal warmth, and childhood unhappiness (Micali et al., 2017; Reid et al., 2019) combined with additional factors including individual psychodynamics, family dynamics, trauma, attachment issues, cultural influences, genetics, and relationship disruptions increase the likelihood of having eating disorder symptoms. Just like the variables in a mathematical equation can be weighted differently and still yield the same sum total, the previously mentioned factors can vary in degree of significance from person to person, but in the end, all add up to the development of an eating disorder.

The Helicopter Story is one way to conceptualize the etiology, function, and treatment of an eating disorder. I developed the analogy many years ago and have told it hundreds of times to professionals, people in recovery, and family members; all have consistently found it to be very helpful. Among other things, it explains how the eating disorder behaviors align with the desperate desire of many who develop eating disorders to stop feeling altogether—to live a Mr. Spock-like existence governed only by rational means and cognitive control, what Levine (2012) refers to as "the fundamental part of an eating disorder" (p. 250).

The Helicopter Story is included in the information provided to the couple at the start of Gottman-RED therapy.

THE HELICOPTER STORY

I would like you to imagine that you are taking a trip by airplane. An interesting fact about you is that you do not know how to swim. This will be relevant later. You buy your ticket and board the plane. Unfortunately, the plane crashes into water. You are the only survivor and, desperate to survive while not knowing how to swim, you grab your life preserver and hold on for dear life. You understand the gravity of your situation. If someone does not come to save you quickly, you will drown or die of hypothermia. Frantically, you scan the skies, hoping and praying someone will appear.

Suddenly, you hear the noise of a helicopter approaching. You wave one hand and the people in the helicopter indicate that they have seen you. You breathe a sigh of relief and eagerly await their arrival as a shiver runs through your body. The water is cold. When they get closer, they announce that the way they are going to rescue you is by taking away your life preserver.

You stare at them, a puzzled, panicked expression on your face, and practically scream, "No, wait a minute! I don't know how to swim!"

They shrug, and say, "Well, we're sorry, but the only way we know how to rescue people is by taking away their life preservers."

Given this information, you realize that you have a very difficult decision to make. You can keep your life preserver and tell them to go away, hoping that someone else will come to rescue you, or you can relinquish your life preserver, trusting these people will actually help you and not leave you to drown. Minutes pass. You shiver again.

The helicopter pilot becomes impatient and says, "Look, we have other people to rescue. We are tired of waiting for you to make up your mind, so we are just going to take this life preserver away from you."

They grab it. You instinctively grab it, too, and an intense power struggle ensues. You want to trust them, but you are scared.

Surprised by the intensity of your response, the pilot says, "OK. OK. There is one other option. Look behind you. We see a rescue boat coming in. Perhaps it can take you to safety."

You reply, "Thank you. I like that idea. I will wait for the boat, but when it comes and I step aboard, I am taking my life preserver with me. If that rescue boat sinks, I want to be sure I survive!" And that is exactly what you do. The rescue boat picks you up and takes you to shore. Shortly thereafter, you take swimming lessons. Only after you have learned how to swim are you willing to give up the life preserver.

Each part of this story represents an aspect of the development and treatment of an eating disorder.

THE PLANE. The plane represents a person's life. This person is moving through life and appears to be managing just fine, but they have limited capacity to cope with intense emotions. Often, this person believes they would look better if they lost some weight or values being thin, but not always.

THE WATER. The water represents intense emotions.

THE CRASH. There is an emotional crash in the person's life. The crash can be caused by one or more of 10 things:

1. **A single traumatic event.** The emotional pain of this event is too much for the person to handle. The most common "last straw" traumatic event before the onset of an eating disorder is the end of a romantic relationship. Other examples include death of a parent, death of a close relative or friend, leaving home for the first time, a significant betrayal of trust, divorce of parents, a serious injury, or a degrading comment.

2. **A 2-to-3-year period of unusual stress or emotional pain.** Too many emotionally painful events happen too fast and the person's ability to cope is short-circuited by the stress and the emotional intensity. If only one of these events had occurred, the person might have been OK, but too many things happened in rapid succession (e.g., parents divorced, best friend moved away, grandmother died, romantic partner ended the relationship, and the person left home for the first time).

3. **An extended period of emotional pain.** The person has lived in a painful situation for a period of years and finally reaches the point where they can no longer tolerate the pain. Examples include growing up in an alcoholic family; growing up with physical, sexual, or emotional abuse; suffering bullying at school or at home; or living for years in an unhappy marriage.

4. **The onset of a mood disorder or anxiety disorder.** Suddenly, the person begins to experience depression or mood swings at a level of intensity they have never experienced. They are not able to understand or control these feelings because they are due to biochemical changes. The onset of symptoms often coincides

with the hormonal changes of puberty. Usually, the person does not understand what is happening, feels scared and out of control, and, hesitant to reach out, does not ask for help.

5. **Being a very sensitive child.** The person is very attuned to emotions yet grows up in a family where feelings are not openly discussed. The child soaks up the pain in the family like a sponge, but then does not know what to do with the overwhelming feelings.

6. **A controlling environment.** The person has a parent or partner who is very controlling. The only way they can survive is by giving up their own identity while trying to please the parent/partner. The person does not want to do this anymore but does not know how to change. The emotional pain this causes is crushing.

7. **Lack of validation of feelings.** The people with eating disorders who have the most difficulty identifying the "reason" why they developed an eating disorder are those who grew up in families and/or entered romantic relationships in which there was no overt abuse but, rather, a very subtle undermining of self-esteem. This person repeatedly experienced lack of validation of their thoughts or feelings.

8. **An isolated incident or repeated incident of sexual abuse.** Following the sexual trauma, the person does not tell anyone and keeps all their emotions inside, while desperately searching for a way to distract or numb the pain caused by the trauma.

9. **Low self-esteem.** Some people seem to struggle with self-esteem throughout their lifetime. It is almost as though they were born feeling insecure, even though they may be talented, attractive, athletic, or intelligent. This protracted sense of inadequacy pervades their thoughts and feelings and causes periods of depression and self-doubt.

10. **Something experienced that is not mentioned here.** This list is not exhaustive. Other experiences not explicitly mentioned here can trigger an eating disorder.

The common thread in all these scenarios is that the person internalizes emotional pain that exceeds the threshold of intensity they can cope with in a healthy way. At the same time, the person is desperately seeking a way to numb these overwhelming feelings. They may also have a genetic predisposition toward either restriction or overeating as a method of self-soothing, as well as a tendency to overvalue weight and shape and its control. All these things together place the person in a very vulnerable state.

These individuals do not necessarily develop an eating disorder. They could stumble upon a different behavior such as abusing alcohol or drugs or developing a sex addiction, but if they turn toward a behavior related to food or weight, they move in a direction that could lead to an eating disorder. If they do ultimately develop an eating disorder, they will subsequently follow one of two paths.

In the first path, the person starts to overeat and finds in food a companion and a source of comfort and calm. Food is consistent and reliable. It is something to look forward to when coming home at the end of the day as well as a source of solace when alone and scared. The person notices that when they eat, emotional pain fades away. However, they also start to gain weight and, sooner or later, most people who gain weight go on a diet, not realizing that dieting is likely to lure them into a diet/binge cycle or a lose weight/ gain it back (plus more) cycle. This person becomes trapped in their relationship with food and is vulnerable to developing binge eating disorder or obesity.

In the second path, the person starts to restrict food, count calories, and/or compulsively exercise and begins to lose weight. As they lose weight, they feel a "high" seeing numbers decrease on the scale and feel stronger when they eat less. Other people notice the weight loss and tend to make affirming comments. In a world that is painful, suddenly there is something that feels good, brings positive attention, and is within their control. The more they focus on counting calories, exercising, dieting, or losing weight, the less they feel the emotional pain. Some people become so hungry that they binge eat. Terrified of weight gain, they engage in a compensatory behavior such as self-induced vomiting, laxative abuse, excessive exercise, diuretic abuse, enema abuse, or chewing and spitting food. It is as though they unwittingly entered a room with a one-way door guarded by the fear of weight gain. This person is vulnerable to developing anorexia nervosa or bulimia nervosa.

Not everyone who overeats, goes on a diet, or restricts food develops an eating disorder; otherwise, we would all have eating disorders. Only those who are emotionally vulnerable, emotionally alone, lacking in healthy ways to cope with intense emotions, and genetically predisposed when they start using these behaviors will develop an eating disorder.

THE LIFE PRESERVER. For those people who develop eating disorders, what starts as an innocent behavior crosses an invisible, malign threshold of which the person has no conscious awareness. What began innocuously as food- or weight-related behaviors has now become a coping mechanism—an ingenious way to survive emotional pain by anesthetizing, distracting from, and distancing the feelings. Just as a life preserver keeps afloat a person who does not know how to swim, the food behaviors enable the person with the eating disorder to survive; however, these behaviors do not allow the opportunity to learn healthy ways to regulate the emotional pain.

When past feelings bubble up, the person can, in essence, stuff them into an imaginary box, with the eating disorder behaviors serving as the lid. The box is buried deep inside, in the hope that with time, the feelings will fade away. Unfortunately, time does not heal all things. Many feelings that are buried are buried alive and do not fade with time. The food behaviors work so well that the original source of the pain is often removed from conscious awareness. These buried feelings will need to be identified, processed, and resolved in order for the person to recover.

Present situations continue to elicit emotions. People with eating disorders are not emotionless. However, their most intense emotions are managed, redirected, or numbed with food-related thoughts and behaviors. For example, a person has an argument with her abusive husband. She immediately binges and purges and feels extremely angry with herself for engaging in this behavior. It is safer for her to be angry at herself than at her husband; besides, consuming thoughts or plans of how to "do better" tomorrow give the illusion of control in a world where otherwise she feels powerless.

Once the food- or weight-related behaviors have become a life preserver, they are very difficult to relinquish or change. They have become necessary for survival, so the thought of giving them up floods the person with an overwhelming yet confusing sense of anxiety. At this point in time, the person is not consciously aware that these behaviors have become their primary way of coping with life; all they know is that they are terrified of letting them go and will hold on even tighter if someone tries to take them away. For the person with anorexia or bulimia, the conscious fear is the fear of gaining weight or being fat, but the real fear runs much deeper and is a fear of living life. For the person with binge eating disorder or obesity, there is often an unconscious fear of being thin—of losing the protection from unwanted attention that a larger body provides, which tends to surface only if a significant amount of weight is lost.

THE PEOPLE FROM THE HELICOPTER. The people from the helicopter represent family and friends who want to help. In our case, this is the partner. Partners want to help in ways that are based upon common sense—and common sense says, if someone I love is engaging in a behavior that is self-destructive, I need to intervene to make them stop. Partners instinctively do things to "take away the behaviors" by trying, usually unsuccessfully, to make the person eat more (AN), gain weight (AN), exercise less, go on a diet (BED), not binge, stay away from the bathroom after meals (BN), throw away laxatives (BN), and so on. "Helpful" actions such as hiding laxatives, throwing away binge foods, keeping binge foods in their car, stowing away the scale, signing their partner up for a weight loss plan, or secretly adding ingredients when cooking that will increase calories may be well-intentioned, but are not well received. Instead of a welcoming response or expression of appreciation for their help, they are met with resistance, anger, deception, or an intense power struggle.

If the partner asks the person with the eating disorder, "Why don't you accept my help? I thought you wanted to change. Don't you want to get better?," it is likely the person will say either "I don't know" (and really not know), or, if they are self-aware and feel safe enough to be vulnerable, will admit, "I am afraid of gaining weight or of being fat" (anorexia or bulimia) or "I am afraid of the attention I get and how my life will change (or will not change) when I am thinner" (BED or obesity). For most, the links to the underlying issues have yet to be made.

THE RESCUE BOAT. The rescue boat represents therapy. When people with eating disorders enter therapy, they do not immediately give up eating disorder behaviors (unless forced to in a treatment facility). In fact, most people are in individual therapy for recovery for 1–5 years. In order to let their behaviors go, the person must resolve the underlying issues and/or past trauma, understand the connection between food/weight and emotion regulation, be confident that they can cope with intense emotion in healthy ways, and learn how to be emotionally connected in intimate relationships. In other words, the person will resist giving up the life preserver unless they have learned how to swim in the waters of intense emotions without it.

We do not yet know if couples therapy will shorten the recovery process for those who achieve full remission. What we do know is that people will not magically change their behavior when they enter couples therapy. Given that eating disorder behaviors dampen feelings, the couple must be prepared for the person in recovery to express more emotional intensity. There is an intervention in Gottman-RED couples therapy called *Tolerating Other's Emotional Storms (TOES)* designed for this purpose. Other issues in the relationship need to be addressed and conversations about difficult topics including the eating disorder must take place before significant change in behavior can be expected. What couples therapy will do is equip the couple for the journey. Whether the end of the story will be full remission remains to be seen.

TREATMENT. There are five variables that affect the likelihood and rate of recovery once a person begins treatment (learning how to swim without a life preserver). The third variable is the focus of the Gottman-RED therapy.

1. **Relationship with the therapist.** Having a strong connection with a therapist who understands eating disorders is essential. This is true for both individual therapy and couples therapy.
2. **Motivation to get better.** People who are not motivated to recover do not recover. Sometimes it takes a long time before a person with an eating disorder decides they are ready to get well. From the time of that decision, it typically takes 1–6 years or more to reach full remission. Some people stop treatment when they are in partial remission and never achieve full remission.
3. **Willingness of the partner to be involved in treatment.** Recovery is facilitated by the involvement of a supportive partner who has learned how to avoid the mistakes of the people in the helicopter. Acting based on common sense does not work; thus, the partner really does need to be part of the treatment. This underscores the importance of couples therapy.
4. **How much pain underlies the behaviors.** People who have more to work through in terms of underlying pain typically have a longer course of recovery. Trauma can be worked on as a couple. The Gottman Institute offers training for couples therapists to learn to treat trauma as part of the couples therapy.
5. **How long the person has had the eating disorder.** Sometime people who have had an eating disorder for a long time recover faster than people who are just starting out and are ambivalent about recovery. One would think it would take longer for someone who has had an eating disorder for 40 years to achieve partial or full remission than someone who has had an eating disorder for 4 years, but that is not necessarily the case. Motivation to get better as well as wisdom from life experience appear to be significant determining factors.

Relational Trauma (Including Bullying and Abuse) in the Etiology and Maintenance of Eating Disorders

A discussion of the etiology of eating disorders would be incomplete without addressing the impact and implications of relationship trauma.

Sexual Abuse, Physical Abuse, Emotional Abuse, Neglect

There is a lack of consensus in the literature regarding the relationship between eating disorders and childhood sexual abuse (defined as unwanted sexual contact that includes being touched in sexual parts or being forced to touch the sexual parts of someone else). Whether or not there is a causal relationship remains unclear (Villarroel et al., 2012). However, it appears that researchers around the world are concerned about the impact of sexual trauma on food-, weight-, and body image- related thoughts and behaviors. In a study of 101 female undergraduate students who had experienced childhood sexual abuse, Ana Villarroel and her colleagues in Spain (2012) found an increase in weight concern, which is a risk factor for the development of an eating disorder, but no significant evidence of other eating disorder attitudes or behaviors.

In a different study of 371 undergraduate women, Samantha Holmes at Yale and her colleagues (2019) found a clear association between interpersonal trauma (sexual abuse, physical abuse, emotional abuse, neglect) and disordered eating. Jessica Breland and associates in the VA health care system (2018) studied 407 female military combat veterans and found that 66% reported military sexual trauma, 33% reported combat exposure, and 15% met criteria for an eating disorder. Combat exposure was not associated with eating disorders; however, military sexual trauma was. Asian women veterans with sexual trauma were more likely to develop an eating disorder than were white women veterans. Older women veterans exhibited more eating disorder symptoms than the younger women (age range 18–70).

Nicole Moulding of Australia (2015) interviewed 14 women with a history of abuse and noted that sexual, physical, and emotional abuse have all been correlated with the development of an eating disorder, with emotional abuse being more strongly predictive than the other types of abuse. It is thought that eating disorder behaviors, particularly binge eating and purging, are attempts to regulate the emotions of guilt, shame, powerlessness, and self-loathing that often follow abuse experiences. The women who recovered cited developing noncontrolling relationships, personal empowerment, and self-nurturance as key variables that supported recovery.

In a longitudinal study of almost 6000 women in the UK now at mid-life by Nadia Micali and colleagues, childhood sexual abuse was prospectively associated with all binge/purge type disorders (Micali et al., 2017). Deborah Mitchison and associates in Australia (2019) found that a lifetime history of sexual abuse was associated with increased risk of obesity, binge eating, extreme dieting, and decreased risk of being underweight and concluded that people with eating disorder symptoms were 47% more likely to indicate a history of sexual abuse.

Bullying

Mitchison's group (2019) also studied bullying in a representative sample of 3000 people. They found that those who had a lifetime history of bullying had an increased risk of obesity, extreme dieting, purging, and the core psychopathology of eating disorders—the overevaluation of weight and shape and its control (Fairburn, 2013). Bullying, particularly related to weight, led to attempts to change body size through dieting or purging behaviors, whereas sexual abuse was more likely to lead to regulating emotion through binge eating behaviors. These behaviors continued despite the last incidence of abuse or bullying being an average of 20 years earlier. Martha Levine at Penn State University (2012) speculated that it was the loneliness and social isolation often experienced by people who were bullied that led to eating disorder behavior.

Implications for the Gottman-RED Couples Therapist

It is clear that more research needs to be done regarding the relationship between childhood sexual abuse, physical abuse, emotional abuse, and bullying and the development of eating disorders.

For the purposes of this treatment approach, it is important that the couples therapist keeps in mind that there may be an increased likelihood of bullying or abuse in the history of the partner with the eating disorder that has implications when working on issues related to intimacy and may surface as enduring vulnerabilities (Karney & Bradbury, 1995) in the couples work. In addition, there may have been multiple unexpected relationship losses that were traumatic and may affect the person with the eating disorder's capacity for attachment to their partner (Reid et al., 2019). The couples therapist working with relationships with eating disorders will need to carefully assess whether the partner who has experienced bullying, abuse, or relational trauma would benefit from adjunctive individual therapy and if so, make an appropriate referral.

The Four Couples

As mentioned earlier, there are four couples highlighted throughout the book as I illustrate Gottman-RED couples therapy principles or interventions. The person with the eating disorder in each of the four couples demonstrates thoughts and behaviors that represent very different life experiences and food- and weight-related behaviors: Carmen is a Hispanic woman with a history of anorexia nervosa, purging subtype, but now has bulimia nervosa; Ezra is a gay man who moved from obesity/binge eating disorder to anorexia nervosa; Demarcus is an African American man with obesity and binge eating disorder; and Amy is a white woman with restricting anorexia nervosa. Each couple is facing similar but different challenges including increased tension, communication deficits, secrecy, deception, loss of trust, financial stress, health issues, sexual intimacy problems, and infertility. You have already met one couple, Carmen and Luciano, and will learn more about them. You will then meet the other three. As you read their stories, I think you will understand the role of the eating disorder in the life of the identified partner, the uniqueness of the non-eating disorder partner experience, the complexity of their journey toward recovery, and the impact of eating disorder thoughts and behaviors on each relationship.

Carmen and Luciano

Carmen had a traumatic childhood. Her parents immigrated from Mexico before she was born. Her father was a physician in Mexico, but his credentials did not qualify him to practice in the United States, so he struggled to find fulfilling work and began to drink too much. Her mother supported the family by taking odd jobs whenever she could while going to school to become an accountant. Drunk every night, her father was physically and verbally abusive to Carmen's mother, brother, and to Carmen herself. Carmen's parents got divorced when she was ten. Her mother remarried a man who was kind and not abusive.

Life was more stable. Carmen was a healthy weight and rarely thought about body image. Then, when in middle school, Carmen was at a party and a high school boy sexually assaulted her. She told no one. Shortly after that traumatic experience, her eating disorder symptoms began. Horrified by what happened, she could not eat. When she did eat, she threw up. Realizing that vomiting actually made her feel better, she started making herself throw up. The changes in her body as she lost weight made her feel safe. Alarmed that she was losing so much weight so fast, her parents took her to the doctor who recommended she go to a treatment center. You already know what happened next and how she met Luciano.

Carmen and Luciano have been married for four years and have a three-year-old daughter, Luna. Painful memories of Carmen's history of abuse are triggered during conflict, when Luciano is sexually aggressive, and if Luciano has too much to drink. Their relationship has been very tumultuous and is tenuous.

Ezra and Abe

Ezra was always a little heavier than the other boys his age. Food was a love language at home and he enjoyed eating. The adults in his family talked about needing to lose weight, but no one really tried. His was a Jewish family that cherished and honored traditions and celebrations, many of which revolved around food. While in elementary school, other boys started to tease him, calling him "fat." He laughed it off and found that his warm, funny personality resulted in him having many friends. Things began to change when he entered middle school. The teasing became bullying. Ezra became more withdrawn, focusing on schoolwork, where he excelled. Eating was comforting, so in times of emotional distress, he turned to food, but he did not have an eating disorder (yet). By the time he reached high school, his doctor was concerned about his weight gain, but Ezra was focused on things that were more important to him. He had known he was gay for a long time but had been afraid to come out to friends or family. It was not until his senior year that he began openly talking about it. The bullying about his weight had continued and now he risked being mocked because he was gay. Ezra's family was very accepting, as were his two close friends, but there were other boys who were not. The bullying intensified. He continued to eat, consuming large quantities late at night while playing video games; eating muted the intense loneliness he battled. He told no one about the overeating or his emotional pain. Although never diagnosed, Ezra now had binge eating disorder.

When he went to college, Ezra expected things to be different, but he was shocked to find that many young people in the gay community were not very receptive to overweight gay men. His physique did not match the thin, muscular body valued and idealized by some in this community. Ezra began to diet and exercise and lost weight quickly. In fact, he lost so much weight that now his doctor was concerned about him being too thin, and referred him to a local treatment program for eating disorders. A few months later, he went for an evaluation and was diagnosed with anorexia nervosa. After checking out the offerings, Ezra decided against treatment at that center because there did not seem to be anything offered for people who identified as LGBTQ+. Besides, he was not ready to give up his new, thin body and was determined to never gain weight again. The pain of bullying and rejection, once numbed by eating, was now obscured by living in a state of semistarvation and by obsessively exercising.

When he met Abe, his partner, Ezra was lean and muscular. It was not until 6 months into the relationship that Ezra disclosed that he had an eating disorder. Abe was not surprised; he had observed

Ezra's very restrictive eating and compulsive exercise routines. He was concerned about Ezra's secrecy and deception regarding his continuing weight loss and increasingly narrow range of acceptable foods, and he suggested that they get some help. Abe wanted to learn what he could do that would be supportive, since everything he had tried so far had been met with resistance or caused conflict. After a particularly destructive argument, Ezra indicated that he was open to couples therapy. Desperate, Abe began to search for a couples therapist who knew something about eating disorders.

Demarcus and Quisha

Demarcus grew up in one of the suburbs of New York City. His neighborhood was mostly Black professionals; his dad was a doctor at the local hospital and his mom was an attorney. They joked that Demarcus must have been switched at birth because he did not have an academic bone in his body; all he wanted to do was play sports. And that is what he did. He loved football and wrestling, but also went out for basketball and baseball. Demarcus was always at the upper end of the growth curve in height and weight and coaches had their eye on him from a young age. When in high school, professional and college scouts approached him every year. His high school football coach took him under his wing and Demarcus excelled as an offensive tackle. Always having a tendency to gain weight, Demarcus learned how to restrict for a few days to take off the pounds. His weight fluctuated up and down. He ate a lot, but worked out so much that he burned off the extra calories.

His coach became a little too enamored with Demarcus and began inviting him to his home after practice to watch films. One thing led to another and the coach began touching Demarcus inappropriately on a regular basis. Demarcus told no one. This continued until he graduated from high school.

Demarcus was drafted to play professional football right out of high school. Things were going really well until he had a career-ending injury. Deflated and devastated, he stopped working out and turned to alcohol and food. Eating the way he had before the injury, he developed the habit of drinking beer and ordering in large quantities of food every night. Demarcus began to gain weight and was well over 350 pounds by the time he met Quisha. Quisha was instantly attracted to him, always liking big men. They married after dating for 2 years. During this time, he cut back on drinking and, knowing how to diet, he cut back on food as well, and lost about 50 pounds. Their daughter, Kalisha, and son, Tyler, were born. Kalisha is now 20 and Tyler is 14.

Things were stable for many years until a series of hard things happened. Demarcus's father died; Quisha had a cancer scare; Tyler was diagnosed with ADHD; and Demarcus lost his job as offensive line coach for the local NFL team, leaving him unemployed for about 6 months.

This was too much for Demarcus, who became very depressed, started binge eating again, and, over the years, gained back the 50 pounds—plus 50 more. He felt ashamed of his body size and physically uncomfortable, no longer able to move easily even when doing simple tasks like driving the car, walking the dog, or getting down on the floor to play with his kids. The quantities of food he was eating were costing a lot and straining their already tight budget on Quisha's income. He started eating in secret after she went to bed and in his car so she would not see him, lying about how much he was spending. In addition, he started having some health problems and was diagnosed with Type 2 diabetes and hypertension. Demarcus's sexual desire had diminished as he gained weight. Quisha said nothing about his weight changes—she was attracted to large men—but Demarcus's larger size made intimacy more difficult. Quisha was not prepared for the extent of his eating problem. It seemed as if all of the activities in their lives revolved around food. She was becoming increasingly unhappy and began stopping at the casino to lift her spirits, but this did not take away her sadness about the relationship. She told Demarcus that they had to get help or she was going to leave. They had tried couples counseling once before, but the therapist clearly did not understand eating disorders, so they quit. Demarcus, reluctant to try again but desperate to save his relationship, began the search for a couples counselor who could help them.

Amy and John

Amy could not remember ever feeling good about herself, having struggled with self-doubt and insecurity from the time she was a small child. Other than that, her childhood was unremarkable. She did well in school; her parents stayed married; her older brother acted out but not too much; she graduated from high school; and she attended a good university. While in high school, she dated some but never had a serious relationship. Her weight was a little on the thin side but within the normal range and her eating was stable. However, she had a friend who was dieting, so Amy decided to join her and was surprised to find that losing weight felt good. Unfortunately, she restricted a little too much, got way too hungry, and ended up binge eating for the first time in her life. This frightened her, so she began restricting to compensate for the binge eating. She learned to count calories, read food labels, and record her eating in an app on her phone, except on the days she binged; on these days, she did not want to see a graph on her phone showing how much she had eaten. Ashamed of this cycle, she told no one.

In college, she continued this binge/restrict cycle and slowly started to gain weight. This troubled her even more. After being rejected in a romantic relationship, she became obsessed with losing weight, convinced that her boyfriend had broken up with her because she had gained weight. Things got out of control and her weight plummeted, but this did not bother her. Though she did not fully understand her subconscious motivations at the time, she was aware that the pain of rejection had faded since she had started losing weight. About 6 months later, she was diagnosed with anorexia nervosa and hospitalized for 3 months. Forced to gain weight in the treatment center, she left and maintained the healthy weight for a few months, then started losing again.

It was at this time that she met Jeff, her first husband. That relationship lasted 5 years and ended in divorce. Jeff said he left because he could not deal with her eating disorder anymore. This rejection precipitated a severe relapse.

Amy went in and out of treatment centers for the next 10 years, gaining weight while in treatment, sustaining the changes for a while, and then losing it again. By the time she was 37, she decided that even though she gained insight about herself and learned more valuable coping skills every time she went, she needed a break from treatment. Maintaining a very low, barely healthy weight, she was able to perform well at her job as a web designer, maintain friendships, and live a meaningful life. Her eating and exercise behaviors were rigid and ritualistic, involving restriction of certain food groups, chewing and spitting her food, and exercising for a minimum of 3 hours per day. While single, she could do what she wanted without impacting or inconveniencing anyone else. Then she met John, a senior game developer, who worked in an office down the hall. They fell in love and got married. John liked her thin body type, admired her discipline with exercise, and minimized her odd behaviors, literally looking the other way some of the time. As long as he accommodated her, things were peaceful at home.

When John expressed interest in having children together (he had two from a previous marriage), Amy was not excited about gaining weight with pregnancy, but knew how important it was to John, so she agreed to try. However, her weight was so low that they were unable to conceive naturally, and she was unwilling to take fertility drugs because of the risk of weight gain.

Tension was mounting in the relationship. Amy's behaviors started to increase, as did her secrecy and deception. Amy's sexual desire had decreased with weight loss while, simultaneously, John felt less attracted to her at the extremely low weight, so they had not had sex for months. Her weight dropped so low that she was hospitalized again, but left after 3 days. At this point, John, feeling powerless and scared, said they had to get help for their relationship. Neither wanted a second failed marriage. They both started looking for a couples counselor who understood eating disorders.

Concluding Thoughts

Gottman-RED couples therapy builds on the understanding that eating disorders are complex mental disorders that evolve over time in a person's life. What starts innocently as a behavior or habit mysteriously crosses an ill-defined line to become a way of coping with emotional distress and/or relationship challenges. Even more elusive than a definitive explanation of the etiology of eating disorders is the identification of an effective evidence-based treatment for adults. While treatment for adults tends to be somewhat effective, no one mode of treatment stands out as superior to any of the others. Despite the development of innovative and ingenious individual and group therapy approaches and carefully conceptualized and comprehensive treatment facilities, the recovery rate for adults with eating disorders remains dismal, 50–60% at best. Most professionals concur that improvements in treatment for adults need to be made, but scratch their heads, still as puzzled today as was Hilde Bruch, a pioneering psychiatrist in the early days of eating disorder treatment, back in 1978 when she used the word "enigma" to capture the inscrutable nature of anorexia nervosa (Bruch, 1978).

Eating disorders, unlike most mental disorders, are significantly impacted by the body's attempts to compensate for the food- and weight-related behaviors. Thoughts and behaviors directly related to food restriction, purging behaviors, or food overconsumption are different from those that have an emotional or psychological basis. This subset of personality and behavioral manifestations are a consequence rather than a cause of the eating disorder and will not abate until there is substantial behavioral recovery (Keys et al., 1950; Selekman & Beyebach, 2013). It seems to also be the case that many of the dysfunctional relationship interactions are a consequence of the eating disorder behaviors, and not the cause (Selekman & Beyebach, 2013). Thus, there is potential for a vicious cycle and a chicken-and-egg conundrum. Which does one treat first? Or is it even possible to effectively treat one before the other?

In Gottman-RED couples therapy, the couples therapist helps couples in which one or both partners have an eating disorder learn ways to strengthen their relationship while concurrently acquiring skills in talking about delicate issues related to eating disorder recovery and—the even more sensitive topic—the eating disorder itself.

2

Eating Disorders and Couples Therapy: Gottman-RED in Context

Before introducing Gottman-RED couples therapy, it is important to understand some of the barriers to accessing care and to review the couples therapies that have been tried thus far to help people during their recovery journey. This chapter focuses on common stereotypes and gives historical context for these therapies.

Eating Disorder–Related Stereotypes That Are Barriers to Accessing Care

When you hear the word eating disorder, what type of person comes to mind? What are they doing? Take a moment to allow yourself to reflect on these questions and the image that you visualize.

Most people imagine a single person, female, white, young, skinny, alone, compulsively exercising, meticulously preparing low-calorie concoctions, aimlessly walking the aisles of a grocery store, binge eating then vomiting, or repeatedly standing on a scale hoping each time to see a lower number. These are the stereotypes of someone with an eating disorder. As with most stereotypes, there is some truth intertwined with a significant amount of distortion.

Unfortunately, these stereotypes may limit the number of couples who reach out for help even though they could benefit from Gottman-RED (**R**elationships with **E**ating **D**isorders) couples therapy, a new therapy for couples in which one or both partners have an eating disorder, and the interventions designed specifically to help couples address difficult issues related to food, weight, body image, and/or exercise.

Under the best of circumstances, most couples drag their feet when it comes to seeking help. The thought of talking with a therapist about intimate details of their relationship is daunting. In fact, John Gottman has stated that most people wait 6 years too long before they reach out to schedule a couples therapy appointment (Gottman & Gottman, 2018). When one or both partners struggle with food or weight issues, there may be additional obstacles to overcome before taking that first step. Some feel embarrassed or ashamed, questioning if their eating problem is serious enough or is even a problem at all. These individuals may conclude they are not really "sick" when they compare themselves to social media influencers or YouTubers, or they may believe their issues do not matter since they never have or no longer meet the diagnostic criteria for an eating disorder. I have heard many in my practice say that they hesitated to ask for help because they were not skinny enough to deserve therapy, so should just deal with their food problems on their own.

Other factors contribute to the reluctance to seek treatment. Many men are unlikely to identify with having a problem that is portrayed in the media as a woman's disorder. People who are middle-aged or older question if they are too old to have an eating disorder, frequently minimizing and hiding their thoughts, behaviors, and pain. People who are members of ethnic minorities may be hesitant to reach out due to financial constraints, fears of being labeled or stigmatized, and lack of access to care providers (Coffino et al., 2019).

According to a study by Jaime Coffino and colleagues at the Mayo Clinic, help-seeking for eating disorder-specific symptoms is low in general, with 34.5% of those with anorexia nervosa, 62.6% of those with bulimia nervosa, and 49.0% of those with binge eating disorder ever seeking help, with only one-third of those who do contacting a mental health provider (Coffino et al., 2019). Rebecca Bomben and her associates in the United Kingdom (2022) found that three out of four people with eating disorders were managing on their own, living with their disordered eating thoughts and behaviors without actively engaging in professional help. Janet Treasure and colleagues in the UK (2020) also reported that only 20–30% of people with eating disorders actually sought treatment.

Because stereotypes about age, gender, weight, ethnicity and race, relationship status, and severity may be barriers to seeking treatment, a closer examination of the impact of each of them is warranted.

Age

Most people erroneously assume that eating disorders primarily afflict teenagers or college students. It is true that eating disorders often begin during adolescence or emerging adulthood; however, for many, they continue into young adulthood, middle age, and sometimes, for an entire lifetime. Micali and associates (2017) specifically focused on eating disorders in mid-life women and found that full threshold and sub-threshold eating disorders are common, either due to new onset or a chronic disorder, most commonly OSFED or BED, however, few women accessed healthcare. They also found that by mid-life, 15.3% of women had met criteria for a lifetime eating disorder. In the four couples we will be following, Carmen is 33, Demarcus is 50, Ezra is 26, and Amy is 39; however, all engaged in eating disorder behaviors for the first time during childhood, adolescence, or young adulthood.

Gender

Although thought to be significantly underreported and minimally researched, boys and men develop eating disorders (Bomben et al., 2022; Coffino et al., 2019; Malova & Dunleavy, 2021; Reas & Stedal, 2015; Siegel & Sawyer, 2020). Men today are more focused on body size, muscle size, body composition, and weight than in previous generations (Malova & Dunleavy, 2021). Current estimates are that 25–33% of eating disorder cases occur in males and that the prevalence in males has been increasing in recent years (Siegel & Sawyer, 2020). Males present differently, tending to focus more on muscle mass and definition, exercise, and hedonic eating (eating large amounts of food for enjoyment and pleasure). Men, like women, die from consequences of eating disorder behaviors, with male inpatients having a higher mortality rate than females: anorexia nervosa, 12.9%; bulimia nervosa, 11.1%; and Eating Disorder-Not Otherwise Specified (ED-NOS), 6.4% (Quadflieg et al., 2019; van Eeden et al., 2021). The lifetime prevalence of males with anorexia nervosa is quite low at 0.3% of the male population; the lifetime prevalence of males with bulimia nervosa is a little more than 1% of the male population.

Binge eating disorder tells a different story. Of those with binge eating disorder, 40% identify as male, with the lifetime prevalence among males being 2.6% (van Eeden et al., 2021). Although very little is known about eating disorders in men midlife and beyond, it is estimated that between .02% to 1.6% of this population meet diagnostic criteria, with subthreshold behaviors more common. Deborah Reas and Kristin Stedal in Norway studied men aged 40–81 who had reported eating disorder behaviors and found a pattern of early onset of eating issues, periods of relapse and remission, diagnostic crossover of symptoms, and weight cycling. They noted that late life stressors such as death, divorce, medical issues, or change in financial status triggered relapse or resumption of more serious symptoms causing "unexplained" weight gain or loss in men. The stereotype that eating disorders are a problem afflicting young females may result in medical providers or family members minimizing or misconstruing the meaning of these changes (Reas & Stedal, 2015).

Barriers to Treatment for Men

Though eating disorders do affect men, they tend to not ask for the help they need. There appear to be many reasons for this: stigma (eating disorders are known as a woman's disorder); lack of recognition of symptoms by health care providers; diagnostic criteria that work for women but not men; assumptions regarding sexuality; the gendered portrayal of eating disorders in social media; unhelpful responses of significant others; justification of behaviors based upon involvement in sports (e.g., self-induced vomiting or laxative abuse to achieve a required weight for wrestling, compulsive exercise to stay fit for track, bulking up for football); and the belief that men should not talk about their problems (Bomben et al., 2022; Reas & Stedal, 2015). After Bomben and her colleagues (2022) reviewed the literature regarding barriers to help-seeking for men, they concluded that, "primary interventions should center on dispelling gender-specific myths and portraying more diverse representations of eating disorders within health and media domains" (p. 193).

Also concerned about barriers to treatment for men with eating disorders, Ekaterina Malova and Victoria Dunleavy at the University of Miami (2021) designed a fascinating qualitative study in which they analyzed narratives posted on YouTube by men with eating disorders in various stages of recovery. Bullying, drive for muscularity, and self-regulation were identified as the three common factors increasing disordered eating behaviors. Shame, stigma, lack of knowledge/information, and poor doctor–patient communication were recognized as significant impediments to seeking treatment.

In my experience working with couples, it appears that asking for help with food-related issues in the context of couples counseling may be a more acceptable entrée into treatment for men who have chronically struggled with food or weight issues, particularly binge eating, as opposed to seeking individual therapy. We will be following two males with eating disorders in our four couples: Demarcus, who has binge eating disorder, and Ezra, who struggles with anorexia nervosa. Demarcus primarily uses food for self-regulation and enjoyment, while Ezra's restricted and controlled eating was fueled by bullying and drive for muscularity. It is noteworthy that in both cases, it was the influence and encouragement of their partners and/or concern about the future of their relationship that opened the door to therapy. Left to their own devices, neither would have contacted a therapist.

Weight

Most people with eating disorders are not underweight. The only eating disorder with a diagnostic criterion related to weight is the least common, anorexia nervosa (APA, 2022). Amy and Ezra struggle with this eating disorder. Among those with bulimia nervosa or binge eating disorder, many maintain a healthy weight and are highly functional in daily life. This is a blessing and a curse. The blessing is that no one knows. The curse is that no one knows. They can continue behaviors without interference, living a double life while engaging in eating disorder behaviors in secret. Based on outward appearance, no one suspects that there is anything amiss. They fly under the radar, suffering in isolation and silence. Carmen is in this group.

Although not considered an eating disorder but, rather, a medical diagnosis with potential health or relationship implications for some, obesity is diagnosed based upon body mass index (BMI). Demarcus has binge eating disorder and health consequences related to obesity. His high body weight drew the attention of his doctor and his wife; however, unless they asked him the right questions, neither would know that Demarcus struggled with binge eating disorder. Most people with this diagnosis feel so much shame about their behaviors that they keep them secret for as long as possible.

Although being married is thought to have many positive health benefits, it is also correlated with weight gain. Janice Kiecolt-Glaser and her associates at Ohio State University (2015) found that the combination of chronic marital stress, hostile interactions with partners, and a mood disorder history increases the risk of obesity, metabolic syndrome, and cardiovascular disease. For Demarcus, circumstances external to the relationship as well as marital stress have compounded his eating disorder. This is where couples therapy may make a difference. Ying Chen and his colleagues at Harvard University (2018) decided to examine archival data for 2600 married individuals at midlife. What they found was that a supportive marriage was correlated with maintenance of a healthy weight. This does not prove causality, but definitely raises the question of whether Gottman-RED couples therapy could not only improve the relationship, but also open the door to a healthier lifestyle and healthier weight for couples in midlife such as Quisha and Demarcus.

Ethnicity and Race

As noted previously, eating disorders affect people of every race and ethnicity all over the world. In the United States, it appears that treatment utilization for those diagnosed with anorexia nervosa and bulimia nervosa is lower for underserved U.S. ethnic and racialized groups than among the non-Latinx white population, while Black people present more often than white people for treatment of binge eating disorder (APA, 2022).

Of interest is the taboo nature of mental illness in some cultures or racial groups that functions as a barrier to help-seeking (Sim et al., 2019). For example, in a study led by Jessica Saunders in New Jersey (2023), participants commented on how in Latinx/Hispanic families and their culture at large, mental illness was invisible, not acknowledged, and not discussed. Seeking help outside of the family was discouraged. The same often holds true for Asian Americans with eating disorders. Pursuing outside help was a last resort, according to a study by Yuying Tsong and their associates at California State University (2023). They found that Asian Americans, particularly women, were heavily influenced by the Asian thin ideal, which is a more rigorous standard than in the United States, and by the Asian myth of transformation which is the belief that losing weight not only transforms one's body but also improves one's life. Mental health stigma also affects the likelihood of Black Americans to reach out for help, even though Black people are statistically more likely to have binge eating disorder than are other groups. Kevin Rivera in Iowa and colleagues (2021) noted that distrust of the health care provider system; racial inequities; and cultural expectations to solve problems on one's own, with one's family, or through faith-based channels reduced the likelihood of seeking professional help.

In collectivist cultures like these, family involvement is so important that individual therapy or a program where the individual leaves the family for treatment may be hard to embrace. It logically follows that an approach like Gottman-RED couples therapy that emphasizes the importance of working together with a supportive partner/family member to address eating disorder–related issues may be more acceptable, thus opening more doors for underserved populations to receive help and support.

Relationship Status

Contrary to the stereotype that people with eating disorders are single, the vast majority of adults with eating disorders are married or in a committed relationship at a rate comparable to people who do not have eating disorders (Bulik et al., 2012; Maier, 2015). In a study of women with either anorexia nervosa or bulimia nervosa by Andréa Pinheiro and associates (2010), 98% of women reported having experienced intimate relationships and 87% reporting being in a committed relationship. When in a relationship, people experience a whole gamut of emotions: the exuberance of love and happiness as well as flashes of anger, frustration, and loneliness. Eating disorder behaviors can serve as a buffer by numbing and distracting when these intense emotions arise. Janet Treasure and colleagues (2006) noted that, particularly for anorexic individuals, avoidance of closeness in relationships made possible through eating disorder behaviors meant avoidance of all the painful, intense, negative emotions more likely to occur with emotional intimacy. Perhaps one of the more painful emotions to experience while in a relationship is loneliness. People with eating disorders often fear loneliness and would rather not feel at all than risk this emotion; they find that the numbing provided by their behaviors brings welcome relief (Levine, 2012).

Jon Arcelus and his colleagues in the United Kingdom (2012) were intrigued by the fact that relationship therapy had rarely been part of the treatment process for people with eating disorders despite significant research indicating that there was a clear connection between eating disorders and romantic relationships. They decided to review 20 studies of eating disorder behaviors and couples. Subsequently, they concluded that relationship issues and eating disorder behaviors have a direct correlation: when one increases, so does the other, regardless of the eating disorder. Although bidirectional, it was not possible to determine which came first. Regardless, when one partner has an eating disorder, the relationship is stressed, and it is in the best interest of both partners to do all that is possible to support recovery. Arcelus recommended that serious consideration be given to incorporating relationship therapy into the treatment of people with eating disorders.

He went on to report that marital distress played a significant role in the onset and maintenance of behaviors for about 70% of eating disorder cases (Arcelus et al., 2012). Women with anorexia nervosa in relationships reported longer duration of illness, greater numbers of past treatments, and more intense eating disorder behaviors than those who were single (Bulik et al., 2012). Arcelus and his colleagues (2012) also found that as early as 1984, one researcher speculated that late-onset anorexia nervosa appeared to be a response to increasing marital distress. In another study, women with anorexia nervosa were less likely than those with bulimia nervosa to state that they had a partner who provided social support. Women with bulimia nervosa were found to have dissatisfaction with their marriages, to be conflict avoidant, and to lack problem-solving skills. Women with binge eating disorder reported fewer positive interactions and lower marital satisfaction when compared with women with other mental disorders or no disorders. All in all, people with eating disorders were attempting to juggle eating disorder recovery with the management of a struggling relationship. After thoroughly reviewing the 20 studies, Arcelus and his team concluded that couples therapy should be incorporated into the treatment of people with eating disorders.

Since over 85% of adults with eating disorders are married or in a committed relationship and many of them are unhappy in their relationships, couples therapists working with relationships in which one or both partners have eating issues (RED couples) need to understand and be able to recognize the unique issues that these couples are likely to face. Strengthening the couple's bond will hopefully improve the quality of life for both the person with eating issues and their partner. Whether this equates to full behavioral recovery remains to be seen, as eating disorders are one of the subgroups of mental disorders where some remain in partial remission indefinitely, retaining certain behaviors that do not significantly impact day-to-day functioning but that may still affect a relationship.

Not Only People With Diagnosable Eating Disorders Have Significant Food or Weight Issues

People who struggle with eating behaviors, weight, or body image but do not meet the diagnostic criteria for an eating disorder generally fall into one of three categories. First are those who have had health complications related to obesity due to overeating. The incidence of obesity in the United States is estimated to be between 22–35% of the adult population; thus it is likely that relationship therapists will work with couples in which one or both partners are obese. For some couples, this will not be an issue, but for other couples, there will be eating issues or behaviors that affect the relationship and therefore merit discussion.

Second are those thought to have orthorexia nervosa, a condition characterized by an obsession with eating only foods one considers healthy (an unhealthy focus on eating in a healthy way) and systematically avoiding certain foods due to the belief that they are harmful (Valente et al., 2020). This behavior can become so extreme that the person becomes malnourished. The rigidity and obsessive focus on food can have a significant impact on a relationship.

Third is the neglected, nameless group of those who are marginally recovered (in partial remission) yet no longer meet the diagnostic criteria for an eating disorder and those who never quite made the diagnostic cut but are overly focused on food or weight and have disordered eating patterns.

All three of these groups may slip through the cracks, struggling alone in silence even if they are in a committed relationship. Some will struggle with obsessive or intrusive thoughts about food, weight, or body image and others with compulsive behaviors that outwardly appear healthy (e.g., exercise, eating only organic food), yet are driven by an unremitting, secret, inner fire that compels them to act in a certain way.

Approaches to Treating Eating Disorders With Couples Therapy

Traditional treatment for adult eating disorders is individual therapy and/or group therapy, with rates of recovery at the end of treatment for anorexia nervosa being 46%, bulimia nervosa 67%, and binge eating disorder being 50–60% at best (Linville & Oleksak, 2013; Runfola et al., 2018) with posttreatment abstinence rates dropping to 35% for people with bulimia nervosa and most of those with anorexia nervosa having a lifelong struggle (Levinson et al., 2020; Linardon, 2018). As recently as 2020, there has been a reiteration of the need to find more effective treatments. "We urgently need personalized, effective, empirically valid treatments for adults with eating disorders that can promote full eating disorder remission" (Levinson et al., 2020).

Back in the 1970s, there were those who believed that dysfunctional family dynamics were a risk factor for not only developing an eating disorder, but maintaining the symptoms. Over 30 years ago, Blake Woodside and a team of eating disorder treatment specialists in Toronto (1993) challenged this notion that improving eating disorder symptoms would unmask family psychopathology and worsen family functioning and found that not to be the case. They also set out to challenge the same idea for marriages and, noting a deficiency in the literature, wrote the first book about marriage and eating disorders (Woodside, personal communication, February 22, 2024). The bookshelves of eating disorder professionals were replete with excellent resources for individuals seeking treatment for eating disorders and valuable volumes about family therapy with eating disorders, but the section dedicated to couples therapy was conspicuously sparse (Woodside et al., 1993).

When Jon Arcelus and his colleagues embarked on their extensive review of the literature in 2012 to see what had been studied about couples therapy for eating disorders since Woodside's seminal work was published, I can imagine them shaking their heads, a puzzled look on their faces. Although they unearthed significant research supporting a connection between eating disorders and romantic relationships, they were surprised to find that not only had couples therapy rarely been part of the treatment process, but most eating disorder specialists were unclear about the role that a couples therapist could play (Arcelus et al., 2012).

Although well aware that cognitive behavioral therapy (CBT), acceptance and commitment therapy (ACT), family-based treatment (FBT), or radically open-dialectical behavior therapy (RO-DBT) are the frontrunners when reviewing the treatments offered in the eating disorders world, Candace Maier at the University of Iowa (2015) was convinced that couples therapy was needed given that adult mental and physical health was integrally interwoven with what happens in the love relationships of people with eating disorders. In addition, adults with eating disorders often noted significant problems in their marriages or committed relationships. At one time, it was thought that anorexia nervosa developed as an unhealthy way of coping with a marriage that was in crisis. If this is indeed the case, interventions targeting interpersonal dynamics could provide a breakthrough in the therapy for chronic, treatment-resistant anorexia nervosa (Arcelus, 2012; Murray, 2014).

Debra Bussolotti in Italy and her colleagues in Spain (2002) were interested in the relevance of marital status to eating disorder psychopathology. They studied 322 eating disorder inpatients (anorexia nervosa and bulimia nervosa) admitted for treatment. They found an interesting paradox; those who lived with a partner were older, presented with greater symptomatology and exhibited more psychopathology, while at the same time they demonstrated increased motivation for change. Bussolotti and colleagues (2002) concluded that improving interpersonal functioning was an important component of treatment.

A perpetual challenge for inpatient and residential treatment providers has been helping patients transition from treatment to home. Step-down programs including partial hospitalization and intensive outpatient programs have had some success in addressing this problem. Most programs include family weeks when family members and/or spouses travel to the treatment center to receive psychoeducation about eating disorder recovery and attend group sessions as well as conjoint sessions with the person with the eating disorder. Family weeks allow spouses to be involved in the treatment process on a limited basis. Integrating concomitant, consistent couples therapy into treatment protocols may help with the transition to home. With the now widespread acceptance of telehealth, this is a more feasible option even if the spouse is far away. Also, couples therapy may be a viable alternative for people unable or unwilling to go away for treatment; couples therapy allows people to "target symptoms in the context in which they exist," as opposed to working on issues individually and then coming home to work things out with a partner who was not involved in the therapy (Murray, 2014, p. 396). Treatment center providers and individual therapists need to be willing to try a different approach if the current one is not proving to be successful or is not an option. The reality is that long after therapy ends, the couple relationship will continue, so does it not make sense to strengthen this relationship in ways that support recovery?

Interest in developing a couples therapy specifically for people with eating disorders has mushroomed during the past 15 years. Perhaps John Arcelus's team (2012) inspired treatment providers to shift their focus in this direction when they wrote, " . . . the research suggests that concomitant marital, intimate and romantic difficulties are associated with eating disorders and are likely to be a maintaining factor, although the direction of causality is unclear, and that consideration should be given to using relationship therapy for patients with eating disorders" (p. 147). This does not mean that the person with eating issues will jump at the chance to engage in couples therapy that promotes communication about their eating behaviors. A feeling of dread of behavior change coupled with an overarching sense of being unable to live without the behaviors affects both men and women with eating issues. As noted earlier in this chapter, when Rebecca Bomben and her colleagues in the United Kingdom (2021) reviewed the recent literature, they identified that men often resisted seeking help even though they knew their eating behaviors were causing relational problems. However, men do not have a corner on the market when it comes to resistance to seeking help (Bulik et al., 2012); people of all genders drag their feet at the prospect of couples therapy until given an ultimatum by their partner. This characteristic ambivalence about recovery and reluctance to begin the daunting, uphill climb of change presents unique challenges for the couples therapist.

History of Couples Therapy and Eating Disorder Treatment

In preparation for learning about Gottman-RED couples therapy, it makes sense to review other approaches to working with couples in which one or both partners have an eating disorder. As previously stated, there is a paucity of research regarding the effectiveness of couples therapy in the treatment of adults with eating disorders (Linville et al., 2015; Linville & Oleksak, 2013; Maier, 2015; Murray, 2014). The number of evidence-based interventions for couples with eating disorders is extremely limited (Linville et al., 2015). Of course, even if there were more research, it would need to be carefully evaluated as there is a tendency for proponents of a particular approach to look for data that supports its effectiveness. As Hilde Bruch (1978) wrote many years ago, "The more an investigator is convinced of the importance of their own theory, the more they are inclined to use their particular findings as explanation for the whole picture" (p. 6). The author of this book is no exception.

Back in 2010 or so, Cynthia Bulik, Don Baucom, and Jennifer Kirby of the University of North Carolina, Chapel Hill, took up the charge and developed a suite of innovative couples therapies that started out specific to anorexia nervosa and binge eating disorder and have since become more generalized. Their research and pioneering work was inspirational to me when developing Gottman-RED couples therapy.

Let us review the approaches utilized to date when working with couples in relationships with eating disorders before introducing Gottman-RED interventions. Seven relationship therapies documented since 2000 are summarized: two for anorexia nervosa, three for binge eating disorder, and two for eating disorders in general, without specifying.

Anorexia Nervosa

An assortment of treatment approaches exists for anorexia nervosa and all promote some change and movement toward recovery, but none is ideal. Among people with anorexia nervosa, 35–42% relapse within 12–18 months of discharge from treatment (Bulik at al., 2012). Couples therapy may be a viable alternative or addition to future treatment protocols; however, "the most effective way to incorporate a partner into treatment is unknown at present" (Baucom et al., 2017). As aptly noted by Hunna Watson of Australia and Cynthia Bulik, for adolescents with anorexia nervosa, Family-Based Treatment (FBT) is the treatment of choice; for adults with anorexia nervosa, there is no treatment of choice (Watson & Bulik, 2013).

UCAN: Uniting Couples in the Treatment of Anorexia Nervosa

Uniting Couples in the Treatment of Anorexia Nervosa (UCAN) is a manualized, cognitive-behavioral treatment approach that integrates cognitive behavioral therapy for anorexia nervosa with cognitive behavioral couples therapy (CBCT). UCAN is considered an augmentation treatment, meaning it is part of a multidisciplinary approach that includes individual therapy for the person in recovery and close collaboration with other treatment providers.

The literature regarding the effectiveness of FBT for teenagers with anorexia nervosa was the inspiration for the development of this couples approach (Kirby et al., 2016). The pilot study results were promising, demonstrating that addition of UCAN to the treatment plan resulted in people with anorexia gaining more weight and reducing a greater number of eating disorder symptoms than with traditional individual treatments (Murray et al., 2014). However, Cynthia Bulik and her team (2012) noted that introducing a couples-based intervention is complicated when the person with the eating disorder is conflicted about recovery. In this type of intervention, the partner's role is to support changes, so a person ambivalent about recovery can easily misconstrue the partner's comments as attempts to control.

UCAN has a twofold focus: (1) teaching skills that provide couples concrete ways to collaborate when facing issues related to anorexia nervosa and (2) reducing the stress of chronic relationship distress to support recovery (Kirby et al., 2016). UCAN helps the couple "develop a clear blueprint of how to engage the partner meaningfully in treating anorexia nervosa" (Bulik et al., 2012, p. 22).

Just like therapists implementing Gottman-RED, those administering UCAN need to understand how anorexia nervosa affects the relationship *and* how the relationship affects eating disorder recovery, thus need training in eating disorder treatment as well as couples therapy. Bulik noted that often a therapist will be trained in one but not the other; UCAN therapists need to be willing to learn about the other half of the equation (2012, p. 22).

With UCAN, the non-eating disorder partner is viewed as an ally in promoting treatment consistency, a member of the treatment team, a safety net and extra support, and an additional source of information about struggles and progress during the time between sessions. The UCAN therapist assists couples in addressing difficult topics related to eating disorder behaviors or recovery that may have been avoided in the past.

UCAN uses couple-based interventions; however, this is *not* the same as couples therapy. The interventions take one of three forms. The first two do not presume there is relationship distress.

1. **Partner-assisted interventions.** The partner acts as a coach/support to help the person in recovery to make changes necessary for recovery.
2. **Disorder-specific interventions.** The relationship is the focus of treatment but only in areas where issues relate to the eating disorder (e.g., decisions about going out to dinner). Partners are not responsible for monitoring weight or eating.

3. **Couples therapy.** This form is for couples who have relationship distress and is not part of the UCAN manualized treatment. It is particularly helpful if relationship stress is thought to be a maintaining factor for the eating disorder. Typical issues facing couples in which one partner has anorexia nervosa include: sexual functioning, relationship distress, and communication (Kirby et al., 2016).

Strategic Couples Therapy (SCT) in Adult Anorexia Nervosa

In strategic couples therapy (SCT), there is the assumption that the symptom (in this case the eating disorder) is maintained due to the "valuable interpersonal, communicative, and protective function" (Murray, 2014, p. 393) that the behavior serves in the family. The couple may be ambivalent about change because of these inadvertent benefits of the eating disorder and its behaviors. Consequently, the therapy focuses on releasing the symptoms from this systemic function.

Stuart Murray (2014) in Australia, like Cynthia Bulik, was concerned about the poor rates of treatment outcomes for adults with anorexia nervosa and was influenced by the success of FBT with adolescents. Turning his attention to conjoint therapy, he studied SCT to see if it would improve outcomes. He described the anorexic symptoms as offering both partners a simultaneous sense of power and disempowerment relative to each other. For example, the person with anorexia could secretly restrict when feeling controlled by their partner, thereby creating the illusion of control at a time when they felt powerless. Murray believed CBT or insight-oriented therapy would not effectively address or induce relational change. In his case study of a 36-year-old male with chronic anorexia nervosa, the presence of anorexia nervosa was closely tied to conflict regulation in the marriage. Detriangulating the presence of anorexic symptoms from couples interactions with a therapy like SCT was necessary for this person to recover. SCT utilizes interventions that destabilize the homeostasis in the relationship, such as defiance-based paradoxical prescriptions, with the belief that small changes lead to bigger and more meaningful changes. The couples therapist needs to create an environment where change is possible and celebrated. SCT is not insight based; the focus is on the present and action-based change (Linville & Oleksak, 2013).

Binge Eating Disorder

Since 30–50% of overweight adults pursuing weight loss treatment have binge eating disorder (BED), 70% of the adult population in America are overweight or obese as reported by the CDC, and 77% of adults with BED are married or living with a partner, the likelihood of working with a couple in which one or both partners have BED is very high (Runfola et al., 2018). Because tension or stress in a relationship often triggers binge eating, it seems prudent to involve the spouse in treatment (Whisman et al., 2012). As aptly stated by Amy Gorin (2019) from the University of Connecticut and her colleagues, "Weight gain occurs during marriage, yet obesity treatment is focused on individuals" (p. 137).

CBT for Binge Eating Disorder With Couples in Groups

CBT for BED with couples is a group therapy for couples in which one partner has BED (Gorin et al., 2003). Amy Gorin teamed up with Dan Le Grange and Arthur Stone to develop a manualized group treatment for couples intended to decrease binge eating and promote weight stabilization. Strategies used included daily self-monitoring, regular eating, identifying triggers for binge eating, and a relapse prevention plan. Exercise was encouraged. The goal for the spouse was increased knowledge of BED and understanding of coping resources. It was hoped that the therapy would result in both partners feeling confident as a couple in being able to address BED. At the beginning of each group therapy session, the partner with BED checked in about progress and then the non-eating disorder partner set behavioral goals intended to help the person with BED binge less often. Marital partner agreement on the goals was necessary.

In their study of 94 couples, Gorin and her team (2003) found the surprising result that spouse involvement in this approach did not have an additional benefit over CBT alone in terms of decreasing frequency of binge eating. The researchers wondered if spouses were less motivated to be involved in helping change behaviors since many were unaware of the binge eating before the study began and the binge eating had minimal impact on their partner's functioning (unlike alcoholism or chronic pain). This approach might actually be more effective after a therapy like Gottman-RED that works with couples individually to facilitate conversations about the eating disorder and its impact on both partners, thereby laying a foundation for behavior change.

UNITE-BED (United Couples in the Treatment of Eating Disorders-BED)

This couples therapy focuses on BED psychopathology, co-occurring symptoms, and relationship functioning while working closely with other members of the eating disorders treatment team (Runfola et al., 2018).

Cristin Runfola (2018) led the team at Chapel Hill in the development of UNITE-BED, a 22-week manualized treatment that incorporates CBT principles for treating BED symptoms and improving emotion regulation. In their pilot study of 10 couples (Runfola et al., 2018), results were encouraging, with an 80% abstinence rate and decreased beck depression inventory (BDI) scores (attitudes and symptoms of depression) for the eating disorder partner at the end of treatment. Non-eating disorder partners learned how to offer support and accountability that increased the likelihood of the partner with the eating disorder continuing in treatment, demonstrated improvement in discussing issues related to BED, and practiced providing support when their partner felt tempted to binge eat.

Unfortunately, non-eating disorder partners did not show change in emotional well-being. Since Gottman-RED couples therapy interventions are designed to address the emotional well-being of the non-eating disorder partner in a way that results in improvement, it could be used as an adjunctive therapy with UNITE-BED.

Weight Loss Program for Couples: TEAMS (Talking About Eating, Activity, and Mutual Support)

Amy Gorin and her team (2019) noted that body weights in spouses rise and fall in synchrony, with couples typically gaining weight during the first year of marriage. In addition, people tend to marry a partner with a similar weight status, and mixed-weight couples often experience judgment, prejudice, and discrimination (Collisson et al., 2017). Thus, if the weight of one partner changes significantly, resulting in a noticeable disparity between body sizes, the couple may encounter a new and unexpected social stigma that may impact the relationship. However, a supportive marital relationship is associated with a healthier body weight in midlife and thus may serve as a protective factor for long-term health (Chen et al., 2018).

Gorin and her team were baffled by the reality that despite the evidence that the marital environment affects body weight, almost all weight loss programs continue to focus on the individual. Weight loss approaches that have included spouses are typically focused on one participant in a weight loss program, with the spouse along for the ride to support behavior change (Gorin et al., 2017; Gorin et al., 2019). Consequently, they developed and studied the program called Project TEAMS: Talking about Eating, Activity, and Mutual Support.

The study included 64 married couples, half in a behavior weight loss program and the other half learning about "autonomy-support" in the TEAMS method. The behavior weight loss program relied on directive support from the participants' partners; this included reminders regarding eating, not eating, or exercise. The autonomy-support group members, on the other hand, learned to ask what is helpful, respond with empathy to struggles and setbacks, and validate with respect one's partner's choices and attempts to change. Finding that autonomy-support was more effective than directive support, they concluded that it behooves couples therapists to introduce the concept of autonomy-support into work with couples around weight loss issues and, perhaps, around eating disorder issues as well (Gorin et al., 2019).

In a subsequent analysis of the data from the same study, Theodore Powers, Amy Gorin, and their associates (2022) found that autonomy-support not only benefited the partner wanting to lose weight, but also the partner providing the support. Both partners experienced improved weight-management outcomes and male support providers experienced enhanced relationship satisfaction.

Talea Cornelius at Columbia University and her associates (2018) studied the effect of psychoeducation regarding prescriptive support (directive support) versus indirect social control (autonomy support) on weight loss. Indirect social control (autonomy-support) by the partner was associated with greater weight loss (about 15 pounds), while pressure to change (directive support) by the partner resulted in no weight loss. They speculated that the stress induced by pressure from a spouse employing criticism or direct control offset any progress made in the direction of weight loss. Speculating that educating partners regarding how to deliver support could be a missing piece in weight-management approaches, they recommended further study of this concept.

Eating Disorder Generic

Integrated Eating Disorder Treatment for Couples (IEDT-C)

Melanie Linville and Nicole Oleksak of Oregon (2013) developed an approach to outpatient couples therapy called the integrated eating disorder treatment for couples (IEDT-C) that integrates work on behavior change with work on emotion regulation. In this method, the theory and techniques of solution-focused therapy (SFT) are combined with those of emotion-focused therapy (EFT). The goal of the treatment is to strengthen the attachment bonds in a couple in which one person is in eating disorder recovery. The developers of this approach noted that proponents of systemic thinking about eating disorders have moved away from viewing family dysfunction as a causal and significant, if not primary, maintaining factor of the problem to seeing the family as a resource that can help recovery.

Linville and Oleksak (2013) noted that UCAN for anorexia nervosa treatment is limited in effectiveness when clients have difficulty with emotion regulation, particularly when discussing topics related to sexuality or body image. As a result, they drew upon the resources of EFT to address attachment needs and regulate emotional distress. They also noted that CBT for couples speaks to communication skills but fails to address trauma that has impacted the relationship. Creating emotional safety within the couple system and strengthening the couple bond, thereby increasing security in the relationship, appears to enhance the eating disorder recovery process as does adding the focus on strengths and resources for change from SFT (Linville et al., 2015).

Acknowledging that attachment needs are often met through eating disorder thoughts and behaviors, IEDT-C therapists work to shift the attachment to the partner. This is not an insight-based model. Change is present-oriented in current interactions and present situations. When processing trauma, the focus is on the coping/ survival strategies used, not on the pain connected to the trauma. When applied to the eating disorder, the focus is more about the strengths the person in recovery has demonstrated rather than on the pain they have experienced. The couples therapist is viewed as a collaborator and validator with the therapy being client directed.

Feminist-Informed Emotionally Focused Couples Therapy (FI-EFCT) for Eating Disorders

Candace Maier of the University of Iowa (2015) also noted that despite the documented associations between relationship quality and eating disorders in the literature, few people had explored the treatment of eating disorders with couples therapy. Despite improved awareness of the increased incidence of eating disorders in men, the vast majority occur in women. For this reason, Maier (2015) felt strongly that viewing eating disorders through a feminist lens was essential, acknowledging that our patriarchal society has imposed a thin-ideal for women and has overemphasized women's appearance. Education about patriarchal messages that maintain eating disorder symptoms; the impact of mood swings; and the complex relationship between emotional distancing and shame, feeling fat, guilt, or engaging in bulimic behaviors is beneficial. FI-EFCT emphasizes maintaining factors that support eating disorder symptoms using a systemic, experiential approach to therapy while acknowledging that women with eating disorders are likely to have insecure or anxious attachments to parental figures that may make closeness to a partner challenging (Linville & Oleksak, 2013; Maier, 2015).

The effectiveness of this therapy depends upon the eating disorder partner's willingness to talk about her eating disorder and the couple's willingness to explore sociocultural variables that encourage weight loss and body-control strategies. Maier recommended that there be a randomized clinical trial of FI-EFT to determine if the treatment helps reduce eating disorder behaviors.

What Does This All Mean and How Is Gottman-RED Different?

The implications of this review of the literature regarding relationships with eating disorders and couples therapy are summarized here:

1. Eating disorders affect both men and women.
2. Eating disorders affect people of all ages, including those in midlife or beyond.
3. The vast majority of people with eating disorders are in romantic relationships.
4. Most people with eating disorders are not dangerously thin.
5. It may be through couples rather than individual therapy that men take first steps toward getting the help they need for eating-, exercise-, or weight-related issues.
6. People from collectivist cultures or groups that stigmatize mental illness may find a couples approach more acceptable than individual therapy.
7. Marital stress often increases food-related behaviors and vice versa.
8. Although they may become maintaining factors, interactions between partners in relationships with eating disorders are not believed to be causal.
9. The search for an effective therapy for relationships with eating disorders has begun but is in its infancy.
10. Eating disorder professionals are confused about, but not opposed to, integrating couples therapy into treatment proto-

cols; thus, education and promotion of this valuable addition to current treatment approaches is necessary.

The seven couples therapies developed to date all have value. Time will tell which will make a significant difference for people with eating disorders and their partners. Now, added to the list is Gottman-RED couples therapy. Unlike UCAN, SCT for anorexia nervosa, UNITE-BED, CBT for BED, and TEAMS, but akin to IEDT-C and feminist informed EFCT, the Gottman-RED therapy interventions are transdiagnostic. However, they are not only transdiagnostic, but also flexible and adaptable enough that they can be incorporated into any of the other therapies. For example, our couple Amy and John might have sought out UCAN for help with anorexic symptoms, completed the program, and then, with guidance from their therapist, added several of the Gottman-RED interventions to further improve their relationship. Similarly, Ezra and Abe might benefit from SCT for anorexia nervosa and enhance their treatment with interventions from Gottman-RED couples therapy. Demarcus and Quisha might have tried UNITE-BED or TEAMS, then followed these programs with Gottman-RED. Longer term couples therapies like IEDT-C might work for Carmen and Luciano. In this case, Gottman-RED interventions would be incorporated into the therapy over time. The interventions can also supplement couples therapies focused on improving the relationship but not specifically addressing eating disorder issues, such as Gottman method couples therapy, emotionally focused couples therapy, or cognitive behavioral couples therapy.

Gottman-RED differs from the seven therapies reviewed in another critical way. Gottman-RED considers the journey of the partner of the person with the eating disorder to be equally as important as that of the identified patient. Thus, the primary measures of success of the therapy are improvement in quality of life for *both* partners, however they define that to be; improved communication regarding the needs of both members of the couple; and more effective conflict management for the relationship, both in general and regarding eating or weight issues in specific. If remission or partial remission of eating disorder symptoms results, so much the better. The interventions are constructed with this perspective in mind.

In all their books about couples, John and Julie Gottman have stressed how in loving, lasting relationships, both partners take the time to understand the inner world of the other before attempting problem solving. In fact, after 45 years of research, they felt so strongly about this principle that they wrote a book, *Eight Dates,* in which they prescribed eight conversations designed to deepen each partner's understanding of the other (not solution seeking) regarding sensitive topics (Gottman et al., 2019). Time and again, in workshops and in writings, they have repeated the mantra "understanding before problem solving." Seeking to understand helps build trust, commitment, and friendship, making the effective management of conflict possible. In the throes of an argument or when immersed in a crisis, this idea often flies out the window and one or both partners enter problem-solving mode, to the detriment of the closeness in the relationship.

Strangely enough, this principle of understanding preceding problem solving often flies out of the window for relationship therapists as well. Therapists are helpers. It is what we do, and even though we know better, we often measure our effectiveness by the relational stability of our couples. When the relationship is rocky, we are vulnerable to jumping into problem-solving mode and sometimes even tell our couples what to do. This is particularly true when a relationship is really struggling or when a partner relapses. Understanding the perspectives of both partners in a relationship where one has an eating disorder is foundational for effective couples therapy. Much attention in the literature has been given to the thought processes and needs of the person with the eating disorder, but relatively little to the thought processes and needs of the non-eating disorder partner. In this next chapter, we will seek to better understand this relatively neglected partner's perspective before learning about a therapy intended to help both partners improve their relationship.

3

The Non-Eating Disorder Partner Experience

Quisha walked into the TV room waving a piece of paper, a scowl on her face. She stared at Demarcus, who was sitting on the couch watching TV with their son, Tyler.

"What is it now?" Demarcus asked, knowing by her expression that he had done something that upset her.

"Look at this bill!" Quisha's voice was rising.

"Go hang out with your sister now, Tyler. Your mom and I are having a conversation." Tyler got up and gladly left the room. He knew what was coming.

"We cannot afford this, Demarcus! Ten fast food charges on this bill, plus takeout!" Quisha was yelling now.

"You know I can cover it. I am making good money, so what is the big deal?" Demarcus retorted. He had recently been hired as assistant football coach for the nearby major university.

"That's not the point! We need that money for other things, like Tyler's school," Quisha replied.

"You promised me you were not going to get any more fast food. Your words mean nothing!"

"I'm sorry, Quish. I don't know what's wrong with me. I meant what I said. It's like the car just went there on its own."

"Well, we don't have one of those self-driving cars! I am sick of this, Demarcus. Things need to change. I am getting migraines from the stress of it all." Quisha, on the verge of tears, quickly left the room before she started sobbing.

Demarcus could hear her crying in the kitchen.

He just sat there, confused, feeling ashamed and defeated. He knew she was right. He needed to stop the binges, but no matter how hard he tried, he could not do it for more than a few days. Every night, he resolved to have a "good" day the next day, but, more often than not, by the late afternoon he would start eating; and once he started, he could not stop.

Quisha wished she could be totally honest with Demarcus about how this was affecting her, but every time she tried, they ended up in a fight. The amount of stress she had experienced since marrying him was taking a toll on her mental and physical health, plus she was going to the casino more often and knew this was not good.

People in eating disorder recovery have repeatedly noted that the presence of a supportive partner is an important, if not *the* most important, variable that impacts recovery. However, as desirable as that may sound, the magnetic pull of the eating disorder behaviors in a direction away from intimacy complicates this connection. Way back in 1991, Geneen Roth wrote a bestselling book titled *When Food is Love*. It was clear that she understood this ambivalence when she wrote, "I thought I wanted to be thin; I discovered that what I wanted was to be invulnerable . . . . I didn't know how to engage myself deeply with a person, only with food . . . . Food was my lover for seventeen years and it demanded nothing of me. Which was exactly the way I wanted it" (p. 2). Roth went on to explain how her behaviors that consisted of binge eating and dieting and losing weight and gaining it back created drama and emotion that was absorbing and exciting, so absorbing that another human being did not, or maybe could not, get emotionally close to her. Many people who develop eating disorders enter relationships desiring closeness and connection yet have no clue how to build this kind of relationship. Having little or no experience in managing conflict, they also tend to be conflict avoidant, which limits intimacy (Blok, 2002). These tendencies, combined with the rigidity, unpredictability, up-and-down nature, peculiarity, and intractability of the eating disorder behaviors affect the partner in a way that makes connection difficult and, at times, downright impossible.

The couples therapist must maintain a neutral stance even when it would be tempting to take the side of one partner or the other. Understanding the non-eating disorder partner's viewpoint makes it possible for the couples therapist to facilitate conversation, to assist with conflict management, and to maintain objectivity.

There is an overwhelming amount of material written and posted about the eating disorder experience from the perspective of those who currently have or have had an eating disorder and the professionals who treat them. There is relatively little content focused on the experience of the non-eating disorder partner. The Gottman-RED couples therapist needs to understand not only the basics about an eating disorder and the fundamentals of a healthy relationship, but also the layers of complexity in a relationship when one person has a chronic mental health disorder as serious as an eating disorder. Learning about the non-eating disorder partner experience will equip the couples therapist and enhance their effectiveness. Remember, understanding precedes problem solving both for couples and for therapists.

The Non-Eating Disorder Partner Experience

Let us look more closely at the non-eating disorder partner experience in each of our four couples.

Luciano is totally confused and frustrated. He has no idea what an eating disorder is or what the implications are for their relationship. Abe knows enough about eating disorders to know that persistent restriction and weight loss is serious and that help is needed, but has minimal understanding of the long-term potential impact on a relationship or of how to be supportive. Quisha does not realize that Demarcus has an eating disorder. In fact, she has never heard of a man having an eating disorder. She attributes his overeating and weight gain to lack of self-control and laziness. John knows quite a bit about eating disorders since his sister has one, but Amy's rationalizations for her behaviors and low weight are so convincing that he questions his own better judgment. He has an inkling that being the partner of someone with an eating disorder is very different from being the brother, but he is not quite sure how.

The partner of someone with an eating disorder is given the opportunity to learn about a syndrome that for many, like Luciano, Abe, and Quisha, is uncharted territory. An attitude of curiosity rather than judgment is an asset, with open-mindedness being the golden ticket to a better relationship. Prior to entering a relationship with someone with an eating disorder, it is likely that most non-eating disorder partners had minimal understanding of eating disorders, perhaps breezing through a chapter about them in a general psych textbook or occasionally hearing about them on social media or the news. Like most people, they may have been judgmental of the behaviors, or even repulsed by some of them, mistakenly assuming they were about losing weight, looking a certain way, lack of self-control, or keeping up with media influencers or celebrities. As the relationship progresses, partners become increasingly aware of the complexity of these enigmatic mental disorders and, hopefully, develop empathy for their partner's struggles and pain.

Being in a relationship with someone with an eating disorder is like joining with someone who is a foreign correspondent. As a partner, you have three choices: staying home while letting them travel alone, traveling with them without learning about the culture or speaking the language, or taking trips with your partner and being committed to learning about the culture and the language. Clearly, the last option increases the likelihood that the relationship will thrive.

Partners of people with eating disorders may experience a roller coaster ride of emotions due to the complexity and unpredictability of the disorders. This smorgasbord of feelings includes fear of long-term dependency, confusion about deception, loneliness when pushed away, anxiety about physical health consequences, sadness and grief due to lost opportunities, joy when steps are made toward recovery, disappointment during periods of lapse or relapse, happiness when treatment ends, frustration if it again becomes necessary, guilt and self-blame, or anger at manipulation, secrecy, or deceit (Bulik et al., 2012; Chen & Kaye, 2018; Highet et al., 2005; Schmit & Bell, 2017). Recovery is a long-term proposition that, for most, takes years, not months.

Many non-eating disorder partners feel drained and less hopeful as time goes on, feeling more powerless and inadequate when recovery spans years (Chen & Kaye, 2018; Highet et al., 2005). In addition, the toll on the non-eating disorder partner is moderated by the type of eating disorder, the severity of the behaviors, and the stage of recovery. Thus, the frequently neglected mental and physical health of the non-eating disorder partner that is often sacrificed while attending to the needs of the person with the eating disorder must be monitored as well. The Gottman-RED couples therapist may be the only professional to have any consistent contact with the non-eating disorder partner, and so needs to be vigilant, watching for signs that this partner might benefit from individual therapy in addition to the couples therapy.

In this chapter we will view the relationship through the lens of the non-eating disorder partner with regard to burden, exclusion, and stages of growth.

Burden

Burden can be thought of as the weight of responsibility carried by the partner of someone with a mental health disorder (Perkins et al., 2004). When a couple comes for Gottman-RED couples therapy, the couples therapist will assess and monitor the level of burden felt by the non-eating disorder partner. Since burden develops over time, the non-eating disorder partner may or may not feel burden at the beginning of the therapy.

Quisha is feeling burden. Demarcus's issues with food have lasted long enough to have emotional and physical ramifications. Some couples I see in my practice come for therapy after being married for more than 25 years and one of the partners has struggled with food, weight, or body image issues for all that time. In some cases, they never talked about the impact of these issues until they started Gottman-RED couples therapy. They are tired, not of each other, but of the persistent presence of the eating issues.

There are two types of burden: subjective and objective (Perkins et al., 2004).

SUBJECTIVE BURDEN. *Subjective burden* refers to the extent to which the non-eating disorder partner feels like they are carrying a heavy load. Subjective burden encompasses economic burden, the worry about financial security due to the actual or potential cost of eating disorder treatment. Nicole Highet and her associates in Australia (2004) launched a study of people caring for someone with anorexia nervosa or bulimia nervosa and found subjective burden to be higher than objective burden, particularly when helping someone with anorexia nervosa. Some partners felt they could no longer cope with the burden, with mealtimes and food-related activities being particularly challenging. Fear of long-term dependency was reported as the most distressing part of the experience. Eating disorders are among the top 15 causes of nonfatal disability in girls and women (Highet et al., 2005); consequently, the risk of physical consequences for the person with the disorder that would significantly impact the non-eating disorder partner as well is real. Dramatic changes in levels of sexual and emotional intimacy take a huge toll, with non-eating disorder partners questioning the viability of the relationship while, at the same time, feeling that it would be wrong to leave a relationship when someone is struggling with an illness. The decrease in social interaction due to the strong need to control food and exercise placed an additional strain on the relationship. Needless to say, the mental health of the non-eating disorder partner was negatively impacted (Highet et al., 2005).

Quisha is experiencing subjective burden and both John and Abe are feeling a twinge of worry about subjective burden in the future if their partner's health does not improve. Carmen is high functioning despite her eating issues, so it is unlikely that Luciano will experience subjective burden.

Eating disorder treatment can be very expensive. (Bulik et al., 2012; Linville & Oleksak, 2013; Watson & Bulik, 2013). Fortunately, many people can use insurance to cover a portion of the cost. Even so, the cost for a 30-day stay in a treatment facility averages about $30,000, with many people needing 3–6 months of care or more. Luxury treatment centers can cost up to $80,000 per month for individual care in a spa-like environment. This cost does not include ongoing outpatient therapy following residential, partial hospitalization, or intensive outpatient care. Typically, treatment for anorexia nervosa, in particular, has a chronic course with relapse common for 35–42% within the first 18 months following discharge from a treatment facility (Bulik et al., 2012). Readmissions increase the financial burden. Needless to say, the cost of treatment significantly affects the finances of a couple and is a potential source of tension and stress (Linville et al., 2015).

> *While none of our couples are in this situation at the start of couples therapy, there is the possibility that Carmen, Ezra, or Amy could need to go to a treatment facility while in couples therapy. Demarcus, although likely to benefit from treatment, is less likely to find a place that accommodates the needs of a middle-aged man with binge eating disorder.*

OBJECTIVE BURDEN. *Objective burden* refers to the disruption in the partner's life due to the person with the eating disorder's condition. These disruptions may include hiding food, buying particular foods, reduction in income during the time the partner with the eating disorder is in treatment, limited choices for eating out, not eating meals together, having to prepare separate menus, diminished sexual desire or frequency, financial strain due to buying food, rigid rituals around eating and food preparation interfering with plans, excessive or obsessive exercise, concerns related to body image, limitations on activities due to physical consequences of the eating behaviors, or lost opportunities for socializing with others.

> *All four partners in the couples we are following are experiencing objective burden. Luciano is getting tired of reassuring Carmen that she is not fat, waiting for her to come out of the bathroom, being confused by the lack of sex, going to the refrigerator for food he wants to eat only to find that it is not there, and discovering*

evidence of vomiting in the house. Abe is frustrated by the lim-
ited options of restaurants when eating out, Ezra's rigidity around
exercise, and the need for separate home-cooked meals even when
eating together. Quisha is overwhelmed by the financial strain, the
constant preoccupation with food and eating, the food wrappers in
the car and TV room, and the inability of Demarcus to help around
the house due to his size and health. John is losing patience with
Amy's chewing and spitting her food, the increasingly restricted list
of acceptable foods, the expense of the specialty foods and supple-
ments, the rigidity around exercise and how it affects their time
together, the disruption to their sex life, and the possibility that they
will not be able to have children together.

Sarah Perkins and her colleagues at the Institute of Psychiatry in
London (2004) noted that although there had been many studies
about the impact of caring for individuals with mental disorders,
there was very little research about the impact of caring for someone with an eating disorder. They interviewed 20 people in a relationship with a person with bulimia nervosa and found that they
experienced considerable distress. Among the non-eating disorder
partners they interviewed, common experiences included worry
about doing or saying the wrong thing; tiring of constantly encouraging and building up the person with the eating disorder; concern
about neglecting the needs of other family members; stress at mealtimes about deciding what to eat; and feeling powerless to help.

Samantha Schmit and Nancy Bell of Texas (2017) focused
specifically on non-eating disorder partner perspectives. They
interviewed 12 partners (10 men and 2 women) of people with disordered eating, 6 of whom had initiated recovery and 6 of whom
had not. Prior to the relationship, all had minimal understanding
of eating disorders and had no idea how serious they could be yet
did not reach out for information, feeling embarrassed, reluctant,
and even reticent to talk to anyone about the situation. As in other
studies, these partners were significantly impacted by the secrecy
that limited conversations about the eating disorder and the social
isolation from family and friends that resulted from these behaviors. Alone with their own feelings of fear of health consequences,

worry, frustration, and confusion, they were continually anxious, walking on eggshells, concerned they were doing more harm than good by saying or doing the wrong thing. If the person with the eating disorder initiated recovery, partner reactions ranged from feeling relieved to feeling responsible to make sure their partner kept moving toward health (Schmit & Bell, 2017).

Exclusion

Feeling excluded is painful and lonely for the non-eating disorder partner whether it be exclusion from their partner's eating disorder thoughts, feelings, and behaviors; exclusion from treatment and information; or both.

SECRECY. Of all the challenges faced by the non-eating disorder partner, the most damaging to the relationship is the trust shattering secrecy and deception; however, secrecy, deception, lying, and manipulation related to eating disorder behaviors is commonplace, regardless of diagnosis (Bulik et al., 2012; Gorin et al., 2002; Huke & Slade, 2006; Kirby et al., 2016; Perkins et al., 2004; Schmit & Bell, 2017). The reason for withholding information from a partner varies and may not be the same from person to person. Our four couples illustrate this point.

Carmen hides her behaviors from Luciano because of shame and dread of his criticisms. She hides her thoughts from Luciano because she is not ready to give up her eating behaviors and fears he will leave her if she reveals that truth. Ezra did not hide his behaviors from Abe when they first met but is starting to become more secretive as Abe expresses concern and is pushing for treatment. Ezra's intense terror of gaining weight drives him to go underground with his behaviors in order to lessen Abe's concern and vigilance. Demarcus fears Quisha's disapproval. He feels guilty about breaking promises to Quisha and hides his behaviors to avoid disappointing her and to avoid conflict. Amy is secretive because she knows how important it is to John to have a baby and understands that her fear of weight gain makes getting pregnant difficult and prevents her from seeking fertility treatment. Consequently, she does not want him to see her when she is doing things that will result in weight loss. Amy hates disappointing John, has a hard time not being a perfect wife, and is terrified of the conversations that follow any time he sees her engage in an eating disorder behavior. Unfortunately, this secrecy and deception create a wedge between the two partners, weakening the friendship and leaving both lonely and longing for more emotional connection.

When the person with the eating disorder subsequently uses eating disorder behaviors to cope with feelings of loneliness in their relationship and/or to meet attachment needs, the desperation to use behaviors fuels the deception and secrecy. When the non-eating disorder partner "discovers" that the partner with the eating issues has been using certain behaviors, they end up feeling frustrated, disconnected, and overwhelmed (Linville et al., 2015). It is the shame regarding the eating disorder behaviors or the embarrassment from breaking promises to the non-eating disorder partner to cease certain eating disorder behaviors that frequently underlies the secrecy (Maier, 2015). Unfortunately, this shame is compounded by the impact of the deception on the partner, who, feeling deceived and betrayed, becomes angry and upset, leading to conflict and distance in the relationship (Arcelus et al., 2012; Bulik et al., 2012). The person with the eating disorder then reaches for eating disorder behaviors to cope with the conflict and distance, and the couple is off to the races; a vicious cycle has begun.

Amy froze. She knew what was coming. It was too late to hide. The sequence of events that had just occurred was so unlikely. What were the chances? Amy was reminded of the game Mousetrap she played as a kid.

They were eating dinner at the table. John went to get matches to light the candles. When he sat back down, he knocked over his water glass. Fortunately, there was just a little water in it. When he reached for the napkin to mop up the water, his fork, that was still on the napkin, landed precariously on the edge of the table. When he finished mopping the water and sat back down, his elbow bumped the fork and it fell on the floor, landing under the table. He had to crawl under the table to pick it up and happened to glance at Amy's lap . . . . A mound of food-soaked napkins were piled there. Their dog, Scruffy, was lying next to her chair, licking his lips and waiting. When John got back up to his chair, he stared at Amy, a disgusted look on his face. She knew what was coming. "What are you doing?" he stammered.

"What do you mean?" Amy was shaking, but her voice was calm. She had years of practice.

"I thought you told me you didn't do that anymore." John's tone was accusing and angry. He was referring to chewing and spitting her food into a napkin or feeding it to the dog.

"I don't." She lied to hide her shame. Being caught in the act of sneaking a behavior was humiliating. She feared John would be disappointed in her and she hated that. Their conversation right before dinner had been tense and, somehow, this behavior was soothing at times like these, but she knew John would never comprehend that.

"Then what is that pile of tissues on your lap? And why is Scruffy over there by you?"

"It's my napkin—just leave me alone." She stood up, the wad of paper in her hand, and left the table. "I'm not hungry anymore." Scruffy followed, looking up at her with hopeful eyes.

"I don't know what do to, Amy. I can't help you if you aren't honest with me about what is going on."

"I don't want your help, John. I just want you to understand. You just don't get it!"

John sat at the table, shaking his head. He knew he shouldn't have gotten angry, but he felt so frustrated. Not only did the secrecy bother him, but the behavior itself was hard for him to stomach. Now, she wasn't going to finish her dinner. That scared him. Her weight was way too low already. He felt helpless, so he filled his wine glass and drained it as if he were taking a shot of whisky, then poured another.

Secrecy can obscure the reality of the seriousness of the eating disorder, keeping it out of view, creating the illusion that things are better than they are, and giving the couple a break from thinking about the challenges that they face. Regardless of the reason, the cloud of secrecy complicates efforts by a couple to work together to address eating disorder–related issues (Gorin et al., 2002; Kirby et al., 2016; Reiff & Reiff, 1999).

As noted by Cynthia Bulik and her associates (2012), couples therapy allows the cards of the eating disorder to be laid on the table, so that it is no longer "a solitary and secretive disorder" (Kirby et al., 2016, p. 242). It teaches couples to have conversations about eating-related issues characterized by listening, validation, and empathy, rather than by the Gottman Four Horsemen of criticism, contempt, defensiveness, or stonewalling (Gottman & Gottman, 2018). The couple practices in the presence of the Gottman-RED couples therapist until they are ready to have these conversations on their own.

EXCLUSION FROM TREATMENT. Although serving an essential role in providing support and care, many non-eating disorder partners felt their distress was exacerbated when treatment professionals excluded them from discussions about progress and treatment planning for the partner with the eating disorder (Bulik et al., 2012; Highet et al., 2005; Linville et al., 2015; Winn et al., 2004). This lack of inclusion, coupled with the unspoken implication that talking about the eating disorder was off-limits, potentially silenced non-eating disorder partners and unwittingly contributed to maintaining the eating disorder.

Traditional approaches to eating disorder recovery involve hospitalization, partial hospitalization, or residential or intensive outpatient treatment in a program, followed by outpatient group and/or individual therapy, where, in the name of confidentiality and HIPPA, nothing is shared with the non-eating disorder partner unless the person with the eating disorder signs a release of information (ROI). Partners are included in family weeks, specific days when spouses are invited to participate in psychoeducation sessions and therapy but are not privy to what has been addressed in individual or group therapy sessions regarding things like changes in weight, dietary or exercise recommendations, or meal planning unless the person with the eating disorder shares this with them (Bulik et al., 2012). Lacking information, the non-eating disorder partner lacks confidence when talking about the eating disorder behaviors and often stays silent. The risk inherent in this situation is that the eating disorder "mutes them and rules the relationship" (Bulik, 2012, p. 25). Although confidentiality and privacy are to be respected, there may be a middle ground that allows non-eating disorder partners to learn enough to avoid unrealistic expectations by better understanding the etiology of eating disorders as well as the "three steps forward, two steps backward" nature of recovery (Bulik et al., 2012).

> *Carmen and Luciano were on the waiting list for couples therapy. All along, Carmen had been in individual therapy with Dr. Foster and, unbeknownst to Luciano, had been attending eating disorder group therapy as well. One night, Luciano surprised Carmen by saying, "Hey, have you told Dr. Foster about your eating problem?"*
>
> *"Yeah, she knows."*
>
> *"What did she tell you to do?"*
>
> *"Nothing."*
>
> *"Nothing? We are paying her all this money and she tells you nothing?" Luciano was feeling frustrated. This was the second time he had gone to the cabinet for a few chocolate chip cookies, only to find there was only one left in the entire bag.*
>
> *"That's not what I talk to her about."*
>
> *"Well, what **do** you talk to her about?"*
>
> *"I don't want to talk about it."*
>
> *"Great," Luciano sighed. "Well, I am going to call her next week. I need to know what is going on."*
>
> *"Stay out of my treatment, Luciano. I haven't signed a release so she can't tell you anything." Carmen felt scared, just like she did as a teenager when her mother wanted to talk to her therapist. She wanted to feel on the same team with Luciano, but in this moment, she felt like they were on opposite sides and that she was playing defense.*
>
> *"Well, how am I supposed to know what to do? Everything I*

say is wrong. This isn't just about you, Carmen. I feel like I am going crazy."

"Just wait for the couples therapy, OK?" Carmen snapped back at him as she left the room in a huff.

Gottman-RED and other approaches to couples therapy for people with eating disorders bring the partner into the inner circle and facilitate communication about the eating disorder and its impact on the relationship. It is the job of the therapist to create a safe space for couples to talk about these sensitive issues that potentially trigger deep feelings of shame or guilt.

LACK OF ACCESS TO CREDIBLE INFORMATION. Partners are typically confused about the etiology and treatment of eating disorders. As already mentioned, most partners lack knowledge about eating disorders prior to the relationship. As they learn more, there is a slowly growing realization of the magnitude and gravity of the problem (Schmit & Bell, 2017). It is very hard for someone who has never had an eating disorder to understand why a person cannot simply stop certain behaviors and modify others if they just put their mind to it (Kirby et al., 2016). As a result, most partners are highly motivated and desire to learn more about their partner's eating disorder. Unfortunately, they often experience frustration in determining which sources are reliable or credible especially with the vast array of online information, what their own role is in the recovery process, what recovery entails, and signs of lapse or relapse (Arcelus et al., 2012; Huke & Slade, 2006; Linville et al., 2015; Schmit & Bell, 2017). They likely also desire information detailing different treatment approaches (Winn et al., 2004), support groups, and services they can access to address their own mental health needs (Highet et al., 2005). Information about couples therapy for people with eating disorders is scarce since so few professionals currently specialize in this aspect of treatment.

Burden and exclusion engender a myriad of emotions in the non-eating disorder partner and are very challenging. Some, like Amy's first husband, will choose to leave the relationship. Those who are committed to the relationship will stay and find that they move through a series of predictable stages.

Stages of Growth Experienced by Non-Eating Disorder Partners

Partners of people with eating disorders or disordered eating issues are often very successful in their careers and/or excel athletically, so expect that they should be a recovery partner superstar as well. Most have high expectations of themselves and may even be perfectionistic. Understanding and absorbing the implications of an eating disorder disclosure or diagnosis is a process that takes time. Learning how to talk about very sensitive, food-related issues in a way that promotes closeness rather than distance is a skill that takes practice, persistence, and patience. Seeking professional help is an indicator of wisdom, not failure.

There are six stages non-eating disorder partners move through after learning that their partner has an eating disorder as they process their feelings and consider the implications of this reality for their future and the future of the relationship (Reiff & Reiff, 1999). It usually takes the non-eating disorder partner from one to three years to move through these stages.

Stage 1: Denial

Denial is real. Denial occurs regardless of how the person learns about the eating disorder. Sometimes the non-eating disorder partner suspects their partner of having an eating disorder and introduces the idea; other times, the person with the eating disorder initiates the conversation and confides in their partner about the problem. It makes no difference. Denial is the first stage. Denial is a complex phenomenon. It is thought to be an unconscious process that serves as a wall of protection, shielding a person from a reality they fear or are emotionally unprepared to face. Denial can be frustrating for the person with the eating disorder because it may seem like their partner does not take their eating problem seriously enough; the person with the eating disorder may not realize that their partner's minimizing the severity of the problem is a form of denial. The rate at which denial fades depends upon the non-eating disorder partner's self-esteem, self-awareness, emotional safety, and emotional stability.

When a person in a relationship has an eating disorder, denial may take one of two forms. In the first, either partner or both can be in denial that one or both has an eating disorder. When this occurs, it will take time before the wall of denial is pierced. Eventually, both will be able to come to terms with the reality, but it probably will not be at the same time or in the same way. When denial takes this form, it is doubtful that a Gottman-RED couples therapist will come in contact with the couple, as the need for couples therapy to help with eating disorder–related issues will remain unrecognized until both partners are no longer in denial.

The other form of denial is denial that addressing issues in the relationship will help with recovery or improve the quality of life for both partners. When this wall of denial breaks down, the couple is likely to reach out for help and be open to relationship therapy.

Even after a non-eating disorder partner is no longer in denial and accepts that their partner has an eating disorder, they may simply be ignorant of the fact that the disordered eating usually indicates significant emotional problems. When this reality sinks in, the non-eating disorder partner, acting out of fear, ignorance, and panic, tries to problem solve, fix things, and make the behaviors stop.

Stage 2: Fear, Ignorance, and Panic

Fear, ignorance, and panic are a potentially dangerous combination. These emotions create a sense of urgency that often propels the non-eating disorder partner into problem-solving mode, vacillating between desperate attempts to control and self-sacrificing accommodation: they typically want to help but are often unsure what to do (Baucom et al., 2017; Schmit & Bell, 2017). Witnessing the devastating effects on one's partner of starvation, binge eating, or binge eating followed by purging while feeling powerless to do anything about these dire consequences has a significant psychological impact on the non-eating disorder partner. These feelings of helplessness and hopelessness are exacerbated when there is comorbid alcohol use, drug abuse, and/or self-harm (Highet et al., 2005; Huke & Slade, 2006; Winn et al., 2004). Despite persistent efforts to help, partners sometimes question if they are hindering recovery when they do not see the person with the eating disorder getting better (Schmit & Bell, 2017).

CONTROL: WHY CAN'T YOU JUST STOP? With the best of intentions, non-eating disorder partners will employ a wide variety of tactics to change or control eating disorder behaviors, unaware that they may be doing more harm than good. When efforts do not produce changes, non-eating disorder partners may intensify their efforts, responding to the continuation of behaviors with anger, condemnation, or even more suggestions for change, thereby exacerbating the problem. What one would do based upon common sense rarely works (e.g., stopping someone who wants to throw up from entering the bathroom, hiding all binge foods, sneaking higher calorie foods into the dinner, throwing away boxes of laxatives, disposing of the scale), but instead engenders a rebellious, resentful attitude on the part of the person with the eating disorder.

> *Ezra felt frantic. "They have got to be here," he thought. "I put them in this drawer last night." But they weren't there. He feverishly rummaged through that drawer and the other two drawers in the cabinet. No sign of them. "Maybe Abe put them somewhere."*
>
> *Ezra raced downstairs and found Abe making coffee in the kitchen. "Abe, have you seen my laxatives?"*
>
> *Abe startled and spilled some coffee on the counter. While wiping it up, he cringed inside, then answered, "Yes. I threw them away."*
>
> *Ezra just stared at him. "What? You threw them away? Why?"*
>
> *Abe replied, "Because I am worried about you, and they are bad for you. Why can't you just stop?"*
>
> *Ezra was shocked. Abe had never done something like this before. All he could articulate was, "Don't ever do that again!"*
>
> *Abe just stared at him. He didn't know what to say next.*

Ezra walked toward his car. As he drove to the drugstore, his desperation to get there as fast as possible resulted in him driving way over the speed limit. He was focused on identifying the best hiding place he could so that Abe would not find the laxatives next time. He missed the police car parked, waiting on the side of the road and recording his speed, until it was too late.

Other common controlling responses include logical reasoning about eating behaviors, forcing the partner into treatment, becoming angry, nagging, shaming, or being critical of the behaviors. These responses, like Abe's, typically backfire, creating distance in the relationship. Sometimes issues of control surface with the person with the eating disorder clinging more tightly to their behaviors. The question, "Why can't you just stop?" circulates unspoken and unanswered in the air, like a moth circling a flame.

Monitoring the behaviors of the person with the eating disorder—in essence, being the "food police"—has negative consequences for the relationship. However, partners may feel responsible for making sure eating disorder recovery happens, even if they know that this sense of responsibility is not realistic (Schmit & Bell, 2017). When the spotlight is turned on them, non-eating disorder partners have reported feeling pressure, often self-imposed, to model healthy behaviors by eating regularly, not skipping meals, regularly exercising, matching their partner's portion sizes, and avoiding dieting or food restriction (Linville et al., 2015; Schmit & Bell, 2017).

At this point, there is minimal understanding by the non-eating disorder partner of the psychological, relational, or emotional functions of the behaviors. From the outside, it looks like their partner either lacks discipline in eating, is simply trying to lose too much weight, or is being obstinate. The irrationality of the eating disorder behaviors becomes extremely frustrating to an outside observer who thinks the problem is all about food or weight. Often, the person with the eating issues has limited insight into why they are doing what they are doing or why they cannot stop, and so they cannot explain it. Most have tried to stop many times without success.

Even if the non-eating disorder partner comes to the realization that there is no magic bullet for recovery from an eating disorder, they may keep trying to fix things, believing if they just say or do the right thing, their partner will be able to magically stop their behaviors. It is a pattern analogous to the pursuer-distancer pattern that often occurs during conflict in which the pursuer keeps talking and asking questions when the distancer shuts down emotionally, sometimes following them from room to room, hoping that if they just say the right thing, the distancer will come closer again emotionally and connection will be restored. Both of these patterns, so easy to fall into and so hard to stop once they have started, only make things worse in a relationship.

ACCOMMODATION. Resignation to the reality that the behaviors are not going to stop overnight often leads to accommodation. Once a pattern of accommodation starts, it is difficult to change. Common ways of accommodating include eating separately, only going to restaurants the eating disorder partner likes, letting the eating disorder partner choose the food to be prepared, secretly snacking, not buying desserts or snacks, allowing the eating disorder partner to control what foods are brought into the home, eating what the eating disorder partner specifies, eating according to the eating disorder partner's schedule, leaving the house so the eating disorder partner can binge, or going along with the eating disorder partner's diet. Some non-eating disorder partners, in an effort to help recovery or decrease conflict, have sacrificed their own health, gaining weight by eating with the person who needs to gain weight, succumbing to pressure to eat foods prepared by the person with the eating disorder even when not hungry, or discontinuing exercise if their partner cannot exercise. Accommodation by the non-eating disorder partner is understandable but, in the long run, perpetuates the eating disorder by allowing the eating disorder partner to comfortably continue their behaviors or view them as normalized while oblivious to the fact that they may be negatively impacting the health of the non-eating disorder partner. This only fuels resentment in the non-eating disorder partner.

Stage 3: Increasing Realization of the Psychological Basis for the Eating Disorder

As non-eating disorder partners understand more about the psychological aspects of the eating disorder, some begin to question if they might have had a role in the development or maintenance of the eating disorder (more about this in Chapter 4). If the non-eating disorder partner feels guilty, the guilt feelings may motivate efforts to help the eating disorder partner recover. Healing requires letting go of the need to find someone to blame and focusing instead on understanding the process of recovery. As non-eating disorder partners learn more about eating issues, there is a growing realization that there is no quick fix and that recovery is a long-term proposition. Issues that are complex and take time to resolve such as perfectionism, low self-esteem, unresolved grief, childhood trauma, the relentless pursuit of thinness, or the overvaluation of weight and shape and its control greatly impact the rate of recovery (Fairburn, 2008; Reiff & Reiff, 1999).

Non-eating disorder partners need to learn how to create a safe environment where their partner can talk openly about their eating disorder and practice appropriate responses to food- and weight-related behaviors. One of the most challenging things for partners to do is refrain from commenting on weight or looks, about the person with the eating disorder or anyone else. This means not even saying "you look good" if their partner who is too thin has gained weight or if their partner who is on a diet has lost weight. Rachel Calogero at the University of Kent and her colleagues at the University of South Florida (2009) recognized that little was known about the impact of compliments about appearance, so they asked 220 college women. What they found is that appearance compliments, a phenomenon they named complimentary weightism, offered with the motivation to affirm can have detrimental consequences for women's self-objectification and body image. They concluded it is better to say nothing at all about changes in appearance. It is not the compliment itself that is the problem; rather, it is the way it reminds the receiver that others are noticing or evaluating their appearance. For some with binge eating disorder who have lost weight, a comment can trigger resumption of binge eating and weight gain. For others with anorexia nervosa working on weight gain, a comment can trigger restriction and weight loss. Thus, to err on the side of caution, it is advised that non-eating disorder partners cease making any comments about changes in appearance of the eating disorder partner, themselves, or anyone else.

Stage 4: Impatience/Despair

The initial surge of hope experienced by the non-eating disorder partner when the couple decides to work together toward recovery may begin to fade when progress treads water. The realization that the eating disorder overshadows everything, draining time and energy away from the relationship while being all-consuming in the life of their partner, can be overwhelming for the non-eating disorder partner and evoke feelings of despair (Highet et al., 2005). Dreams and hopes for the future may feel squashed.

The frustrations and sense of powerlessness experienced by the non-eating disorder partner often lead to feelings of impatience and anger at the person with the eating disorder that may be expressed indirectly through emotional distance, detachment, absorption in work or other activities, or turning toward another person for emotional connection or support. According to a study by Reiff and Reiff (1999), the most common reasons included the dishonesty and deception, the expense of treatment, believing their partner was not trying hard enough to get well, feeling helpless, the limitations on socializing with other people, believing the eating behaviors to be unfair to the rest of the family, the fact that although the partner could die from the behaviors they kept doing them, and feeling cheated out of a "normal," happier marriage.

Some partners found individual therapy to be helpful, whereas others did not feel it to be necessary (Winn et al., 2004). Partners may be resistant to examining their own issues and how they relate to recovery. Ironically, the non-eating disorder partner often struggles with the same underlying issues as the person with the eating disorder, creating blind spots that limit empathy and tolerance. For example, a partner who is a perfectionist may not see that lowering expectations or learning to view mistakes as opportunities to grow is a positive step.

As mentioned earlier, the Gottman-RED couples therapist should be on the lookout for signs that the non-eating disorder partner could benefit from individual therapy in addition to the couples therapy. When non-eating disorder partners become willing to work on themselves and the relationship, both partners become healthier. "In any relationship, both people contribute to the strengths and problems of the relationship. Although it is not possible to control the person with the eating disorder, it is possible to make changes in oneself" (Reiff & Reiff, 1999, p. 421).

Stage 5: Hope

During this stage, things are starting to look up. Eating behaviors have lessened and communication in the relationship has improved. Family interactions and gatherings centered around food are becoming more normal. Non-eating disorder partners feel better about themselves due to their own insights and personal growth. If a partner initiates recovery, non-eating disorder partners view themselves as influential and feel empowered by the transition toward recovery (Schmit & Bell, 2017). The person with the eating issues is less dependent on the food behaviors and more available for intimate connection, which is possible due to the work on the relationship done by both partners.

SELF-CARE. It is during this stage that the non-eating disorder partner has the mental space to consider the importance of preserving their own mental health, physical health, and self-care. Concerns regarding the physical health of the person with the eating disorder may have taken priority, but now the non-eating disorder partner can think about the potential long-term consequences of the stress of the eating disorder on their own health and on the relationship and take steps to protect themselves (Bulik et al., 2012; Highet et al., 2005; Linville et al., 2015; Perkins et al., 2004; Schmit & Bell, 2017). The necessity of taking on additional tasks related to cooking, buying food, pet care, or child care when the person with the eating disorder was away in treatment may have left some depleted (Bulik et al., 2012; Kirby et al., 2016). Still others may have turned to their own self-destructive behaviors such as drinking, smoking marijuana, playing video games, gambling, pornography, binge-watching favorite shows, or spending more time at work. Now there is time to take stock and make healthy changes.

Luciano, who has struggled with sexual addiction, started watching pornography again. Quisha was having physical symptoms from the stress—migraines and fatigue—and is gambling more. Abe gained weight hoping that Ezra will eat more if he eats more. John started drinking too much to cope with his feelings of loneliness and powerlessness.

Non-eating disorder partners need to acknowledge unhealthy behaviors and addictions and need to replace them with a variety of healthy coping strategies to deal with the challenges of being with someone with an eating disorder, including thinking positively, staying optimistic, using humor, accepting the problem, maintaining their own interests, and leading as normal of a life as possible (Linville et al., 2015; Perkins et al., 2004). In a study by Linville et al. (2015), it was found that spending time pursuing individual interests and having time apart resulted in a more positive experience for both partners.

When self-care for the non-eating disorder partner involves weight loss or exercise, things become a little more complicated. Dieting and the behaviors that go with it such as restricting calories, eliminating certain food groups, taking medication to aid weight loss, refusing to eat foods prepared by the person with the eating disorder that do not align with the new eating plan, or frequent weighing can be potential triggers for the person with the eating disorder (Linville et al., 2015; Reiff & Reiff, 1999). The same is true when a partner wants to increase exercise or become more physically fit.

Her phone buzzed. Amy answered.
"Hey, Amy. I am going to stop at the store on the way home.

Just wanted to see if you need anything," John asked, sounding upbeat and in a good mood.

"How did it go at the doctor?" John had had his yearly physical.

"Pretty good. Blood pressure up, so she wants me to exercise more and lose about 10 pounds."

Amy froze and could not speak.

There was a long silence.

She did not know why she froze; all she knew was that the thought of John exercising more and losing weight scared her. She immediately started planning ways to increase her own exercise and to further restrict her food intake, even though she knew she was not supposed to do that. Her reaction confused her. She felt that familiar feeling of shame and knew she could never share her thoughts or feelings about this with John.

"I'm at the store now," John commented.

No response.

"Amy? Are you there?"

Regardless of the reaction of the person with the eating disorder, the non-eating disorder partner needs to make choices that do not sacrifice their own well-being or physical health. It is important that the couples therapist understands that these situations can be difficult for a couple when one partner has an eating disorder, and will need to assist the couple when talking about or processing feelings that arise.

ADDITIONAL SUPPORT FOR THE NON-EATING DISORDER PARTNER. Social support appears to help ameliorate the non-eating disorder partner's distress (Winn et al., 2004). However, professionals typically focus on securing help for the person with the eating disorder and not for the partner, even though the majority of non-eating disorder partners are very stressed, often questioning if their feelings and reactions are normal for someone in their circumstances. Validation and empathy for their position and reactions are very important (Linville et al., 2015). Most non-eating disorder partners only feel comfortable confiding in a very small group of people, typically some family members or close friends. Both partners reported that feelings of shame and a desire for privacy limit disclosure to others, leaving the non-eating disorder partner feeling isolated (Linville et al., 2005; Winn et al., 2004). In addition, the social stigma surrounding eating disorders inhibits non-eating disorder partners from reaching out for help (Bulik et al., 2012). Given that most recovery journeys last for years, non-eating disorder partners need succor to combat the weariness of providing long-term support and reassurance to the person with the eating disorder (Reiff & Reiff, 1999; Schmit & Bell, 2017) but are limited in their options for finding it.

SUPPORT GROUPS. Some non-eating disorder partners will be more open to attending a support group than going to individual therapy. It is a good idea for the couples therapist to mention this valuable resource to the couple. Many non-eating disorder partners have turned to support groups where they can talk with people who can relate and share similar experiences (Huke & Slade, 2006; Perkins et al., 2004; Schmit & Bell, 2017; Winn et al., 2004). Some indicated it would be helpful to have separate support groups based upon different stages of recovery, or separate groups for parents and partners given that their needs are different (Schmit & Bell, 2017; Winn et al., 2004). Others mentioned the value of disorder-specific support groups, noting that they felt only those with direct experience of bulimia could understand what it was like to live with someone with this eating disorder (Winn et al., 2004).

Stage 6: Acceptance/Peace

Painful emotions regarding the eating disorder have been released and resolved. The partner has had a chance to grieve for what was lost because of the eating issues. Focus shifts to what has been learned, how the relationship has improved and grown, and plans for navigating the future together. Both partners are more accepting of each other and have relaxed their perfectionistic worldviews. The Gottman-RED couples therapist will help couples talk about their future together and how their plans, hopes, and dreams may need to be modified based upon the progression of the eating disorder.

Sadly, there are times when this stage is not reached, and the relationship does not survive. The pain may run too deep in the relationship, with lack of forgiveness and absence of repair for regrettable incidents. Unless both partners are willing to change, the relationship may not survive the recovery journey. Under these circumstances, most non-eating disorder partners have accepted that recovery must come from the person with the eating disorder and there is nothing more that they can do (Schmit & Bell, 2017).

Concluding Thoughts

Thirty years ago, Blake Woodside and his colleagues at the University of Toronto (1993) stated the obvious, namely that even though the age of onset of an eating disorder is typically in the teen years or early adulthood, many of these young people grow up without recovery, bringing their eating disorders with them into their relationships. Few eating disorders treatment professionals at the time considered the implications of this astute observation. This is the case for Carmen, Ezra, Demarcus, and Amy. Some will recover while in a relationship; others will not. In the latter scenario, the partner can either choose to stay and accept the reality of the chronicity of the eating disorder or leave the relationship.

During the course of couples therapy, both partners are navigating the complex interplay of individual choices with relationship development. Finding the balance between the needs of each partner and the needs of the relationship is dynamic, complicated, and challenging. I have been a Star Trek fan forever. As I write these words, I am reminded of Mr. Spock's famous line in *The Wrath of Khan*, "The needs of the many outweigh the needs of the few," to which Captain Kirk added, "or the one." Kirk then reversed the logic when he rescued Spock in *The Search for Spock* and said, "The needs of the one outweigh the needs of the many." The Gottman-RED couples therapist helps the couple discuss each partner's needs *and* the needs of the relationship, viewing all three as equally valid.

In a couple where one person has an eating disorder, the needs of the non-eating disorder partner and/or the needs of the relationship are often overshadowed by those of the person who is struggling with the disorder. Understanding the non-eating disorder partner's perspective gives the Gottman-RED couples therapist the insight necessary to work effectively with the couple to strengthen their relationship. Now it is time to dig a little deeper and unravel the complexities of a relationship when one or both partners have eating issues or an eating disorder history.

4

Equipping the Couples Therapist to Work with Relationships with Eating Disorders

As therapists, we learn to be very comfortable with the idea of digging deeper. When engaging in individual therapy, we ask probing questions, make observations, offer therapeutic interventions, give empathetic responses, and reflect feelings in ways that help our clients have new insights, realizations, and deeper understanding of themselves and their relationships. As couple therapists, our job is significantly different. We are focused on helping each partner learn how to get to a deeper level of understanding of the other partner by teaching them how to do for each other many of the things that are second nature to us. We are *not* teaching them to be each other's therapist, but we *are* teaching them how to ask deepening questions, listen, validate, and show empathy. For many, this is like learning a foreign language.

To do this effectively when working with couples dealing with eating disorder issues in addition to all of their other relationship dynamics, couples therapists need to have a deep level of understanding and insight regarding the nature of relationships when one person has an eating disorder. This chapter and the next is all about equipping you to effectively work with this unique couples population. Often, it will be up to you to introduce topics for **R**elationship with **E**ating **D**isorder (RED) couples to process in session, particularly those related to timing and maintaining or protective factors.

One of my favorite analogies when working with couples is that of the underground parking garage. I encourage you to use it or one of your own when facilitating meaningful conversations. I introduce it when teaching the Gottman-Rapoport intervention.

THE PARKING GARAGE STORY

Imagine that you need to park your car in an underground parking garage. Think about how the ramps circle around and around as you drive your car lower and lower (downward spiral hand motion). It may feel a little scary the lower that you go. In fact, there is word for this. Tingchechekuphobia is the fear of parking garages. Most couples like to keep conversations more superficial, staying at Levels A or B—the safer, less risky place to be—or not enter the parking garage at all, meaning avoiding all but necessary conversations. When you are the listener in a conversation, your goal is to ask deepening questions in a sensitive, open-ended way that creates a safe space for your partner to open their heart to you at Levels E, F, or G.

When you both share at this level, there will be a deeper level of understanding, insight, openness, and vulnerability in your relationship. This is where empathetic engagement and a shift in perspective can occur. It is where you reveal your enduring vulnerabilities to each other. Even if you have been together for 25 years or longer, you are likely to learn something new about your partner when you get down to these deeper levels.

The underground parking garage analogy speaks to the process of deepening understanding of each other in a relationship; however, it can be applied to couples therapists learning Gottman-RED couples therapy as well. We will be venturing into the depths of the parking garage of relationships in which one or both partners have an eating disorder or eating behavior issues in order to achieve a more profound level of insight into the complexities of these relationships, and how to best help such couples. Some therapists are wary of working with people with eating disorders and others are wary of working with couples, so combining the two may seem like an insurmountable hurdle. But it is not. My hope is that the more you understand about RED couples, the more confident you will feel about your effectiveness, and the more you will want to work with them. As we seek to untangle the complexity of these relationships, it is hoped that both eating disorder therapists who have never worked with couples and couples therapists new to the world of eating disorders will develop an appreciation of the challenges of this work. Even if you are a seasoned couples therapist or have extensive experience working with people with eating disorders, it is my hope that you will learn something new that will inform your treatment of RED couples.

When an eating disorder is part of the equation, the eating disorder behaviors and obsessions consume such a high percentage of emotional functioning that marital intimacy, openness, and satisfaction are substantially compromised (Highet et al., 2005; Maier, 2015). As noted previously, the burden of care experienced by the non-eating disorder partner may negatively impact both the marital relationship and the course of eating disorder recovery. Thus, the relationships that include an eating disorder require more work than most other relationships (Highet et al., 2005; Schmit & Bell, 2017).

The impact of the eating disorder on the stability of the relationship is affected by many variables, including severity of the eating disorder, stage of recovery, timing of disclosure, level of functioning and health of the partners, and expectations regarding recovery. Couples in which one partner has an eating disorder experience increased distress, fewer positive interactions, and more negative communication than couples without eating disorders (Murray et al., 2014). Accommodating to eating disorder behaviors and/or avoiding saying anything that has the potential to cause tension or conflict may be the path of least resistance (Hibbs et al., 2014; Reiff & Reiff, 1999; Schmit & Bell, 2017). Non-eating disorder partners are usually unaware that they are using accommodation "as a strategy to reduce both the patient's and their own distress" (Weber et al., 2019, p. 920). The presence of the eating disorder is so pervasive, dominating all aspects of the relationship, that it has been likened to having a third party in the relationship (Linville et al., 2015). Some non-eating disorder partners have described feeling like their partner is having an affair due to the secrecy, obsession with, and furtiveness regarding the eating disorder thoughts and behaviors.

The damage to the relationship can be significant. Hence, the earlier in the recovery journey that couples therapy can begin, the better (Bulik et al., 2012). As noted by Bailey et al. (2015), there appears to be "growing evidence that issues associated with dieting and body image, often conceptualized in the clinical literature as problems operating at the intrapsychic level, also need to be understood in the wider context of intimate relationships" (p. 767). Issues surrounding sexual intimacy appear to be closely linked to feelings about body image. Although not unique to those with diagnosable eating disorders, body image concern is an area of particular sensitivity for those with eating disorders. As previously noted, the literature clearly supports the inclusion of couples therapy in the treatment plan for people with eating disorders.

In this chapter, you will learn about the significance of timing and examine the impact of maintaining and protective factors so that you can facilitate conversations that increase understanding and enable effective planning for a healthier future together. It will be your job to make sure the couple addresses these issues as they may not even be aware they exist.

Timing

Relationships with eating disorders are affected by timing; timing of disclosure, timing of onset of the eating disorder, and timing of recovery. The couples therapist should include discussion of timing in the treatment goals for this couple. Let us look at each of these in more depth.

Timing of Disclosure

Amy's heart was pounding. She had to tell John but was ter-rified of his reaction. Her first husband, Jeff, left because of her eating disorder. The end of that relationship was so traumatic that she swore to herself that she would never tell another man about her food issues. Now, however, things were so bad that she had to tell John. "Thank goodness we got married first," she thought, but knew that was no guarantee he would stay.

John was watching the game. She walked in slowly, taking deep breaths to quell her anxiety, and then sat down beside him.

"John, can we talk for a minute?"

"Did you see that?" He was pointing to the TV screen. "Look at that catch! Unbelievable! There is no way we won't get into the playoffs."

"I mean. About something serious. Could you turn off the game for a minute?"

"Sure. What is it?" John replied while turning off the game but still holding the remote.

"You know how I am afraid of taking the fertility drugs because I might gain weight? Well . . . it's because I have anorexia." She did it; she laid the cards on the table.

John stared at her like he had just seen a ghost. The remote dropped out of his hand. "What? You? You're almost 40. I thought anorexia was a teenage thing. You told me you had it in high school but were over it."

Amy pressed on. "Well, I'm not. It started when I was a teen-ager, but the symptoms never totally went away and they are com-ing back now."

The first thing John said was, "Is it my fault?"

"No, I had it way before I met you. But that's why my weight is so low. It's not because of food allergies, like I said."

"So you lied to me?"

"Well, kind of. I do have some food allergies, but that is not why I lost weight." She looked down, afraid to see his expression.

There was silence. John was thinking, "Can she be serious?"

*"Why didn't you tell me you still had it before we got married?"
He sounded angry. His anger scared her.*

"I was scared to," she muttered, her heart pounding even harder.

*Then came a barrage of questions. "Are you going to see some-
one? I mean for therapy? Can you get over it fast? Why would you
want to be skinny at your age?" He paused, was silent for a few
seconds, then added in a hoarse whisper, "So you would rather be
skinny than have our child? Great."*

*"I can't handle this, John. I was hoping for some compassion
or empathy, but obviously all you can do is think about yourself."
Feeling his anger and disappointment in her was frightening.*

*"Well, it affects me. This is not just about you, Amy." His tone
was cold and distant. The reality was that she could not think
about him; all she could think about was the number of calories she
had just eaten at dinner.*

*John picked up the remote, turned on the game again and stared
at the TV in a futile attempt to erase the conversation from his con-
sciousness. He had no idea what to do with his feelings. Somehow,
watching the intensity of football was distracting enough that he
could begin to calm down.*

Was this disclosure a surprise for John? Yes and no. Shortly after
they were married, he started wondering if Amy still had an eating
disorder. While dating, Amy casually mentioned to John that she
had been hospitalized for anorexia nervosa in the past, but she had
emphasized *in the past* and assured John that she was over it. However, when issues came up about getting pregnant and her behaviors
increased and Amy admitted that it was still a problem, John felt an
odd mixture of emotions: betrayed and deceived by her assurances,
disappointed that she had not told him sooner, worried, and scared
about being responsible in some way for her relapse, and panicked
and powerless about desperately wanting children while now in a
second marriage at age 40 where the likelihood of that happening
was totally out of his control.

Timing is everything—well, almost. Telling a potential partner
or current partner that you have an eating disorder is essential for

transparency and trust in a relationship; however, the person with the eating disorder often feels vulnerable and scared of the possibility of rejection or judgment. The impact of the disclosure varies depending upon the timing. Often the person with eating behaviors will test the waters first, dipping their toe in to see how the temperature feels. If it is warm enough—meaning their partner responds in an accepting and empathetic way without making disparaging comments or immediately jumping to problem solving—the person is likely to share a little more.

Just like we saw with Amy and John, learning that one's partner has an eating disorder elicits a wide range of emotions, ranging from concern to fear to revulsion. More often than not, the person struggling with eating issues has limited capacity to listen to or show empathy for these feelings due to their own sensitivity to the topic. Thus, the disclosure conversation is typically one-sided, leaving the non-eating disorder partner with a mélange of emotions to sort out on their own or, if this seems too difficult, to sweep under the rug.

Disclosure During Dating

When the eating disorder is disclosed during dating, the partner has time to assess the potential impact on the relationship before making a long-term commitment. Although most non-eating disorder partners have an initial emotional response feeling emotions such as powerlessness, helplessness, disgust, fear and/or guilt, they tend to underestimate the seriousness of the problem and may believe that even if no one has been able to do this before, they can jump in and make everything all better (Perkins et al., 2004).

> *Carmen disclosed a little bit about her eating disorder to Luciano before they were married. Luciano, gravely underestimating the complexity of the problem, was convinced that marrying him would be enough for her to leave her eating disorder behind. He was the proverbial knight in shining armor riding in to save the maiden in distress. This fantasy was just that—a fantasy and not real life. Mar-*

rying Luciano did not cure Carmen. Disillusioned, Luciano became less supportive over time. Even after years of marriage, Carmen has yet to disclose the full extent of her eating disorder. She heard the disgust and impatience in Luciano's voice when she revealed a little about her struggles, immediately felt shame and guilt and then, with silent resolve, thought, "I will never tell him everything."

Ezra and Abe are just beginning their relationship. Abe has a more accepting view given his experience with his sister. During her treatment, there was family therapy for her eating disorder, so he understands that eating disorder behaviors become a life preserver to the person with the eating disorder. Although he approaches Ezra with empathy and curiosity, he is adamant about the importance of getting help and is cautious about commitment. When Abe confronted him, Ezra could feel Abe's warmth, empathy, and caring. Although very tentative about therapy and terrified of gaining weight, Ezra is willing to go to couples counseling to preserve the relationship.

Disclosure After Marriage

If the person with the eating disorder discloses the eating disorder after marriage, the non-eating disorder partner may view the choice not to disclose prior to commitment as betrayal (Linville et al., 2015). John and Quisha were negatively impacted by this timing.

Amy, scared to tell John about her eating disorder because of rejection in past relationships, finally builds up the courage to tell him, but as we saw earlier in this chapter, it did not go well. Quisha had no clue that Demarcus used food to cope with emotions when she met him and married him. He was eating in a healthy way, had lost weight, and was working out. But then, when life got tough, he started binge eating. Quisha felt so angry when she saw empty bags from fast food restaurants in the garbage can or found candy wrappers in the car. Feeling betrayed and misled, plus afraid that this might somehow be her fault, Quisha started to compare Demarcus to her friends' husbands and spent increasing amounts of time thinking about leaving the relationship. They had never talked

directly about what was going on with food because even Demarcus
was in the dark. He was unaware that there was a name, let alone
a diagnosis, for what he was doing with food: binge eating disorder.

Ideally, soon after these conversations either John or Quisha would
have reached out for a couples therapist to help navigate a way forward that would be good for their relationship and support them
in getting the help they needed. Rarely do people do that. Couples
wait, hoping they can work things out on their own, and as John
and Julie Gottman (2018) have repeatedly told us, they usually wait
about 6 years too long.

Timing of Eating Disorder Onset and the Impact on Relationship

We had a neighbor who wanted to build a new deck right where a
beloved, majestic fir tree was growing. Not wanting to cut down
the tree, they built their deck around it leaving a hole in the floor of
the deck so the tree was not disturbed. People marveled at the tree
and the hole in the middle of the deck at first, but then got used to
it and just walked around it, enjoying the shade in the summer, and
feeling bothered by the needles that fell in the fall. It soon became
hard to imagine the deck without the tree.

If the eating disorder begins when a relationship is forming,
there is the risk that the eating disorder will become like the tree
with the relationship built around it. If the non-eating disorder
partner knows about their partner's disordered eating, there is the
risk that they will define their position in the relationship or marriage as a caregiver, substituting the closeness of caregiving for true
intimacy (Woodside et al., 1993). The danger of this posture is that
the eating disorder will become a stabilizing factor, with recovery
threatening the homeostasis. The non-eating disorder partner may
worry their value in the relationship will diminish once recovery
is achieved so may unwittingly undermine the recovery process. If
this happens, it will be unlikely the tree will ever be cut down. Of
our four couples, the only person at risk of moving into this position is Abe. He feels very concerned about Ezra and is a naturally
warm and caring person who likes to help and be needed.

When the onset of the eating disorder is some years after marriage begins, the dynamic may be different due to the spouse feeling a mixture of guilt, shame, and self-blame for potentially being responsible for the development of the eating disorder. Unfortunately, if the couple reaches out for help, the current standard of care for eating disorders is individual therapy for the person diagnosed with the eating disorder, not couples therapy. What is really needed is that the couple starts therapy concurrently with individual therapy so that the marital issues can be processed and the impact of the eating disorder minimized.

None of the couples we are following fit this profile; however, as just mentioned, Amy relapsed after marriage and that can evoke a similar emotional reaction. Woodside et al. (1993) posited two response scenarios: the dynamics of repair, a more parental role in which the spouse becomes the problem solver and is overinvolved in fixing the problem; or the dynamics of denial, in which the spouse feels betrayed and angry and thus emotionally distances from the partner with the eating issues and may even threaten separation. Some partners vacillate between the two. Neither response is good for the relationship since both revolve around illness and interfere with the non-eating disorder partner's ability to function as a healthy person in the relationship.

Timing of Recovery

Another interesting implication for partners that goes beyond the timing for disclosure is the timing of initiation of overt steps toward recovery. Having the eating disorder out in the open does not equate to pursuing treatment. Even if one does decide to pursue treatment, this effort may not be a constant; some people will be committed to recovery for a while and then either need a break or stop after achieving partial remission, deciding that there has been sufficient progress to allow for adequate life improvement. As noted earlier, there is no quick fix for an eating disorder. Recovery takes time, typically 3 to 5 years of consistent therapy, with the average length of an anorexic episode being 6 years (Treasure et al., 2001). Both partners will benefit from the interventions in Gottman-RED that facilitate constructive conversations related to eating disorder thoughts and behaviors as they prepare for this journey.

In relationships where partners pursued recovery, the supportive partner had a sense of making a difference and felt their influence was accepted (Schmit & Bell, 2015). When the partner did not pursue recovery, feelings about self-efficacy in the non-eating disorder partner were vastly different. Although ultimately coming to a position of accepting that initiation of recovery needed to come from the partner with the eating disorder, these non-eating disorder partners experienced feelings of helplessness, disempowerment, and lack of confidence in their ability to influence change (Schmit & Bell, 2015). Internally motivated eating behavior change is more likely to be long-lasting than externally motivated behavior change; thus if someone changes to please their partner, this change is less likely to persist than if they make the decision for themselves (Cornelius et al., 2018). For example, encouraging someone to lose weight when they are not already engaged in a weight loss program tends to have a negative result and can be experienced as shaming or stigmatizing, whereas eating healthier foods together or exercising together can be perceived as supportive and validating (Cornelius et al., 2018). The former is unlikely to result in behavior change, whereas the latter is more likely to generate steps toward recovery.

Because the focus of Gottman-RED is improving the relationship and is not predicated upon the person with the eating behaviors being committed to eating disorder recovery, the therapy is very helpful for couples in these circumstances.

Maintaining and Protective Factors

Love is the wild card introduced when working with a couple. Love can maintain connection when all else seems to fail; love motivates couples to keep trying even under arduous circumstances; love can be blind or hypervigilant; love fuels forgiveness; love allows us to be there when someone is at their worst. Love can bring healing if channeled through interventions that allow it to be expressed in a way that fosters recovery, vulnerability, and intimacy, rather than destructive behaviors or self-protective distance. The conversations facilitated by Gottman-RED couples therapists are intended to strengthen a loving connection in the relationship, thereby creating a safe environment to have meaningful conversations about eating, food, weight, exercise, or body image-related issues and to process the many regrettable incidents or fights that can occur because of them.

John loves Amy. John regretted how he responded to her in their earlier interaction, so initiated a repair conversation.

> *John could not focus on the game. He knew he had reacted poorly to Amy's disclosure. He got up and walked into the bedroom where she was lying on the bed, looking up at the ceiling. Approaching tentatively, he sat down beside her.*
>
> *"Amy, I did not handle that well. What you shared with me is very important and I want to thank you for being open and honest with me, I am sorry I got angry and was so self-focused. I love you and don't want to hurt you," he said in a kind, gentle voice.*
>
> *Amy sat up and looked at him. He looked sad and truly remorseful. She loved him deeply. As she reached out and stroked his hair, she said, "I forgive you, John. I understand why you reacted. I really appreciate your apology. I don't want my eating disorder to ruin our relationship. I know I need your help. I love you so much."*

The way partners interact in a relationship can be a liability or a benefit when someone has an eating disorder. Eating behaviors or thoughts may increase in order to cope with relationship stress; however, at other times, the relationship can provide motivation for recovery and improved self-concept (Bussolotti et al., 2002; Linville et al., 2015). These interactional patterns can be characterized as maintaining factors or protective factors. In a healthy relationship, maintaining factors are minimized while protective factors are maximized.

Stuart Murray of Australia (2014) wrote an article about his experience working with a patient with chronic treatment-resistant anorexia nervosa. What he experienced in this single case study was so impactful that he subsequently changed his whole approach to eating disorder treatment. Because this patient was unable to make progress until couples therapy was added to the treatment protocol, Murray became convinced of the importance of "targeting symptoms in the context in which they exist" (p. 395). He advocated for including couples therapy in eating disorder treatment, noting that intrapsychic or CBT approaches used in individual therapy were inadequate to identify the key maintaining factors in a relationship that could impede recovery, especially if they were subtle or deeply woven into the fabric of the relationship.

It is important to note that the variables that underlie the development of an eating disorder as outlined in "The Helicopter Story" (Chapter 1) may not be the same variables that perpetuate it. For example, eating disorder behaviors originally functioning to numb the emotional pain following a series of traumatic events in a person's life might resurface 20 years later because that same person found the numbing of emotions and self-soothing of the behaviors also helped with marital stress in the present.

Although a whole book could be devoted to an in-depth discussion of maintaining and protective factors, a rudimentary understanding will suffice for the Gottman-RED couples therapist. We will focus on selected maintaining factors: core beliefs, interactions, marital stress, comments about appearance or weight, and accommodation; and selected protective factors: healthy boundaries, loving and supportive interactions, open communication around sensitive topics, and acceptance of each other. Let us take a closer look at both maintaining and protective factors.

Maintaining Factors

When a relationship is struggling, neither partner wants to be the bad guy. Yet, partners in a relationship often end up blaming each other and thinking, "If only they (pointing the finger at the other) would change, things would be so much better." In emotionally focused couples therapy, there is actually a name for this pattern of interaction called, "Finding the Bad Guy" (Johnson, 2008). The couples therapist encourages the couple to name the interaction and call it out whenever it appears, thereby focusing the work in therapy on changing the interaction and the role both play in maintaining the destructive pattern rather than finding fault with each other.

Avoiding blame opens the door for increased collaboration and decreased defensiveness when discussing maintaining factors, a potentially sensitive topic.

A maintaining factor in a relationship in which one or both partners have an eating disorder can be thought of as a variable, most likely having to do with interactions, that perpetuates the eating disorder, makes recovery more difficult, and results in symptom persistence over time rather than remission.

The interventions in Gottman-RED couples therapy are intended to vanquish some of these maintaining factors thereby opening the door to recovery a little wider. Addressing maintaining factors is not to imply they are causal. The eating disorder treatment field has moved away from thinking that dysfunctional interactions cause eating disorders to thinking of them as a consequence of the behaviors and thoughts that come with an eating disorder (Linville & Oleksak, 2013; Selekman & Beyebach, 2013). However, once they are integral to a relationship, they are not helpful, and need to be challenged and changed.

Core Beliefs as Maintaining Factors

Much has been written about the role of cognitive distortions and destructive core beliefs in the development and treatment of eating disorders. Cognitive behavioral therapy is a key component of most individual or group therapy treatment protocols. These beliefs can significantly impact a relationship.

Christopher Fairburn at Oxford (2008), a highly respected researcher and clinician in the eating disorder treatment field, developed a transdiagnostic treatment approach entitled CBT-E (CBT Enhanced) focused on overcoming binge eating. In this approach, significant others are included for a few sessions so they can learn about the therapy and how to be supportive, but it is primarily an individual self-help therapy. Fairburn identified the core psychopathology characteristic of most people with eating disorders, namely *the overevaluation of weight and shape and its control,* as the most important maintaining factor that needs to change if a person is to recover. The significance of this core psychopathology for relationships is that for many, weight and shape and its control are so highly valued that it is often more important to the person with the eating disorder than the relationship, the well-being of the partner, and/or their own health. Given a forced choice between using a behavior or spending time together, being intimate, or for some, continuing in the relationship, the eating behavior may come out on top, depending upon the stage of recovery. Fairburn identified four additional maintaining factors: clinical perfectionism, core low self-esteem, mood intolerance, and interpersonal difficulties. All four of these are addressed in Gottman-RED couples therapy.

For people with anorexia nervosa or bulimia, the fear of gaining weight may be so strong that they would rather end the relationship than gain weight. This may sound like placing fault on the partner with the eating disorder; however, in the context of a relationship, it is the eating disorder and its impact, not the partner, that is the destructive force. The subtle messages, casual comments, or behaviors of the non-eating disorder partner often feed into or reinforce the other partner's beliefs about weight and shape and its control, strengthening rather than weakening the belief system. Thus, both partners have the potential to play a significant role in the maintenance of the eating behaviors. This phenomenon is discussed more in the next section regarding interactions.

Interactions as Maintaining Factors

Eating disorder behaviors can be maintained by destructive interactional patterns within a relationship. As with all relationships, people become accustomed to predictable ways of reacting and responding such that there is balance, or homeostasis (i.e., the tree in the middle of the deck). When it comes to perpetual problems, partners expect a certain response from each other such that any deviation from this response is unsettling, even if it is a healthier response. This expectation can even carry over into attempts to change behavior. In the story that follows, Demarcus's change was so out of the ordinary that Quisha reacted.

> *Quisha and Demarcus loved going out for brunch to Sunny's Pancake House after church on Sunday. They knew the menus so well that they did not even have to look.*
>
> *"I think I'll get two eggs over easy and toast," Demarcus mentioned to Quisha as they were sitting down at their usual table. He wanted to make a healthier choice for a change.*
>
> *"What?" Quisha looked like she had just seen a ghost, "Eggs and toast? You always get the short stack with bacon and hash browns! Are you feeling OK?"*

Demarcus has a choice. He can reassure Quisha and say he is fine and working to be healthier or he can, sensing her discomfort, change his mind and order his usual breakfast. If he persists with his new behavior and is consistent over time, Quisha will adapt to his new ways. Although this conversation may seem relatively minor, it is a very significant interaction and how Demarcus reacts will affect his recovery from binge eating disorder.

Eating Disorder–Related Interactions as Maintaining Factors

Here I introduce four idiosyncratic, rarely talked about ways of interacting around food and weight on the part of the person with the eating disorder that are unhealthy for the relationship followed by two more commonly noted interactional patterns. The therapist should watch for and ask about these ways of interacting, as discussion will rarely be initiated by the couple. This lack of transparency is underscored by feelings of shame or embarrassment.

VICARIOUS EATING. When in a state of semistarvation, being able to smell, see, or touch the forbidden foods makes the hunger more tolerable. People who severely diet or restrict intake, eating disorder or not, often spend hours reading recipes, watching food shows, looking at food in the grocery store, dreaming about food, or preparing food. Vicarious eating is the phenomenon in which a person who is restricting total caloric intake or excluding certain foods from their diet will prepare these foods for their partner and insist that their partner eat them, although they do not consume these foods themselves. These foods are often high-fat or high-calorie foods, sometimes combined into multicourse gourmet meals, that can lead to weight gain in the non-eating disorder partner unless the partner is able to set limits on this behavior. Frequently, refusal to eat the food causes such inner turmoil and anxiety in the eating disorder partner that they overreact, which in turn leads to an unpleasant argument. Accommodation on the part of the non-eating disorder partner is not helpful, but keeps the peace. *Both Amy and Ezra prepare high-calorie foods for John and Abe, respectively. John and Abe have reached the point where what started out as pleasurable or a special treat is starting to affect their physical health.*

DIVEBOMBING DIETS. When the non-eating disorder partner begins a weight loss diet, the person with the eating disorder may feel competitive or threatened. People who strongly identify with being thin or the thinnest may react irrationally to their partner losing weight and, even if aware they are reacting irrationally, may feel unable to stop this reaction. Having formed an identity around their eating disorder, they may believe "this is my thing" and not want their partner to be engaging in or potentially "be better at" a similar behavior, such as dieting or restricting intake. People with anorexia nervosa may find it more difficult to continue to gain weight or maintain their current weight when their partner is limiting intake, as they may feel competitive or weak when eating more than their partner at a given meal. Sometimes the eating disorder partner will say disparaging things about the diet or even subtly discourage their partner from continuing with the diet. If the partner loses weight, that can also feel very threatening. Some people with restricting eating disorders secretly feel relieved if their partner fails at the diet or gains the weight back. *Carmen has struggled when Luciano has dieted.*

On the other hand, people with binge eating disorder are often in a relationship with someone who enjoys eating rich food with them or may even have binge eating disorder themselves. Dieting can interrupt this ritual of connection such that the partner subtly or overtly encourages the person trying to change behavior to discard their attempts at change. They may say things like, "Just have a bite of this" or, "Let's go to our favorite restaurant and you can just get a salad," knowing that the temptation will be too great and their partner will likely end up eating like they have in the past. *Quisha, as we will see in the vignette later in this chapter, struggles with this. She wants Demarcus to change behavior, yet really enjoys their eating rituals and the tasty, calorie-dense foods that he prepares.*

THE LOOK. Some people with eating disorders are hyperconscious of weight gain in their partner or children and may give a look of disgust at the other person's body. They may have no tolerance of their partner's high body weight but, at the same time, feel threatened if the partner diets or works out intensively. They may or may not make disparaging or discouraging comments (which may be direct or subtle), send links to weight loss diet websites, leave literature around the house about the benefits of losing weight, or overtly encourage weight loss. It is important that the non-eating disorder partner sets limits on this behavior while at the same time encouraging direct and open conversations about topics related to weight and health for both partners.

DISCUSSION DODGING. Another behavior that can impede recovery is dodging difficult discussions due to fear of conflict or upsetting one another (e.g., gridlocked perpetual issues) rather than openly and directly raising issues of concern (Kirby et al., 2016). In reality, avoiding difficult conversations in a relationship due to fear of slowing eating disorder recovery actually *can* slow recovery (Reiff & Reiff, 1999). *Carmen, Demarcus, Ezra, and Amy all tend to dodge difficult discussions, feeling particularly hesitant to address topics related to food or weight.* Engaging couples in empathetic conversations rather than dodging them is a key component of Gottman-RED.

MONITORING THE PARTNER'S EATING BEHAVIORS. When an eating disorder is present in a relationship, both partners have a heightened awareness of food, weight, and eating behaviors. While the motivation for this behavior will differ between the partner with the eating disorder and the non-eating disorder partner, the hypervigilance exists for both. In a study of romantic relationships and eating regulation led by Charlotte Markey (2008) at Rutgers University in New Jersey, it was determined that partners often do monitor each other's eating behaviors, particularly women who are dissatisfied with their partners' body size. Men and women who were unhappy with their partner's physique and whose partners were relatively heavy were more likely to try to regulate the eating behaviors of their partner. It was unclear whether the motivation was the health of the partner or displeasure with the partner's appearance. Men were receptive to women's attempts to regulate their eating behavior and responded by eating in a healthier way, but women were not positively impacted by men's attempts to regulate their eating behaviors. The researchers concluded by expressing the hope that the power of the relationship could be harnessed for positive change, thereby becoming a protective factor that encouraged healthier eating behaviors.

Eating disorders tend to be maintained within relationships in which control has been substituted for security and attachment or in which the autonomy of the person with the eating disorder has been compromised by allowing the other partner to regulate their eating, exercise, or weight-related behaviors (Woodside et al., 1993). Psychologist Dana Harron (2019) wrote a book about loving someone with an eating disorder that focused on helping the non-eating disorder partner understand, support, and connect with their partner. She identified being a food cop, strong-arming, or nagging as unhelpful ways of interacting around food-related issues. Janet Treasure and her colleagues (2013) developed a cognitive interpersonal maintenance model in which they posited that there were elements of accommodating or enabling behaviors that were maintaining factors. These behaviors were modifiable with skills-based interventions and these modifications yielded a positive impact on the relationship for the person with the eating disorder.

Symptom separation—in which the non-eating disorder partner

disengages from management of the eating disorder symptoms—may destabilize this type of relationship, particularly if the eating disorder was present at the time of the marriage. In reality, some partners actually like being the rescuer or knight in shining armor and are threatened by recovery if it means giving up that role, while others are subconsciously afraid that the partner with the eating disorder will leave them once recovered (Harron, 2019). This fear is not totally unfounded, given that the desire for healthier, more open, and more sexually intimate relationships often comes with recovery. Sometimes this does mean ending the current relationship (Schmit & Bell, 2017). However, engaging in a therapy like Gottman-RED couples therapy that allows for in-depth discussions to clarify thoughts and feelings about these issues before making this decision would be prudent.

UNDERMINING BEHAVIOR CHANGE ATTEMPTS. Maintaining factors can include actions on the part of the non-eating disorder partner, who may inadvertently or unconsciously undermine behavior change or accommodate unhealthy behaviors that need to change for the person with the eating disorder to recover (Selekman & Beyebach, 2013). Undermining behavior change may look like buying binge food for someone with binge eating disorder or bulimia, making positive comments about being thin to a person with anorexia nervosa, making disparaging comments about someone else's weight gain, subtly encouraging a partner to go off their diet, or interfering with their partner's attempts to exercise less. A non-eating disorder partner who accommodates unhealthy behaviors may join their eating disorder partner in overeating or excessively exercising or may ignore the fact that their partner is chewing and spitting food or inducing vomiting.

Resistance of a partner to admit to or identify their own issues, eating or otherwise, that may contribute to the maintenance of the eating disorder may slow recovery. Identifying these behaviors may sound like pointing the finger at the non-eating disorder partners; however, once again, the person with the eating behaviors is not merely a bystander. Often, they will cajole their partner into buying the binge foods, plan excursions involving going to favorite restaurants, ask "Do I look fat?", or buy foods to overeat together.

> *Quisha and Demarcus loved watching movies on the weekends. It was Saturday night. Quisha was out running errands and was going to drive by their favorite restaurant. They both loved Mexican food. She decided to surprise Demarcus and bought takeout: chips, salsa, chicken fajitas for her and a chimichanga with guacamole and sour cream for Demarcus—his favorite. She knew he had been eating healthy all week, so thought something special would be a great reward. She had also picked up a cheesecake at Costco for the kids. Unfortunately, Demarcus would have a hard time resisting this.*
>
> *Demarcus had been "eating well" all day. He had eaten oatmeal for breakfast and a homemade turkey sandwich for lunch, just mustard and no mayo. When Quisha got home, he was pretty hungry.*
>
> *"Hey, honey. Close your eyes." Quisha came in and set up the dinner on the table near the TV, so they could eat while watching the movie.*
>
> *"That smells delicious!" he commented with his eyes still closed. "I hope it's what I think it is!"*
>
> *Demarcus was delighted. She had brought home his favorite meal, not realizing how caloric and high in sodium it was. The chips were a trigger for him. Once he started eating them, he could not stop. The portion sizes from this restaurant were huge, so they would end up overeating together—a ritual of connection they both looked forward to on Saturday night.*
>
> *Quisha had unwittingly undermined Demarcus's efforts to change his behavior. Demarcus took their dinner dishes into the kitchen and there was the cheesecake. He loved cheesecake. Thinking, well, I will start over again tomorrow, Demarcus cut a piece for himself and one for Quisha.*
>
> *"Here you go, baby," he said as he handed her a good-sized piece. Quisha looked at him and smiled.*
>
> *"Are you sure you want to eat this?" she asked, taking the first bite. "Oh, this is good!"*

"Yeah. It's Saturday night. I'll start over again tomorrow," he reassured her.

Quisha had no intention of undermining Demarcus's progress. She simply enjoyed the ritual of connection that they had shared for years of eating favorite foods while watching TV on Saturday night and wanted to feel close to him.

Marital Stress as a Maintaining Factor

If we look once again to the review of the literature of RED couples by Jon Arcelus and his colleagues (2012), we see the consistent finding that marital, intimate, and romantic problems are related to eating disorders and are most likely a maintaining factor, with the direction of causality undetermined. Schmidt and Treasure (2006) proposed that anorexic behaviors are maintained by positive and negative responses from close others that are evoked by the physical appearance and behaviors associated with the disorder. For example, saying, "You look so good, you've gained weight!" to a person who is dangerously thin may trigger weight loss, whereas saying, "You look so good, you've lost weight!" to someone with binge eating disorder who has lost weight could trigger weight gain. When non-eating disorder partners engaged in deleterious behavior, it was usually inadvertent and due to ignorance of what is actually encouraging and supportive (Schmit & Bell, 2017). In other words, when non-eating disorder partners make comments like this they think they are being helpful when, in reality, they are not. The Gottman-RED couples therapist will assist non-eating disorder partners, helping them learn what is useful and not useful to say and how to initiate a repair conversation when a mistake is made.

Luciano and Carmen just got home from having dinner with their friends, Armen and Cynthia.

"That was really fun! It sounds like Armen is really excited about his new job," Carmen commented. *"It has been about a year*

since we last saw them, hasn't it?" she asked as she took off her coat. She was feeling a little full, but thought she could handle it. They had eaten more food than she usually did for dinner, plus drank some alcohol and shared a dessert. Throwing up the dinner had crossed her mind, but she really did not want to.

Luciano walked into the kitchen where Carmen was now standing and said, "You know, they have both gained so much weight, especially Cynthia. I almost didn't recognize her. She used to be really fit, like you. . . . They say everyone gains weight after marriage, and they sure have." He checked the time. "It's still pretty early. What do you want to do now? Want to watch that movie we talked about seeing?"

Carmen tensed, her jeans suddenly feeling tight around her waist. She had stopped listening after Luciano mentioned weight gain. Feeling fat and ugly, she grabbed a full water bottle and walked toward the bathroom. "I am going to take a shower," she announced to Luciano.

Sensing a change in her mood, Luciano asked, "What just happened? Are you in a bad mood now?"

"I'm fine," she replied, but she was not fine. The fear of gaining weight was ignited by his words and all she could think about was getting the food out of her stomach as fast as she could.

Luciano sat down in front of the TV, flipping through channels, feeling confused. He could hear the sound of the shower running in the distance. About 30 minutes later, he heard the door to their bedroom close and he knew Carmen had gone to bed. He grabbed a beer and watched TV late into the night—alone.

When relationships are characterized by interpersonal fights, disagreements, or uncertainty about the future of the relationship, eating disorder recovery becomes more challenging due to the tendency to use eating disorder behaviors to cope with the tension, uncertainty, and pain of marital conflict (Fairburn, 2013; Linville et al., 2015; Murray, 2014).

A vicious cycle ensues in which the couple has a fight; the anxiety of the person with the eating disorder increases; the eating disorder partner uses eating disorder behaviors to cope with the feelings; the non-eating disorder partner's anxiety increases; the non-eating disorder partner uses an unhelpful strategy or makes an inflammatory gesture or comment; and the cycle begins again. Unhelpful behaviors on the part of the non-eating disorder partner include: nagging or criticizing, doubting the chances of behavior change or recovery, giving more money if overspending on binge foods; cleaning up the bathroom after purging, making up excuses for changes in plans or absences due to the eating disorder to tell family or friends; commenting on weight, appearance, or food choices; making critical comments about the eating disorder partner's body or someone else's; taking eating disorder behaviors personally; acting impervious; making light of the eating disorder; oversimplifying; trying to convince; and guilt-tripping (Harron, 2019; Selekman & Beyebach, 2013).

That is exactly how Carmen felt in the vignette from Chapter 1 after the fight with Luciano. She felt alone, rejected and hurt by him, but the cookies were there to comfort and soothe her.

Whenever Luciano stonewalled, Carmen panicked. She hated the distance. It took her back to childhood when her mother would not speak to her for days if she did something wrong. The taste of the cookies pierced the memory. She liked the taste. It was pulling her back to the present. There were four cookies left and she put them in the microwave. Now they were warm with the chocolate chips melted and they tasted even better. While they were heating, she got out the ice cream and other food for the binge. It was never enough. She knew the relief that would come when she purged and then her thoughts would be consumed with worry about how many calories were still in her body, whether she was going to gain weight, and planning how she could eat like a "normal person" when around Luciano the next day. His aloofness would not matter anymore.

Then she heard him coming upstairs. What to do now? She stuffed the food into the dishwasher, knowing he would not open it. He never helped with the dishes.

"Hey, I'm sorry I went off on you. Can we talk more tomorrow, and just hang out tonight? Let's watch our show!" His voice was calmer and he was reaching out.

He never does this, she thought. What do I do now? I am in the middle of a binge. It is so hard to stop in the middle. Flooded with a mixture of emotions—anger that he was taking her away from the food, fear that she could not purge, shame about the ice cream melting in the dishwasher—she hesitated, torn between the food and her lover, the safety of the distance versus the prospect of repair, vulnerability and connection. Well, maybe I can do it. Be with him and just deal with the discomfort!

About to say, "OK. I would like that," she noticed his eyes had locked onto something. It was the open door to the microwave. Her heart started beating faster. She knew he would see the four cookies and he did. He tried to hide his reaction and said nothing, but the look of disapproval and disgust on his face was unmistakable. Carmen felt the shame of the adult as well as the pain of the little girl.

"Not tonight, Luciano," she managed, then added, "I really do appreciate your apology, though."

But he didn't hear the second part, having walked away after her first three words.

Luciano did make a repair attempt but the timing resulted in the repair failing since unbeknownst to him, Carmen was in the middle of a binge episode when he approached her. Regrettable incidents like these need to be processed in couples therapy.

Accommodating as a Maintaining Factor

Accommodation occurs when a person responds to the distress in their partner by giving reassurance or adapting their own behavior in a way that minimizes the distress of one or both partners. There are times in every relationship when accommodation occurs and is innocuous. For example, one partner may be panicking due to poor time management and their partner offers to help complete a task for them. If this is a repetitive behavior, this may be an issue; but if it is occasional, it is a loving and kind act. If the accommodating behavior perpetuates dysfunctional behaviors, it is problematic and needs to be addressed. Typically, accommodating behaviors are modifiable, meaning that they can be changed (Hibbs et al., 2014).

Accommodating behaviors of the non-eating disorder partner that may maintain the eating disorder include adjusting schedules based on eating disorder rituals or exercise routines; allowing the person with the eating disorder to control the food that is bought; eating high-calorie foods made by the person with the eating disorder; protecting the person with the eating disorder from consequences of their behaviors; gaining weight when it is not necessary or healthy; not attending social functions if the person with the eating disorder does not want to go due to fears about food being served or embarrassment about being seen due to body image issues; being with the person with the eating disorder continually; being afraid to express honest feelings; making negative comments about weight, shape, body, or appearance; making it easy for them to binge eat (e.g., leaving the house, bingeing with them, buying binge food); or eating only at restaurants the person with the eating disorder finds acceptable (Linville et al., 2015; Reiff & Reiff, 1999; Selekman & Beyeback, 2013).

It was Ezra's birthday. Abe and Ezra decided to go out to dinner. Ezra chose a local seafood restaurant and Abe agreed to go. They made reservations for 5 p.m.—much earlier than Abe would have preferred, but this was the time that Ezra ritualistically ate dinner every day. Unbeknownst to Abe, Ezra had scrutinized the menu in advance and carefully selected foods for dinner that equaled his caloric allotment.

When they got to the restaurant, Abe pulled the server aside and asked the server to surprise them with a shrimp cocktail, thinking it was a low-calorie appetizer that Ezra would like. Not expecting this, Ezra became very anxious because he had not allowed for these calories. He ate some of the shrimp but felt increasingly uncomfortable. When the main course came, Ezra started pushing it around on his plate. Abe noticed the food avoidance and got upset. The dinner was very expensive.

"Ezra, is there something wrong with the halibut?" Abe asked in frustration.

"No, it's fine."

"Then why aren't you eating it? We ordered it broiled with no sauce, just the way you like it."

"I don't know." Ezra did not want to make an issue at his birthday dinner. He forced himself to eat it but became increasingly anxious.

Then, the server brought a surprise birthday dessert for Ezra with a candle in it. This was too much for Ezra. Abe saw the reaction and could not help himself from saying, "Ezra, you are so thin—it wouldn't hurt you to eat a little cake on your birthday! What is wrong with you? Can't you make an exception for once, just for me?"

Ezra abruptly excused himself to go to the restroom.

Abe, not wanting there to be a scene in the restaurant, thanked the server for the special dessert and asked if they could box it up and take it home to eat later. He paid the bill, got up from the table, texted Ezra that he would meet him in the car, and went outside. Ezra quickly joined, sat in the front seat, glanced at Abe, then looked down. Abe said nothing. They drove in silence.

Common reasons for accommodation include fear the person with the eating disorder will die of health complications; fear of an angry or defensive response; fear the person will attempt death by suicide; fear the person with the eating disorder will lose or gain more weight; and fear of inhibiting recovery. However, there is another reason for accommodation that needs to be addressed by the Gottman-RED therapist and that is that accommodation to eating behaviors reduces the stress for the non-eating disorder partner. In other words, sometimes the tension, defensiveness, or conflict that results from introducing a sensitive topic related to food, body image, or weight is not worth it in the short term, even if the result of this avoidance is maintaining eating disorder symptoms in the long run (Hibbs et al., 2014; Sepulveda et al., 2009; Weber et al., 2019).

Occasionally, the non-eating disorder partner decides that saying nothing—in essence, accommodating—is the path of least resistance and the path of least conflict, calming the waters of the relationship for both. It can also be a way of decreasing stress in the eating disorder partner. As aptly stated by Weber et al. (2019),

"It is reasonable to expect partners to become emotionally aroused themselves upon witnessing the patient's emotional arousal and then accommodate to alleviate both their own and their partner's negative emotions" (p. 922). Keeping binge foods out of the house will decrease the stress for the eating disorder partner but will not help them learn self-regulation when these foods are present. So, what happens when the non-eating disorder partner likes their partner's binge food and wants it in the pantry or refrigerator (e.g., chips, ice cream, or cookies)? If the non-eating disorder partner buys it, there will be a fight. If the non-eating disorder partner does not buy the food, the number of fights will decrease, an apparent benefit for the conflict-averse non-eating disorder partner.

Hiding the scale from the person with anorexia may decrease their anxiety about weight gain but will not help them learn to deal with their anxiety about seeing changes in the number on the scale. It will, however, decrease the number of emotional conversations about the scale or feeling fat, which could benefit the non-eating disorder partner if coping with these discussions has become difficult. There is an intervention called *TOES (Tolerating Others' Emotional Storms)* that the Gottman-RED therapist will introduce to help couples manage situations like these without accommodating.

When Things Do Not Work Out

When a partner with an eating disorder decides not to pursue recovery, the non-eating disorder partner will need to decide if continuing in the relationship is in their best interest. The Gottman-RED intervention called *Co-Constructing the Eating Disorder Narrative* helps couples clarify relevant thoughts and feelings. The couples therapist facilitates the emotionally sensitive processing of what was decided that could potentially mean dissolution of the relationship.

Occasionally, negative emotions experienced by partners at the time of discovery persist over time, with some non-eating disorder partners reaching the point of feeling as though they are going crazy or are unable to cope with the stress of the eating disorder (Perkins et al., 2004). Sadly, there are circumstances when the impact of the eating disorder on the relationship and the partner with the eating disorder is so great that the non-eating disorder partner feels as though they are together with a different person and may choose to end the relationship (Highet et al., 2005).

By definition, recovery necessitates change and transformation, not only in the person with the eating disorder but also in the non-eating disorder partner and in the relationship. If the non-eating disorder partner is unwilling to engage in introspection or take responsibility for confronting their issues, the relationship is unlikely to survive the recovery process. In this case, the person with the eating disorder will have a very difficult decision to make: get well and lose the relationship or stay sick and maintain the relationship (Reiff & Reiff, 1999). In emotionally focused therapy couples (EFCT), rigid patterns of interaction that are self-perpetuating and create distance in a relationship are referred to as a dance (Johnson, 2008). If the partners have identified a dance and want to improve their relationship, they will need to learn a new way of interacting that builds connection. However, both partners must learn how to do the new steps together—it is a pas de deux, not two people doing a solo. For example, if the partners were interacting in a conflictual way that they called Dance A and decided they needed to learn a new way called Dance B, both must learn the new moves in Dance B. If one is not interested or does not put in the effort to learn Dance B and continues doing the steps from Dance A while the other is trying Dance B, their movements will be awkward and out of sync. The relationship will stay distant.

If the presence of the eating disorder is so intertwined with the interactions that disengaging from the eating disorder is impossible for the non-eating disorder partner (e.g., no longer locking cabinets or the refrigerator, not hiding food or the scale), recovery is unlikely unless the marriage dissolves (Woodside et al., 1993).

Protective Factors

You may notice that this discussion of protective factors is much shorter than that of maintaining factors. In the field of psychology, despite the introduction of positive psychology in 1998, we still tend to focus research on psychopathology and relationship dysfunction, rather than on mental health and relationship satisfaction. John and Julie Gottman (2018) did embrace a more positive perspective when they studied relationships that succeeded, seeking to identify the characteristics of people who were masters of relationships. The results of this research led to the development of a theory of what made marriages succeed or fail (Gottman & Gottman, 2017). Gottman-RED evolved out of the Gottmans' theoretical orientation and focuses on enhancing friendship, communication, trust and conflict management in RED couples in ways that add to the somewhat shabby list of protective factors.

Relationships that are loving, supportive, and healthy can serve as a protective factor, motivating positive change (Linville et al., 2015). In fact, people who have recovered from eating disorders have indicated that having a supportive relationship, particularly one characterized by patience and flexibility, significantly helped them move forward in their recovery process (Bulik et al., 2012; Linville et al., 2015). A relationship that offers a message of unconditional, positive regard and consistent love counteracts the conditional nature of eating disorder thoughts that place stringent stipulations on acceptability and worth (Linville et al., 2015). A strong relationship can improve self-esteem, decrease concerns about shape and weight, and reduce stress, thereby increasing the likelihood of recovery (Fairburn, 2013).

Tiffany Brown and Pamela Keel of Florida State University (2015) studied the effect of relationship status on eating pathology in 51 bisexual or gay men (BG) and 522 heterosexual men and found that being single or experiencing lower relationship satisfaction resulted in restrictive eating pathology and increased drive for thinness in BG men, but not in heterosexual men. BG men who were in satisfied relationships seemed to be protected from the gay male ideal of being thin and muscular, and were thus less vulnerable to eating abnormalities. Thus, a healthy relationship appears to be a protective factor for bisexual or gay men. It will be important for the therapist working with Ezra and Abe to talk about this; however, Ezra's situation is complicated by his history of being bullied for being overweight. After the tense situation in the restaurant,

Abe initiated a repair attempt that was successful. This speaks to the strength of their relationship. Being able to effectively repair is a protective factor.

> *After driving in silence for 20 minutes, Abe pulled into the driveway and turned off the motor of the car. He turned to Ezra and said, "I did not handle that well. I feel badly that I walked out of the restaurant without you. Will you forgive me?"*
>
> *Returning Abe's gaze, Ezra said, "Of course I will forgive you. I am so sorry that I reacted to the birthday dessert. I know how hard you worked to make this dinner special for me. I really want to get over this eating disorder. Having you in my life gives me courage and hope."*

Gottman-RED therapists introduce couples to interventions that foster a positive, accepting, open relationship that allows for difficult conversations around sensitive topics, repair after conflict or regrettable incidents, as well as building trust and friendship while strengthening commitment.

Positive Impact of the Relationship

Relationships with healthy boundaries related to food, comments about body size, food preparation, eating, and cleaning up messes facilitate recovery, as do relationships characterized by good communication skills, a strong friendship, effective conflict management, healthy food-and-body philosophies, trust, commitment, and effective support skills (Gottman & Gottman, 2018; Harron, 2019). Understanding partners' triggers, accepting all foods, and engaging in non-food-related rituals of connection are also supportive behaviors (Harron, 2019). Avoiding comments regarding body size or appearance has a significant positive impact (Azmy, 2019). A relationship that is close and accepting may support recovery by increasing self-esteem, reducing worries about shape and weight, and decreasing stress in general (Fairburn, 2013; Linville et al., 2015). Many people seeking treatment for an eating disorder see their partners as vital to the recovery process (Maier, 2015).

Understanding of behaviors and their functions opens the door for the relationship to be "a source of happiness, security, and growth toward the recovery of an eating disorder" (Maier, 2015, p. 159).

Positive Outcomes

Psychologists have long been interested in understanding growth following adversity. In his famous book, *Man's Search for Meaning*, Victor Frankl wrote about the importance of making meaning out of unavoidable suffering (Frankl et al., 2006). Richard Tedeschi and Lawrence Calhoun (1996), coined the term posttraumatic growth, referring to the transformation following trauma experienced by those people who see positive growth after enduring psychological struggle. Many people who have recovered from eating disorders have written autobiographical accounts of their journey toward health and how having an eating disorder helped them to grow and change for the better. It is my belief that the non-eating disorder partners can also experience positive changes, or, if you will, post-disorder growth if their partner recovers or positive personal transformation even if the partner does not. There is also the potential for growth as a couple—synchronous growth—when two people experience the same stressor, in this case the eating disorder, and come through the process with increased individual and relational resilience and positive personal and relational transformation.

Sharing life with someone with an eating disorder can have positive outcomes. Perkins et al. (2004) noted that some partners experienced personal growth, becoming a more empathetic and caring person, developing resilience and strength in the face of hardship, and learning to cope with uncertainty and anxiety. Others believed that dealing with the eating disorder brought them closer to their partner and increased openness, communication, and trust (Linville et al., 2015; Perkins et al., 2004). Still others identified becoming more compassionate of others with problems (Highet et al., 2005). In a study of 22 women with eating disorders and their spouses, self-reported marital satisfaction by the partner with the eating disorder increased following treatment that reduced their eating disorder behaviors. The ratings of intimacy by the non-eating disorder partner were not affected by the treatment of the eating disorder, suggesting the good news that moving toward recovery does not necessarily destabilize the relationship (Woodside et al., 2000).

Some couples concluded that coping with the eating disorder helped both people reflect upon health and attitudes toward food in a good way (Linville et al., 2015). Non-eating disorder partners who realized that they needed to maintain balance and "reclaim their own lives" were able to tend to the needs of the partner with the eating disorder and let go of a desire for the relationship to return to the place that it was before the discovery of the eating disorder. They enhanced the relationship in other ways such as engaging in sexual and physical intimacy comfortable for both, improving communication regarding eating disorder behaviors and related issues, and working through difficulties related to social interactions with others involving food (O'Connor et al., 2019). As mentioned earlier, there is an exercise in Gottman-RED couples therapy that helps couples dialogue about their future together in light of the eating disorder and the recovery process. As we learn more about Gottman-RED, we will spotlight the four couples introduced in this book, discuss their progression through couples therapy, and highlight the synchronous growth most experienced throughout the process.

Concluding Thoughts

Irvin Yalom, a gifted writer and master clinician, wrote about psychotherapy as if describing a work of art (Yalom, 2003). He was skilled at leading his clients deep into the parking garage, building a strong therapeutic alliance peppered with self-disclosure, authenticity, gentle confrontation, and here-and-now conversations around difficult relational and existential topics. Although our field is now very focused on scientific and evidence-based practice, I, like Yalom, view therapy as an art. For couples therapy to be effective, the therapist needs to go deep into the parking garage with their couples, facilitating the interactions that they will one day have on their own. When working with eating disorder couples, lack of understanding of the impact of the eating disorder can result in sessions spent following bunny trails leading to dead ends or even worse, the more superficial levels A and B where it is easy to focus on behaviors, food, or weight. In this chapter, we began the downward drive. In the next chapter, we will go even deeper. It is this understanding that will ultimately allow us to engage with the eating disorder couple in a way that is authentic, real, and relationship transforming.

5

Perplexing Problems and Empathetic Engagement: Digging Deeper When Working with RED Couples

No one likes being around a reactive dog. This is the dog that barks or growls at anything that moves or makes noise, be it a car, machine, delivery person, landscape tool, living creature or, perish the thought, another dog. In fact, owners of a reactive dog spare no effort in their attempts to calm their dog—giving the dog treats, removing the dog from any inciting circumstances, keeping the dog away from other dogs, keeping the dog inside all the time away from windows and doors, and even paying a small fortune for a skilled trainer to work with their dog. There are scores of books, trainings, and videos that suggest methods used by owners and trainers to decrease reactivity including distraction, verbal commands, sounds, and rewards, with varying degrees of success.

Worse than one reactive dog are two reactive dogs. One barks and the other responds, escalating the intensifying interaction that grows louder and louder, each working the other into a frenzy. Only distance and time can stop the oral altercation. If not restrained by a leash, a dog fight can ensue. However, while one reactive dog passing a calm dog may become dysregulated, the reactive dog will not become as dysregulated as it would with another reactive dog, and it will return to baseline sooner.

The same holds true for emotionally reactive people. Although movies and videos are filled with reactive humans because people seem to find drama and emotional intensity engaging and spellbinding, most people do not like living with it. When in an emotionally reactive state, people are flooded with stress hormones and say or do things that can hurt, physically or emotionally. People who develop eating disorders tend to feel things deeply. They have found that behaviors that began innocently such as a diet, purge, or a binge actually help them down regulate emotions, but they pay a high price for using these behaviors. Ironically, the eating disorder–related behaviors that calm one partner are often the same behaviors that fire up the other. Talking about emotional reactivity may help RED couples understand the importance of developing a non-anxious, calmer internal and external presence.

In this chapter, we are going to seek a deeper level of understanding of the complexity of couples relationships when one or both people have an eating disorder or disruptive eating behaviors and learn ways the Gottman-RED couples therapist can use this understanding to help these couples improve the quality of their relationships.

Perplexing Problems That Can Affect Chronicity

As mentioned in Chapter 4, Gottman-RED couples therapy emphasizes the importance of helping couples work together such that the relationship is a protective factor and not a maintaining factor for the eating disorder. This does not guarantee recovery but removes obstacles and creates the opportunity for growth and change. In order to be effective as a couples therapist with this population, the therapist must be aware of the issues RED couples typically confront. All couples have perpetual problems, issues that keep resurfacing without a satisfactory resolution due to individual differences in personality or lifestyle needs. In fact, John and Julie Gottman (2018) have found that 69% of all conflict conversations in any marriage are concerning perpetual problems. RED couples are no exception; however, in addition to the run of the mill, perpetual problems that all couples face, these couples have an additional layer of issues. The problems unearthed in this layer are not only perpetual, but perplexing. They are the kinds of problems that cause partners to scratch their heads, to repeatedly react in the same way, and to feel caught in a vortex unable to explain why. By the time people enter couples therapy, many will have already tried to change these dynamics without success. If they do not ameliorate, it is likely that non-eating disorder partners will experience burnout, eating disorder partners will follow a chronic course, and the relationship will deteriorate. It is at this point that couples often reach out for help and search for a couples therapist who also understands eating disorders.

In preparation for helping couples, the Gottman-RED couples therapist will benefit from understanding four concepts that underscore these perplexing problems. The anacronym BEAR is a helpful mnemonic device: **B**idirectional nature of the eating disorder, **E**motion regulation, **A**ccommodation, and **R**elational turbulence. Teaching partners to say the phrase, "BEAR with me as I work to understand and change" may be advantageous when helping these couples.

B = Bidirectional Interaction of the Eating Disorder and the Relationship

Here we find another chicken-or-egg question. It appears that eating disorder behaviors and couples dynamics may have a reciprocal relationship. Deanna Linville's (2015) curiosity about this possibility of reciprocity in eating disorder couples led her and her team of researchers to study 17 couples in which one person currently identified as having an eating disorder or having recovered from an eating disorder. They found that as people felt more stable in their relationships, eating disorder symptoms and the impact of the eating disorder on the relationship decreased; likewise, as people felt less stable in their relationships, eating disorder symptoms and the impact of the eating disorder on the relationship increased. This is not to say that the responsibility for recovery lies with the health of the relationship or that one partner is to blame if recovery is slowed, but it is noteworthy that the eating disorder and the relationship appear to feed off each other. The findings from Linville's study bear enumeration and attention. One cannot assume that what is true for 17 couples will be true for all RED couples; however, from the literature reviewed so far and from clinical observation, it appears that the relationship and the eating disorder become intertwined to varying degrees.

Kristen Morrison and her colleagues at Texas A&M University (2009) wondered if the bidirectionality was only present in couples where there was a diagnosable eating disorder or if it would be characteristic of couples with subclinical disordered eating as well. After interviewing 88 heterosexual couples, they found that even among women with subclinical eating disorder symptoms, there is a bidirectional relationship between eating, weight, and shape concerns and romantic relationship satisfaction. Thus, heterosexual romantic relationships in which men affirmed and accepted the woman's body served as a protective factor against developing an eating disorder. However, a relationship in which men gave negative feedback about their partner's body increased eating, weight, and shape concerns and drive for thinness, leaving the woman more vulnerable to developing an eating disorder.

Morrison and her colleagues also found if a partner suggested a woman lose weight, that woman reported lower relationship satisfaction. This could be due to the tendency for men who are unhappy with their partner's body to invest less in the relationship over time, to participate in fewer positive interactions in the relationship, and to be more aware of potential affair partners (Morrison et al., 2009). It is worth noting that the impact on the relationship was the same whether the man wanted the woman to be thinner or heavier; thus it was the absolute value of the difference between the real and the ideal that impacted the relationship (Morrison et al., 2009). This latter observation points couples therapists toward the importance of facilitating conversations about eating, weight, and shape concerns in all relationships where food- or weight-related issues exist, regardless of body size or seriousness of eating disorder symptoms.

E = Emotion Regulation

> "Emotion regulation can be fostered or thwarted
> by romantic partners." (Fischer et al., 2017, p. 304)

Emotion regulation can be thought of as, "the ability to influence the occurrence, duration, and intensity of emotions" (Fischer et al., 2017, p. 304). Deficits in the ability to regulate emotion are considered to affect mental health and may result in psychopathology or relapse. Ulricke Schmidt and Janet Treasure (2006) noted that some non-eating disorder partners avoid discussing eating disorder behaviors and act in ways that actually serve as maintaining factors when they express anger, hostility, or criticism toward the person with the eating disorder or respond with comfort or reassurance when the eating disorder partner is distressed.

Very aware of the role emotion regulation can play in mental health, Marsha Linehan developed dialectical behavior therapy (DBT) in the late 1970s, a therapy focused on helping people, particularly suicidal women and those with borderline personality disorder. This therapy utilizes change-based strategies involving emotional regulation and interpersonal effectiveness in combination with acceptance-based strategies including distress tolerance and mindfulness (Linehan, 1993). Clearly well received and desperately needed, DBT has since become a household word for therapists, is regularly taught in graduate psychology programs, and has been adapted for use with other diagnoses including eating disorders. Because of Linehan's influence, therapists regularly employ mindfulness practices and relaxation exercises to help clients manage intense feelings and weather emotional storms.

People who develop eating disorders are inclined to reach for eating disorder behaviors rather than people including their partners to moderate the intensity of their emotions, particularly negative emotions (Weber et al., 2019). This does not equate to preferring to channel feelings into food behaviors, but food seems like their safest most reliable option. For example, when people with anorexia nervosa find that they experience a reduction in anxiety with restriction and severe weight loss, they learn to rely more on individual emotion regulation that they can control, namely using behaviors, rather than seeking support from the non-eating disorder partner who may be less dependable or available (Fischer et al., 2017). Likewise, maintaining a thin appearance allows for a reduction of social anxiety, as does control over foods available in social situations (e.g., checking menus in advance, bringing safe food to potlucks, giving reasons why certain types of dishes should not be served at meals when visiting friends' or relatives' homes). The same holds true for people with bulimia nervosa and binge eating disorder who seek refuge in their behaviors that calm, soothe, and distract from difficult emotions without having to be vulnerable with their partners.

There is some evidence that people with eating disorders enter relationships with an insecure attachment pattern, simultaneously drawing a partner close while using food behaviors to push them away, which is both confusing and hurtful for the non-eating disorder partner (Azmy, 2019). Sometimes, attachment needs that are unmet in the relationship are met with food instead (Maier, 2015). The idea put forth by Geneen Roth back in 1991 that food can supplant love or that there are times "when food is love" is consistent with this viewpoint:

> As long as my attention was consumed by what I ate, what size clothes I wore, how much cellulite I had on the backs of my legs, and what my life would be like when I finally lost the weight, I could not be deeply hurt by another person. My obsession with weight was more dramatic and certainly more immediate than anything that happened between me and a friend or lover. When I did feel rejected by someone, I reasoned that she or he was rejecting my body, not me, and that when I got thin things would be different . . . and then I met Matt. . . . I realized I didn't know how to engage myself deeply with a person, only with food. (pp. 1–2)

The Gottman-RED couples therapist assists couples in talking about how to change this pattern—using interventions such as *The Aftermath of a Behavior* that teach the non-eating disorder partner how to be supportive after a behavior has been used with the hope that over time, the person with the eating disorder will reach for their partner for support before using a behavior.

OVERCONTROL. Thomas Lynch (2018) noted that therapies focused on helping people struggling with emotional dysregulation have been in the limelight, potentially eclipsing the needs of those struggling with emotional overcontrol (OC). These individuals, including a subgroup with restrictive anorexia nervosa, struggle with emotional loneliness, not emotional dysregulation. Excessive inhibitory control, or overcontrol, impacts their capacity to have a close, supportive romantic relationship. Intense restrictive eating causes physiological responses that conserve energy including the down regulation or numbing of emotions and reduction in pain sensitivity. Lynch posited that the body actually modifies the response to flooding, phasing out the fight-or-flight response in favor of the "freeze" option. These heroic efforts by the body increase the likelihood of survival of the individual but decrease the likelihood of survival of the relationship; the concomitant flattened affect negatively impacts intimacy. Unfortunately, some with anorexia nervosa discover that the flattened affect has secondary benefits—a Mr. Spock-like visage that no longer reveals emotions, thereby creating the illusion of invincibility and invulnerability, much like the higher body weight of some with binge eating disorder. This emotionless countenance leaves the non-eating disorder partner unable to read their partner's facial expressions, keeps interactions more superficial, and severely limits emotional connectedness. Lynch (2018) developed an individual therapy called radically open-dialectical behavior therapy (RO-DBT) that can be adapted to work with couples. The couples therapist can encourage people with anorexia nervosa to build intimacy with the non-eating disorder partner by focusing on congruence of emotion and facial expression to start (Hempel et al., 2018), then doing activities together like the Loving-Kindness Meditation that will help them move toward recovery and emotional health (Lynch, 2018).

EMOTION CO-REGULATION. Whether emotions are dysregulated or overcontrolled, RED couples desirous of a strong relationship need to learn how to manage them together. Danielle Weber and her associates at the University of North Carolina (2019) defined emotion co-regulation as the bidirectional linkage of emotions between partners that optimally results in homeostasis for both (Weber et al., 2019). In healthy couples, co-regulation can help with emotional stability because both benefit from the parallel emotional responses and from the emotional grounding of one partner when the other is experiencing distress. Co-regulation can also allow for empathy and promote bonding. Some people are better at self-soothing, whereas others look to friends or family to assist in regulating their emotions, finding responses of reassurance or offers of assistance helpful. Ideally, partners will work together to manage intense emotions. However, not all couples have the skills to regulate emotion conjointly. When a relationship is unhealthy in this area, interactions can serve to prolong or intensify emotions, thereby inhibiting effective regulation (Weber et al., 2019).

In couples where one or both struggle with mental health disorders, interactions can be challenging. For example, when one partner has an eating disorder and becomes emotionally distressed and is in a relationship with a partner who is highly reactive, the non-eating disorder partner matches the level of arousal, with both likely to become flooded. This often leads to the non-eating disorder partner acting to reduce the level of emotional distress of the eating disorder partner because doing so will decrease their own distress as well.

The sequence may go like this:

1. **Eating disorder partner becomes upset.**
2. **Non-eating disorder partner reacts.**
3. **Eating disorder partner becomes more upset.**
4. **Non-eating disorder partner acts to reduce the distress by accommodating/giving in.**
5. **Eating disorder partner calms.**
6. **Non-eating disorder partner calms.**

Weber was intrigued and so delved deeply into the topic of co-regulation and found when a person with an eating disorder partnered with someone who is highly reactive, conversations about sensitive topics were challenging. If the couple lacked healthy coping skills, both were vulnerable to using maladaptive behaviors.

Quisha had had a stressful day at work, so decided to stop at the casino. She and Demarcus had been fighting a lot lately, so she was in no rush to get home. She had not intended to spend much, but luck was smiling on her, and she actually walked out with more money than she had when she started. She would have kept going, but ran out of money on the debit card, so took that as a sign that she should stop.

Demarcus had also had a stressful day at work, so decided to swing by the local fast-food restaurant and have a snack. He, too, was in no rush to get home. Just as he had many times before, Demarcus pulled into the drive thru line and ordered, then handed the attendant his debit card.

"I am sorry, sir, but the card was not approved, so I cannot place your order," the attendant said calmly, smiling.

"What?" Demarcus was shocked. "Can we try it again?" He had just put $100 on the card that morning. Unfortunately, he did not have a credit card or any cash with him. This time, he punched in the pin very slowly, but the message was the same. The transaction was declined.

Embarrassed and disappointed, Demarcus drove home in a huff, marched into the house, found Quisha in the kitchen and, without even saying hello, confronted her, waving the card in her direction.

"Quisha!" his voice was raised and demanding. "Why is there no money on the card?"

Quisha was making dinner and looking forward to Demarcus coming home. She was in a good mood and excited to tell him about her winnings. Shocked by the unexpected intensity of his emotions, feeling her blood pressure rising, she immediately went on the defensive.

"Don't talk to me like that Demarcus. What is wrong with you?" The intensity in her voice matched his.

"I just went to get some food and the card was declined. Were you at the casino again?"

"What if I was? It is none of your business, "she snapped.

"It sure is when there is no money left for me!" He was yelling now.

She hated when he got upset like this and she knew it was because he was not able to get his food fix on the way home. What she wanted to say was, "Oh, so you can spend money on your stress reliever, but I can't on mine?" but instead, willing to do anything to make his anger go away, said, "Fine. I will order in your food. I know exactly what you were going to get!"

She actually started to calm down because she knew she was doing something that would settle things. Her tolerance for the tension was very limited. It brought back too many childhood memories.

Demarcus said nothing, grabbed a bag of chips, then flopped on the couch, and turned on the TV. The combination of the crunch of the chips and the knowledge that the food was coming were soothing to him. He felt himself calming down as well.

By accommodating to Demarcus's behaviors, Quisha soothed the waters at the expense of talking about her deeper feelings.

Weber and her team (2019) were particularly interested in studying emotional co-regulation in couples with binge eating disorder before and after couples therapy. Before treatment, they found that non-eating disorder partners with high levels of accommodation were more reactive and became emotionally aroused when the eating disorder partner was upset. After treatment, they were less reactive, as were the partners with the eating disorder. In other words, the emotional intensity in the relationship was toned down.

Melanie Fischer and colleagues (2017), also at the University of North Carolina, were also intrigued by the phenomenon of emotion co-regulation in couples with anorexia nervosa and sought to determine if this could be a maintaining factor for the eating disorder. They found that people with anorexia tended to fly solo when it came to emotion regulation, withdrawing from their partners and limiting emotional sharing, using food behaviors and thoughts rather than people to down-regulate emotion. Fischer recommended using couples therapy sessions as exposure therapy of sorts in which the person with anorexia practiced sharing eating disorder–related experiences with their partner, thereby learning to tolerate increasing levels of emotional arousal that arose in the process (Fischer et al., 2017).

A = The Allure of Accommodation

In Chapter 4 and in the previous section on emotion regulation, we introduced the idea of accommodation and how easy it is for the non-eating disorder partner to become entangled in this web of least resistance. One of the most important tasks facing the Gottman-RED couples therapist is increasing the couple's awareness of tendencies toward accommodation, dodging difficult discussions, and conflict avoidance. Although accommodation may allow the couple to avoid feelings of helplessness and anger in disputes regarding food-related behaviors, it can lead to subsequent feelings of guilt, self-blame, anxiety, disgust, and frustration on the part of the non-eating disorder partner (Sepulveda et al., 2009).

COVARIATION AND COUPLING. Involuntary changes in voice when experiencing emotional distress may be the first clues that enter the awareness of one partner that something is brewing at an emotional level for the other. The response of the partner, covariation, may mediate the level of distress or match it, a phenomenon known as coupling (Fischer et al., 2017; Weber et al., 2019). Coupling is different from co-regulation in that in co-regulation the response of the partner has a dampening effect, whereas in coupling or covariation, the response of the partner amplifies the emotions and moves the couple away from a homeostatic balance.

In Melanie Fischer's study (2017), people with anorexia nervosa responded to their partner's level of arousal by coupling. As their partner became more upset, they became more upset, with emotional intensity escalating such that it took both longer to return to baseline. The level of severity of anorexic symptoms made no difference. Of interest is the additional finding that unlike people with an eating disorder, people with obsessive-compulsive disorder did not couple, remaining unaffected by the arousal level of their partners. In summary, for people with anorexia nervosa, there was a consistent pattern of emotion coupling.

In their discussion, Fischer's team (2017) made a remarkable observation and recommendation. They noted that although at first glance it might seem that working with RED couples to minimize covariation or coupling of emotional responses would be a good idea, the danger in so doing is inadvertently encouraging the non-eating disorder partner to accommodate by responding such that the person with the eating disorder is less dysregulated, just the way Quisha interacted with Demarcus. It is likely better to take a different approach, given that accommodation by the non-eating disorder partner is associated with chronicity and poorer outcomes for the person with anorexia nervosa. The same appears to be true in couples with binge eating disorder. Weber's team (2019) noted that non-eating disorder partners who were emotionally reactive themselves discovered that accommodation to the behaviors of the eating disorder not only reduced the distress of the eating disorder partner but reduced their own distress, not realizing that accommodation could in the long run be detrimental for both and perpetuate the eating disorder. This is exactly the dynamic that Ana Sepulveda and her team at King's College in London (2009) were attempting to measure when they developed the Accommodation and Enabling Scale for Eating Disorders (AESED) to measure modifiable elements of non-eating disorder partner behaviors. The AESED is one of the assessment tools used in Gottman-RED couples therapy.

More often than not, efforts to help such as providing reassurance when a partner is anxious, buying binge foods, supporting a partner in restriction, only going to acceptable restaurants, keeping binge foods out of the house, or adapting schedules to accommodate excessive exercise reinforced behaviors that preserved harmony and decreased distress in the moment, thereby postponing resolution of issues that must be confronted in order that the person recovers and/or the relationship grows. Because the non-eating disorder partner's primary motivation for accommodation may be to alleviate their own distress, they may feel less of a need to accommodate when their own emotions are more stable (Weber et al., 2019). In these cases, individual therapy for the non-eating disorder partner may not only be warranted, but extremely helpful.

It is a delicate balance. Essential discussions of eating-related issues, weight, or food as well as topics such as physical affection and sexuality are likely to elicit emotion dysregulation for the person with the eating disorder and the non-eating disorder partner, thus the couples therapist needs to guide the RED couple through these conversations and help them with coupling, co-regulation, and a tendency to accommodate in the face of strong emotions (Bulik et al., 2012; Maier, 2015). Both partners may benefit from learning coping skills to manage negative emotions (Linville et al., 2015), learning to tolerate increasing levels of emotional intensity, and knowing how to take a break when flooded (Gottman & Gottman, 2018). Introducing the RED couple to an exercise called *TOES (Tolerating Others' Emotional Storms)* teaches them how to listen to each other while minimizing co-regulation, emotional coupling, or accommodation. As the non-eating disorder partner learns to avoid the temptation to minimize distress by accommodating and the eating disorder partner learns to avoid the temptation to minimize distress by hiding behind eating disorder behaviors, emotional connection increases, with great benefit to the relationship.

R = Relational Turbulence

I have always enjoyed traveling in an airplane, except during turbulence. "This is your captain speaking. Flight attendants, please be seated. Passengers, return to your seats. Fasten your seatbelts. We will be encountering turbulence up ahead." The warning creates anxiety in me, but also helps me mentally prepare. Evidently, turbulence is inevitable when flying, given that it is precipitated by mountains, jet streams, and storms. Sometimes the turbulence is quite intense and sometimes not as much. Regardless, I always feel relieved when it is over.

When reading about airplane turbulence, I learned that pilots are not afraid of turbulence. For them, it comes with the territory in aviation and is to be expected. My friend who is a flight attendant agreed and told me that she knew what to do to stay safe and ride out the rough patches until things were calmer again.

Relational turbulence is inevitable as well. John and Julie Gottman (2024) advised couples to expect conflict, learn to manage it rather than avoid it, and focus on becoming masters of repair. People who have learned to avoid conflict may be caught unawares by relational turbulence, feeling confused and mystified by it, and try to stop it. People who grew up in families where there were angry fights between their parents or explosive outbursts in public places may not only react negatively to raised voices or yelling, but also bristle at even a hint of conflict or disagreement. The potential disruption of emotional connection creates anxiety and sometimes panic in one or both partners. Unfortunately, there is no pilot to warn that relational conflict is coming, *unless* there is a couples therapist helping the two partners, announcing that there will be a bumpy ride up ahead and helping them to prepare.

The Gottman-RED couples therapist learns that this turbulence is a normal part of the change process for RED couples and helps them navigate through it. Just like an airplane pilot, therapists understand it, teach couples about it, and normalize it for them. Relationships encounter **mountains**—really hard times and problems related to the relationship (e.g., affairs, domestic violence, regrettable incidents), **jet streams**—strong winds of change (e.g., transitions such as eating disorder behavior change, faith shifts, substance use behavior change, deployment, parenthood, empty nesting, retirement), and **emotional storms**—strong emotions expressed by one or both partners. Let us look at relational turbulence in more depth.

Relational turbulence theory states that romantic partners can influence each other in ways that either facilitate or interfere with the accomplishment of personal goals depending upon how they cope with the loss of predictability that comes with change (Knobloch et al., 2020; Solomon et al., 2016). Relational turbulence can be caused by feeling doubts or relational uncertainty (fueled by fear about what changes will mean for the relationship) or by interference or undermining the pursuit of individual goals, preferring the status quo and current rituals of connection (also fueled by fear about what changes will mean for the relationship). Relational turbulence is a normal part of relationship development; however, in healthy relationships, as partners become more interdependent and intimate, interference in achievement of goals is expected to lessen (Theiss et al., 2016). Thus, the capacity of partners in relationships with eating disorders to support and survive alterations in eating disorder behaviors is influenced by the level of healthy interdependence of each partner at the time of the change.

Looking through the lens of relational turbulence theory, Jennifer Theiss and her colleagues (2016) explored the potential impact of a romantic relationship on weight loss goals. Although this study focused on couples in which one partner wanted to lose weight, the results are relevant and can be extrapolated to RED couples in which one partner determines to change food-, exercise-, or weight-related behaviors as part of recovery. Theiss studied 122 people who were actively involved in a weight loss plan while in a committed relationship to determine if their partners extended facilitating or interfering behaviors. They qualified their results by noting that people in satisfying relationships tended to make more positive attributions to their partner's behaviors than did those in unhappy relationships. The study focused on the impact of a partner on the pursuit of a specific goal, noting that ambivalence about achieving the goal might increase susceptibility to partner interference. Thus, people ambivalent about eating behavior change would be more likely to stop trying when encountering partner interference whereas someone determined to make the change might be undeterred.

Theiss's team (2016) also found that the following facilitating behaviors were perceived as supportive: the partner enabling the diet, the partner providing motivation and encouragement, exercising together, and dieting together. Interfering behaviors that were perceived as unsupportive included lack of partner support in planning healthy meals or controlling the food environment (e.g., how food is prepared, what foods are brought into the house), the partner preventing or discouraging exercise, the partner continuing to buy favorite desserts or doughnuts for the dieting partner, or the partner communicating emotional or relational discouragement. *For example, when Quisha brought home Demarcus's favorite meal, she was unwittingly interfering with his efforts to change behavior.*

The researchers discovered that some partners even made unkind, unsupportive, or discouraging comments that hurt the partner and the relationship including one man stating that a person at a healthy weight is too skinny and that he would not like it if his partner got that small. Undermining remarks are not the sole province of partners dealing with weight loss or binge eating disorder. They are transdiagnostic.

> *For example, Luciano has repeatedly told Carmen that he wants her to get over her eating disorder but continues to make disparaging comments about women who are overweight and tells her he is so happy that she is thin.*
>
> *Every summer, Carmen and Luciano went to a beautiful hotel at the beach for 2 weeks. Unbeknownst to Luciano, Carmen had set a goal for herself to stop restricting and purging while on the trip this year. She was doing well until the afternoon of the second day when Carmen heard Luciano whistle at her. She had just come out of the pool wearing a new bikini.*
>
> *"You look amazing! Your body is perfect! Let's go see if the beds are made in our room!" Luciano was staring at her with admiration as he started gathering up his belongings.*
>
> *Carmen smiled, but her mind was reeling. She grabbed a towel and wrapped it around her. She had eaten a big breakfast and lunch, so now knew she had to be careful at dinner or throw it up. Her thoughts were racing. "I can never gain weight. Not after what he said. Why does he keep saying things like that when I have told him over and over again to stop?"*
>
> *Luciano knew that Carmen was working on recovery and that might mean exercising less or gaining weight. He wanted her to get better, but he did not want her to change. Embarrassed and guilty for feeling ambivalent, he was concerned about how changes in her physical appearance would affect him and his desire for his wife. He was attracted to a very specific body type and size in a romantic partner. He sighed and thought, "I can never share this with her!"*

What is most important for the Gottman-RED couples therapist to understand about relational turbulence theory is that the interfering reactions of the non-eating disorder partner are fueled by fear of and uncertainty about what changes or transitions will mean for the relationship. Educating the couple about relational uncertainty and interdependence as well as teaching communication strategies for minimizing relational turbulence is recommended (Knobloch et al., 2020). In addition, the Gottman-RED couples therapist needs to warn the couple about impending turbulence and help them "sit down and fasten their seatbelts" so that they can talk about and prepare for changes up ahead. This theory embraces the idea that well-timed counseling interventions can promote relational well-being and resilience (Solomon et al., 2016). Conversations like those suggested in the *OWL (Orchestrated with Love) Conversations Assessment* (explained in Chapter 7) help RED couples navigate the periods of turbulence necessary for recovery and emerge from them with a stronger bond.

Identifying Perplexing Perpetual Problems

The most common perplexing perpetual problems that affect people in relationships with eating disorders include confusion about how to talk about food-, weight-, exercise-, or shape-related thoughts and behaviors; inability to successfully navigate added stress, tension, or conflict; difficulty making plans around food or preparing meals; frustrations related to restricted social life and other lifestyle issues; and struggles related to sexual intimacy. Let us look at each of these in more depth.

Food-, Weight-, or Shape-Related Thoughts and Behaviors

Whether a person's behaviors meet the full diagnostic criteria for anorexia nervosa, bulimia nervosa, or binge eating disorder, better fit under the umbrella term, other specified feeding or eating disorder (OSFED), or persist at a sub-clinical level, the disordered thoughts and behaviors around food, weight, and shape will impact the relationship. The effect varies depending upon the eating disorder behaviors and the severity of illness; nevertheless, the presence of the disordered eating related behaviors will be felt, albeit experienced differently by the two partners. Both struggle with being open, vulnerable, and honest with the result being a heap of "things not talked about."

The person with eating and related issues struggles to be transparent while feeling caught between their love for their partner and their preoccupation with food-, weight-, exercise or body image-related thoughts and behaviors. The non-eating disorder partner also struggles to be transparent, caught between their love for their partner and their hatred for the all the suffering and complications these issues have added to their lives. Winn and several colleagues in London who have extensively researched the needs of non-eating disorder partners (2004), noted that partners of people with anorexia nervosa and bulimia nervosa reported feeling that the eating disorder came between them and their partner, sometimes making it hard to think about the eating disorder partner without also thinking about the eating disorder. These individuals wanted to make a positive difference, thus needed and desired clear, practical guidance regarding how to interact constructively and be supportive as well as how to cope with the more challenging behaviors associated with the disorder. This is one of the primary focuses in Gottman-RED couples therapy.

Cognitive impairments caused by malnutrition due to restriction or excessive purging that affected mood, reactivity, and the ability to make wise choices about food and other aspects of life complicated interactions (Murray, 2014). Partners of people with bulimia nervosa may also need to learn to cope with comorbidities, given that 50% of people with bulimia have a concomitant history of impulsive behaviors including deliberate self-harm, suicide attempts, shoplifting, sexual disinhibition, or alcohol abuse (Perkins et al., 2004).

Partners of people with binge eating disorder reported difficulties discussing the eating disorder with their significant other and noted a marked lack of emotion regulation in their partners with an eating disorder. Emotional volatility and a high incidence of depression in people with binge eating disorder can make consistent effective communication unlikely (Gorin et al., 2003; Runfola et al., 2018). Use of food to regulate strong emotions and for self-soothing is so ingrained for many people with binge eating disorder that the non-eating disorder partner plays second fiddle. As aptly stated by Geneen Roth (1991), food does not talk back, leave, or have a mind of its own, but people do.

Some non-eating disorder partners questioned if their partner really needed their help given the high level of functioning of most people with binge eating disorder. To further complicate things, the secretiveness of the person with the eating disorder can so effectively cloak binge eating behaviors that the non-eating disorder partner may wonder if the eating disorder really exists.

Partners of people who have OSFED, orthorexia, or subclinical eating disorder tendencies may feel in the dark, with resources and educational materials difficult to find. They know that their partner is wrestling with something related to food, weight, exercise, or body image, but cannot find a name for it, making it more difficult to discuss. The same holds true for the partner with the symptoms. They also know they are wrestling with something, but often deny the seriousness of it because they do not meet *DSM-5-TR* diagnostic criteria. Consequently, neither knows how to talk about "it," so do not, but "it" still strains the relationship, causes anxiety in both partners and, ultimately, creates distance between them.

One of my clinical supervisors liked to use the analogy of the splitting wedge to describe the impact of "things not talked about" that were never discussed. As you may know, the woodcutter drives the splitting wedge down into the piece of wood. The deeper the wedge goes, the more the wood splits apart until eventually it splits into two pieces.

In a relationship, something not talked about, whether it be an awkward moment, an irritating event, a thought, or a regrettable incident is just like the splitting wedge. Not talking about it drives it lower. The longer it is there, the deeper it goes, and the more distance it creates. It can potentially drive the two people apart, and in the worst-case scenario, they grow so far apart they are emotionally disconnected, if not permanently separated. The only way to remove the wedge is to talk about the painful issues and repair and restore the emotional connection that was lost. Assisting couples in processing these events is another one of the many jobs of the Gottman-RED couples therapist.

Added Stress, Tension, and Conflict

For many, the eating disorder feels like a cloud hanging over the relationship. Just as the sun is obscured on a cloudy day, the joy and fun in a relationship can be obscured by the seriousness and pervasiveness of the eating disorder. Non-eating disorder partners reported continually feeling scared of saying the wrong thing and, ironically, frequently did say the wrong thing (Linville et al., 2015). Trying to find the right words to provide continual reassurance and encouragement was exhausting.

Balancing the needs of the person with the eating disorder with those of other family members, particularly if the couple have children, can be a daunting task since the needs of the person with the eating disorder often take center stage (Linville et al., 2015). If the person in recovery goes to residential treatment for a month or longer, responsibilities of maintaining the family and household fall on the shoulders of the non-eating disorder partner, sometimes resulting in decreased work performance, or illness, or exhaustion. This partner can become angry or resentful and have difficulty showing empathy to the person in recovery due to emotional depletion and prolonged stress (Bulik et al., 2012).

If a couple has children, there is an extra layer of complexity. Some people with eating disorders do not want their children to know that they have an eating disorder, especially when the children are really young. At times, this can put the non-eating disorder partner in the uncomfortable position of bending the truth, avoiding questions, or outright lying to their children in order to respect the wishes of their partner with an eating disorder.

Luna came running downstairs, a worried look on her little 3-year-old face.

"Papá—I opened the door to go potty and Mama was in there

*by the toilet throwing up. She got mad at me and said, 'Go away.'
Is she sick?"*

*Luciano panicked, caught totally off guard. Not knowing
how to respond, he said, "Maybe she ate something her tummy
didn't like."*

Luna persisted, "But why did she get mad at me?"

*What was he going to say now? He was furious at Carmen
for putting him in this position and for not locking the bathroom
door, so their daughter saw her eating disorder behavior. "Probably
because she doesn't feel good."*

*"Can you help her, Papá?" Luna asked. Luna loved her mother
very much and was scared something was wrong with her.*

*"I will check on her in a few minutes. Let's get you back to bed.
Would you like me to give you a back scratch?"*

Luna loved back scratches. Her face brightened, "OK, Papá."

*Carmen and Luciano had a long talk that night that ended in
a fight. In Luciano's mind, it was one thing if Carmen's behaviors
affected him, but when they affected Luna, he had no tolerance.*

Understanding the complexity of situations like this one in relationships with eating disorders empowers the Gottman-RED couples therapist to assist couples in talking about emotionally charged
situations that involve children.

Difficulty Making Plans Around Food or Preparing Meals

Couples reported challenges related to travel, planning or preparing a meal, going to the grocery store, or choosing a restaurant
(Linville et al., 2015; Reiff & Reiff, 1999). Meal planning, something that for most people is routine or requires minimal discussion, often becomes nerve-racking and complicated with multiple,
frequent, stressful conversations about what foods are acceptable
or not, what foods or brands to buy, and what to do about the high
cost of specialty foods (Perkins et al., 2004).

*Amy and John decided to eat in for their anniversary and make
a special dinner. Amy was making the salad and cutting vegeta-*

bles. John was preparing the chicken. They were going to make stir-fry chicken and vegetables and salad with fruit and ice cream for dessert.

Amy was laughing and teasing John, "John, you would look so cute in a chef's hat! I am going to buy you one!"

John laughed and retorted, "I will only wear it if you wear one, too." He paused, then added with a chuckle, "I know. That could be all that we wear!"

Amy laughed and gave him a kiss. She opened the freezer to grab some frozen vegetables and noticed the ice cream for dessert, "John, I thought I told you to get the slow-churned vanilla."

"You did. But they were all out, so I got the regular."

"But you know I don't like the regular because it has more fat in it."

"I know that, but didn't think it would be a big deal for one night."

Amy hesitated. She decided to let it go for now and focused on cutting the vegetables. John was about to start the stir fry. He had the bottle of olive oil in his hand to use in the wok, then noticed the salads Amy made sitting on the counter. Without thinking, he dumped some oil on each of the salads, then added some balsamic vinegar.

Amy stared, horrified. She had no idea how much oil he had just put on her salad and she freaked out.

"John, what are you doing? I hate oil on my salad. I only put vinegar. Now it's ruined. I can't eat that!"

"Are you kidding me, Amy? First, it's the ice cream and now the salad. Are you going to wreck this evening with your stupid food rules?"

The evening went downhill from there. Instead of having a nice anniversary dinner, they ended up eating separately.

Lifestyle

Social life is predictably affected by the eating disorder. Consider this interaction between Ezra and Abe.

Ezra and Abe were invited to go to dinner with friends on Sunday at 5:00 p.m. Abe was excited to go out and do something fun.

Ezra was less enthusiastic. He explained he would still be at the gym, then asked where they would be going. Abe said he would find out. He later informed Ezra that their friends wanted to go to the new local French restaurant.

Ezra mumbled something about needing to think about it and left the room. When alone, he immediately googled the restaurant and scanned the menu, quickly noticing that the limited menu items were quite rich, prepared with sauce, and highly caloric. He panicked. To make matters worse, their friends were big eaters and always wanted him to eat more.

Afraid that Abe would get mad at him if he told the truth, Ezra avoided a face-to-face conversation by texting Abe, "I really don't want to go. You can go without me."

Abe stared at his phone. Here we go again. He is in the next room and he is texting me! *Abe texted back, "All we do is the same thing every weekend . . . and when it comes to food, you eat the same thing every day and if we eat together, I do, too. Why can't we change it up a little?"*

Ezra texted his reply, "Fine, I will go if we can go to the Korean place instead and if we can go at 6:30. Can you ask them?"

Abe had had enough of the texting and walked into the exercise room where Ezra was sitting on the exercise bike and stated firmly, "No, I will not ask them. They asked us and it was their idea. Why can't you be flexible? Can't you shorten your workout for one day?"

Ezra said nothing. He felt paralyzed. He could see how disappointed Abe felt, but he felt powerless to give up the exercise. The fear of gaining weight was too strong.

Ezra was right. Abe felt extremely disappointed, "This is why most of our friends have stopped inviting us to do things. I will just tell them no."

Ezra, still sitting on the bike, pedaled faster as he watched Abe walk out of the room.

When going to a party or a friend's or family member's house, people with eating disorders are often overly concerned about who will be present, what food will be served or available, the body sizes of the people attending, and who will see them eating (Lin-ville et al., 2015). Consequently, the inability to predict or control variables like these result in declining invitations and social withdrawal or isolation from others that leaves the couple alone, with few opportunities for fun or interaction with other couples or family members (Highet et al., 2005; Schmit & Bell, 2017). In addition, rigid schedules with no flexibility regarding mealtimes such as needing to eat dinner at 5:00 p.m. or not eating anything after 6:30 p.m. make getting together with friends challenging, if not impossible.

Sexual Intimacy

In the early 1900s, before bulimia nervosa and binge eating disorder were recognized as distinct, diagnosable mental disorders, mental health professionals struggled to explain the etiology of anorexia nervosa, let alone how to treat it. Psychoanalysis was not effective nor was behavior modification. As hard as it may be to imagine, initial theories posited that women who developed anorexia nervosa believed that sexual intimacy was shameful, frightening, or sado-masochistic. In addition, it was hypothesized that it was their fears of oral impregnation that provided the impetus for the caloric restriction (Kluck et al., 2018).

Understanding of etiology and treatment has evolved considerably since then, with mental health professionals abandoning the oral impregnation theory. However, sexual intimacy remains a complicated issue for most who have an eating disorder history.

In a review of the eating disorder literature, Annette Kluck and other researchers (2018) found that women with eating disorders, regardless of diagnosis, appear to have less sexual enjoyment than those in the general population. However, women who have recovered report more normative sexual functioning; thus the reduced sexual functioning may be a consequence of rather than a cause of the eating disorder (Kluck et al., 2018). Kluck's team was interested in determining if there were some shred of truth in some of the early theories that women who experienced greater psychic conflict about sex, had discomfort with sexual stimulation, and were obsessive about sex were more likely to have disordered eating. They found that intrapsychic conflict, preoccupation with sex, and discomfort with their bodies as objects for intimacy were predictive of disordered eating; however, discomfort with sexual stimulation was not.

Andréa Pinheiro and a group of international researchers (2010) compared data from 242 women with eating disorders with normative data regarding sexual functioning. They found some evidence that personality characteristics more than eating disorder diagnosis determined sexual functioning. It appears that people who are more emotionally constricted and overcontrolled had restrictive sexual functioning as well, whereas people with more emotional dysregulation and under control had more impulsive or self-destructive sexual functioning, regardless of eating disorder diagnosis. However, sexual dysfunction was common across eating disorder subtypes, with low BMI affiliated with loss of libido, with sexual anxiety, and with avoidance of sexual relationships. They concluded that women with eating disorders experienced significant challenges with sexual intimacy and relationships (Pinheiro et al., 2010).

In anorexia nervosa, things are fairly straightforward. Sexual satisfaction is directly related to the degree of caloric restriction, thus, the more weight lost, the less sexual pleasure (Dick et al., 2013; Kirby et al., 2016; Pinheiro et al., 2010; Schmidt & Treasure, 2006). Although lack of sexual desire may feel like rejection to the non-eating disorder partner, the cause is primarily physical, not relational. However, not only people with anorexia have challenges with sexual intimacy. Nearly two-thirds of women with eating disorders indicate loss of libido and have sexual anxiety. This could be due to the co-occurrence of depression in more than 80% of people with eating disorders (Pinheiro et al., 2010). During recovery, women with eating disorders indicated a desire for relationships; however, it is unknown if improved sexual functioning is also a goal or if enhanced sexual satisfaction is a natural consequence of recovery (Pinheiro et al., 2010). Carina Dick and her associates at the University of Alaska (2013) also reviewed the literature regarding eating disorders and sexual intimacy among women in heterosexual relationships and noted that a consistent finding was that non-eating disorder partners were dissatisfied with the sexual aspect of the relationship and believed that the eating disorder negatively impacted the sexual intimacy in their relationship.

What does seem to be the case is that people with eating disorders or disordered eating have complex feelings and thoughts about sex, some due to restriction or purging behaviors, with discomfort concerning their bodies being touched or viewed during sexual intimacy as a persistent theme.

> *Amy regretted getting so upset about the anniversary dinner. She found John sitting on the couch watching TV and snuggled close to him. They had both been looking forward to making love.*
>
> *"John, I am really sorry I got so upset about the dinner. I want to make it up to you." She gave him a long kiss and they began making out on the couch. Soon, they were in the bedroom and all was going well until John touched her stomach. She hated it when he did that, worried he would think she was fat if he felt the soft tissue on her abdomen. She stiffened. He hated when she stiffened. It interrupted the flow for him.*
>
> *"What's wrong?" he asked.*
>
> *"Nothing," she lied. "I'm just really sore from working out." She pretended to relax.*
>
> *He seemed mollified and things progressed, but her mind was elsewhere. All she could think about what how fat her stomach was and that she wanted him to finish so she could put her clothes back on and hide her body.*

Inaccurate beliefs by women that men prefer thinner bodies than they actually do may contribute to body dissatisfaction and affect sexual intimacy (Morrison et al., 2009; Tantleff-Dunn & Thompson, 1995). For many, it is the body image problems, not the act of sex itself, that cause the hesitancy or reluctance to engage in sexual activity (Boyes et al., 2007; Kluck et al., 2018; Morrison et al., 2009). In essence, the origin of the difficulties may not be found in libido or sexual desire, but in insecurity about physical appearance and concerns about what their partners will think if they see their body without clothes (Castellini et al., 2020; Harron, 2019; Kirby et al., 2012; Morrison et al., 2009). This idea was supported in a study by Arcelus et al. (2012) in which it was found that the main predictor of bulimic behaviors among college students was self-consciousness during sexual activity.

Giovanni Castellini and his colleagues at the University of Florence, Italy (2020), noticed that many people with eating disorders reported sexual dysfunctions or risky sexual behaviors. After reviewing 15 articles related to eating disorder psychopathology and sexuality, they concluded that body image disturbance and lack of a sense of embodiment can cause sexual dysfunction and that, "a healthier relationship with one's own body may be the final hurdle in the treatment of patients with eating disorders" (p. 559). They also concluded that good sexual functioning means people recovering from eating disorders will have a better relationship with their bodies in which they can touch their body, look at it, and show it to their partner without shame. The deleterious effect of issues regarding body shame on sexuality among people with eating disorders underscores the importance for RED couples to address these issues. Many RED couples have never talked about any of their thoughts and feelings about sex until entering couples therapy (Kirby et al., 2016). This noticeable absence of conversations about sex is not unique to RED couples but is quite common, particularly in American culture (Gottman & Gottman, 2018). The Gottman-RED couples therapy intervention *RED in Bed* was developed to aid couples therapists as they facilitate conversations specifically related to disordered eating issues and sexual intimacy.

Empathetic Engagement: Working Together as a Team

When partners in a couple work together to help the person with the eating disorder history change attitudes or behaviors related to eating, weight, body image or exercise, there appears to be more success than when the eating disorder partner works alone. Three variables affect the outcome of a team effort: the receptivity of the person with the eating disorder, the nonjudgmental presence of their partner, and empathetic engagement by both.

Receptivity of the Eating Disorder Partner

If a person with an eating disorder is in a committed relationship, sooner or later, they will have to make a difficult decision. Which will come first? The eating disorder or the relationship? The mental tug-of-war can be agonizing, with the relationship pulling one way and the eating disorder the other. If a person trusts their eating disorder behaviors more than their partner to provide dependable comfort, unconditional love, and enduring consistency, they are likely to hold tightly to their relationship with food. Some people with eating disorders, particularly those with binge eating disorder, have learned that love hurts, people leave, and humans deceive or cheat. Choosing the relationship is frightening, because, as stated by Geneen Roth (1991), many with BED have, "taken another lover, one who will never leave. Food" (p. 23). Choosing the relationship means leaving behind the relationship with food that is safe emotionally yet has the potential to hurt the body physically, and risking intimacy with a partner who is safe physically yet has the power to hurt or betray emotionally.

Melanie Linville and her colleagues (2015) determined that secrecy and deception were equated with the eating disorder winning, whereas honesty and openness about struggles and behaviors were equated with the relationship and recovery coming out on top. If the person in recovery thinks like this person who stated, "my eating disorder will never love me like he does" (Linville et al., 2015, p. 334), the pull toward choosing the relationship over the eating disorder is very strong.

The willingness of the eating disorder partner to let the non-eating disorder partner into their world affects how likely the partners are to work as a team toward recovery (Linville et al., 2015). When the person in recovery makes a commitment to be transparent with their partner, it is a turning point, not only for the relationship but for the recovery process. Sometimes, this decision is complicated by wounds from prior relationships.

THE IMPACT OF PAST RELATIONSHIPS. As mentioned in Chapter 4, negative experiences in past relationships can affect the willingness of the eating disorder partner in the current relationship to talk about eating disorder–related issues, especially if there is the potential for long-term commitment. Linville and her colleagues (2015) found that for many, the eating disorder was the main reason a previous relationship had ended. Sometimes, this was due to the inability of the non-eating disorder partner to listen calmly to the eating disorder partner talk about their eating disorder and their behaviors without becoming angry or upset and saying hurtful things. Consequently, there was hesitancy to involve the new partner in the recovery process or to talk openly about the eating disorder experience. In these instances, discussing how enduring vulnerabilities from past relationship traumas impact the current relationship is an important part of the couples therapy.

The Nonjudgmental Presence of the Non-Eating Disorder Partner

If the non-eating disorder partner responds with negative, critical comments, or expresses anger or resentment, it is no surprise that the person with the eating disorder is unlikely to continue to share openly (Bulik et al., 2012; Dick et al., 2013). In Gottman terms, relationships in which the Four Horsemen of criticism, defensiveness, contempt, or stonewalling are running rampant are not conducive to collaboration (Gottman & Gottman, 2024). When a non- eating disorder partner expresses criticism or contempt toward the person with the eating disorder, or with their behaviors, the natural response is to become defensive and protect oneself. In addition to common defensive reactions such as counterattacking, blaming, rationalizing, or playing the victim, people with eating disorders use their behaviors as a shield, retreating into food-related thoughts or behaviors to feel safe.

On the other hand, if the non-eating disorder partner responds with validation, empathy, and compassion to the disclosures, the kind of open communication that promotes recovery is likely to continue (Linville et al., 2015). This is not to say that the non-eating disorder partner cannot express their feelings, but how this is done matters. Listening, minimizing assumptions or judgments, and employing "I" versus "you" statements were more effective than attempts to problem solve or fix eating disorder–related problems (Gottman & Gottman, 2024; Linville et al., 2015). Gottman-RED couples therapists will employ a variety of strategies that help couples have conversations that support recovery.

Empathetic Engagement by Both Partners

Empathetic engagement is fostered by focusing on the eating disorder, not the person, as the problem, discussing expectations about duration of recovery, and having difficult conversations about the impact of the eating disorder on both partners. Empathetic engagement is, by definition, mutual, with the security and well-being of the two partners being equal in importance. Both partners need to learn about factors that promote recovery, then seek to view their relationship through the lens of the other, in essence walking in their shoes for a moment. The non-eating disorder partner works on understanding triggers for eating disorder thoughts or behaviors. The partner with the eating disorder works on understanding what it is like to be the partner of someone with an eating disorder (Linville et al., 2015). Discussing topics identified during the assessment with the *OWL Checklist* can help both partners nonjudgmentally wrap their minds around the perspective of the other. These topics are addressed early in the Gottman-RED couples therapy using the interventions the couples therapist decides best meet the needs of their couple.

Focusing On the Eating Disorder, Not the Person, as the Problem

Cynthia Bulik has a long-standing interest in helping relationships in which one or both partners have an eating disorder. As mentioned in Chapter 2, her team developed disorder-specific couples therapies. She reported that joining together and focusing on the eating disorder as "the problem" rather than identifying the person with the eating disorder as "the problem" strengthened the relationship (Bulik et al., 2016). Conceptualizing the problem, namely the eating disorder, as being between the partners rather than located in one of them allows for progress in both behavior change and supportive, empathetic communication.

Federica Tozzi and her colleagues (2002) studied 66 women in heterosexual relationships with a lifetime history of anorexia nervosa, 90% of whom were recovered, and asked them to rank key factors contributing to recovery. Of the top three most frequently cited, first was having a supportive husband, followed by maturation, and then last, but not least, therapy.

The reader may have noticed by now that there is a recurring theme throughout the literature regarding relationships with eating disorders: the presence of a supportive partner is invaluable and facilitates behavior change. The Gottman-RED couples therapist is tasked with teaching non-eating disorder partners how to offer support, learning how to cope with lapses and relapses. At the start of Gottman-RED couples therapy, the couples therapist will provide psychoeducation regarding eating disorders, eating disorder recovery, and the partner experience.

EXPECTATIONS ABOUT DURATION OF RECOVERY. There is disagreement among treatment professionals and among people who have experienced eating disorders about whether a person can be fully recovered or will always be "recovering," analogous to what is taught in AA about alcoholism. How the partner with an eating disorder conceptualizes recovery affects their expectations of treatment and outcome. Non-eating disorder partners view the treatment and recovery process with different beliefs and expectancies as well, ranging from hoping the eating disorder issues will be resolved within a few months or at the most a few years to believing that full recovery is not an option, thus the eating disorder is a lifetime proposition (Linville et al., 2015). The reality is that each person's journey is different and unpredictable—depending upon motivation, resources, quality of treatment, the relationship with the therapist/treatment team, and trauma history. No one at the outset is able to predict how long recovery will take, or if there will be periods of partial remission or relapse. Beginning the recovery journey is analogous to entering a degree program at a university with no idea or guarantee of the graduation date. Some people will take the risk, but others will never start.

Rarely is recovery fast. Non-eating disorder partners may become impatient with what appears to be lack of progress, particularly during the earliest stages of recovery when a certain amount of personal growth is required before there can be lasting behavior change (Reiff & Reiff, 1999). Repeated stays in residential treatment centers, participating in program after program, and being in therapy for years tests the patience of even the most tolerant of the non- eating disorder partners (Kirby et al., 2016). Couples found that having at least one source of support external to the relationship was very beneficial and released some of the pressure on the relationship (Linville et al., 2015).

In a marriage, there is an additional complication worth mentioning. People tend to marry partners who share complementary psychological issues and similar communication patterns. This means the non-eating disorder partner cannot help with recovery in areas in which they struggle as well and may not recognize change in areas that are blind spots. For example, a non- eating disorder partner who is a perfectionist may not see lowering expectations or learning to view mistakes as opportunities to grow as positive steps (Reiff & Reiff, 1999). On the other hand, the recovery journey can result in synchronous growth, the simultaneous resolution of issues for both partners that occurs when they are working empathetically and collaboratively.

RESPONDING TO LAPSES AND RELAPSES. When Christopher Fairburn (2013) penned the words, "Setbacks are inevitable and they are especially likely during the weeks and months when you are emerging from an eating problem. They are less likely later on. However, they can occur at any time, even years or decades later" (p. 212), he delivered a message that was both encouraging and disheartening. Most people with eating disorders and their non-eating disorder partners want to believe the eating disorder thoughts and behaviors will disappear, never to return. Considering the possibil-

ity that behaviors or thoughts may resurface is, for some, demor-
alizing; for others, this consideration frames recurrence as part of
the journey toward recovery and presents the opportunity and the
time to prepare.

Fairburn goes on to differentiate between a lapse—a setback or
slip—versus a relapse that would equate to going back to square
one in terms of behaviors and thoughts. He emphasized that setbacks are most likely to be triggered by eating-related events (e.g.,
dieting, breaking a dietary rule, binge eating); adverse events,
especially those that threaten self-esteem; clinical depression; or
events related to shape or weight (e.g., comments about body size
or shape of self or others, weight loss due to illness, weight change
after pregnancy). How the couple deals with setbacks is extremely
important. Fairburn recommends being vigilant to spot the problem early; do the right thing, meaning get back on track as soon
as possible; then identify and address the trigger of the setback
(Fairburn, 2013).

Clearly, a setback is an opportunity for the eating disorder partner to risk vulnerability and the non-eating disorder partner to be
supportive and empathetic. In Gottman-RED couples therapy, the
exercise called *The Aftermath of a Behavior* encourages both support and empathy in a structured way that is intended to provide
safety for the eating disorder partner and specific guidelines for
being empathetically engaged for the non-eating disorder partner.
Through using *The Aftermath of a Behavior*, non-eating disorder
partners learn how to support the eating disorder partner after a
lapse. Non-eating disorder partners who learn to recognize triggers and signs of lapses can help the person in recovery notice slips
and implement a relapse prevention plan (Fairburn, 2013; Linville
et al., 2015). Alternately, partners who are critical, hostile, or argumentative may contribute to illness persistence or relapse (Bulik et
al., 2012; Schmidt & Treasure, 2006).

As noted previously, when the Four Horsemen gallop into
a conversation, eating disorder thoughts and behaviors follow
closely behind.

Constructively Discussing Health, Weight Changes, and Body Image

John Gottman has often referenced research indicating that people in committed romantic relationships had better overall health, were less depressed, and were likely to live longer than people who were not in committed relationships, with men tending to benefit more than women (Gottman et al., 2016; Markey et al., 2008). Perhaps this is because romantic partners have the opportunity to influence each other's well-being. However, talking about health, especially if it has to do with weight, can be a sensitive topic for partners with an eating disorder history.

People typically marry partners of similar body weight, with mixed-weight relationships viewed askance. Brian Collisson of Azusa Pacific University and his colleagues (2017) wondered if people expressed prejudice and discrimination toward mixed-weight couples. They queried 233 online participants and found this was indeed the case. Some actually advised people who were dating and in a mixed-weight relationship to display less physical affection in public and to delay introductions to close others. These overt expressions of derision for mixed-weight couples reflects the fact that weight remains one of the most "socially acceptable prejudices to endorse" (Collisson et al., 2017, p. 536).

What are the implications for relationships with eating disorders where frequent weight fluctuations result in episodic disparities in weight between partners, moving the couple in and out of the mixed-weight status? A couple that started out as a same-weight couple may encounter the discrimination or prejudice experienced by a mixed-weight couple (Morrison et al., 2009). This added stress engendered by pressures external to the relationship may impact the couple and cause one partner to feel embarrassed by the change in appearance of the other due to significant weight gain or loss.

Regardless of whether one person has an eating disorder or not, partners do tend to gain weight after marriage, and it may not be at the same rate. A negative response by a partner to physical changes in the weight of the other partner can impact eating behaviors and body image, potentially triggering an eating disorder. Over time, aging and age-related changes in body shape or size may cause increased dissatisfaction with one's own body image for both males and females, increasing the risk for either relapse or the late onset of eating disorders or disordered eating (Linville & Oleksak, 2013).

Weight changes can affect how one feels about one's own body image, how one feels about their partner's body size, and how one feels about being in public together. These feelings can have repercussions for a romantic relationship, particularly regarding touching and sexual intimacy. Partners who respond empathetically regarding changes in body weight foster closeness, whereas those who are critical create distance. A layer of complexity is added if the weight change, either severe weight loss or gain, is caused by eating disorder behaviors and has health implications. For example, when these weight changes cause bone loss, pre-diabetes, hypertension, or difficulties with mobility, there will need to be conversations about the potential impact for both partners.

ONE'S OWN BODY IMAGE. Stacey Tantleff-Dunn and Kevin Thompson (1995) were curious to see how much body image was influenced by the appraisal of romantic partners in heterosexual couples. For women more than men, their perception of their partner's preferred size greatly affected their body image and eating dysfunction. Sadly, their perception did not match the reality. The women believed their partners would be attracted to a smaller, thinner body size than the men actually preferred. There also was a misperception by men who believed their partners would be attracted to a larger, more muscular body size than women actually preferred. The researchers recommended interventions for romantic partners that included psychoeducation regarding body size preferences (Tantleff-Dunn & Thompson, 1995).

Body image is affected by comparison to one's partner weight; thus if one perceives their partner as having a more desirable body size if can affect one's own body image. Lindzee Bailey and associates at Rutgers University in New Jersey (2015) wondered if members of same-sex couples were affected by the body size of their partners. Although gay and lesbian couples tend to be affected differently by societal standards for body ideals (lesbians preferring higher BMI and gay men preferring ultra-muscular ideals), they found that they were affected by social comparison to each other in ways similar to heterosexual couples. Larger individuals who were in relationships with relatively thin same-sex partners were more likely to engage in restrained eating and struggle with body image issues. Bailey et al. (2015) recommended that couples-based interventions be developed targeting healthier eating and more positive esteem building in same-sex relationships where there is a significant disparity in body size. Nagata et al. (2020) noted that transgender individuals have a higher incidence of eating disorders and have elevated shape and weight concerns, thus couples therapists need to be sensitive to these issues in couples that include a transgender person (Nagata et al., 2020).

THE BODY SIZE OF ONE'S PARTNER. As just mentioned, comparisons with the body size of one's partner can lead to restrained eating, eating disorders, and dissatisfaction with one's own body (Bailey et al., 2015). Alternatively, focusing on the body size of one's partner can lead to dissatisfaction with the partner's body size and contribute to dissatisfaction with the relationship. In either case, additional help may be needed. In fact, Jon Arcelus and his associates (2012) noted that, "patients who present with body dissatisfaction may benefit from relationship therapy as a part of their treatment" (p. 150).

Charlotte Markey and her colleagues (2008) were curious about the extent to which romantic partners in heterosexual relationships took things a step further and tried to regulate each other's eating behaviors. They studied what happened when one partner attempted to regulate or control the eating behaviors of the other when they became unhappy with their partners' body size, regardless of partners' weights, and wanted to improve their health and/ or attractiveness. Apparently, women were more likely than men to monitor eating behavior and men were more likely than women to respond positively when their partner attempted to control their eating. Given these results, the researchers expressed hope that romantic partners could learn to work together to help each other become healthier, to eat healthier, and to maintain a healthy body weight, while nondefensively receiving help from each other.

WEIGHT LOSS OR GAIN FOR HEALTH REASONS. When recovery includes weight loss or weight gain for health reasons, there are ways to work together that help and ways that undermine progress. Talea Cornelius joined with other researchers and representatives from Weight Watchers International (2018) to study 130 couples involved in a weight loss program and found that, "feeling obligated to a spouse to maintain health can improve weight-loss outcomes, whereas pressures to lose weight can impede weight loss" (p. 780). They recommended developing couples-based interventions targeted to help spouses more effectively give support.

When one or both partners need to lose weight for health reasons, the interventions that encourage supportive conversations related to food, weight, or body image in Gottman-RED couples therapy could be a useful adjunct to current approaches in weight loss programs. As stated by Gorin et al. (2019), "Our understanding of how to involve spouses in the weight-loss process is in its infancy" (p. 145). Given that obesity is a significant health issue in our country and that 50% of people enrolled in weight loss programs have BED, it logically follows that a therapy that helps couples manage food- and weight-related issues may have value.

Conclusion

Eating disorders are complex problems. There is no universal explanation or clear treatment of choice. There is no cookie-cutter formula for recovery. If a person is single, the behaviors impact their life only. When someone with an eating disorder is in a committed relationship or married, the eating disorder affects both people, and both people affect recovery. Perhaps that is why individual therapy is limited in its effectiveness and recovery remains elusive for over 40% of people with eating disorders.

There seems to be ample evidence in the literature that relationship problems are characteristic of people with eating disorders and that the vast majority of adults with eating disorders are in a committed relationship. Nevertheless, it remains the exception rather than the rule that couples therapy is an integral component of treatment despite the development of several novel couples therapies over the past 20 years that are designed to help people with eating disorders. Most professionals trained to treat people with eating disorders are not educated about the value of a couples therapist as part of the treatment process. In addition, couples therapists who notice someone with an eating disorder or eating disorder history in their practices do not know how to help or how to integrate eating disorder–related issues into their treatment process. One option is for these therapists to continue couples therapy but not address the eating disorder related issues; another option is to stop couples therapy and refer the person with the disordered eating to treatment or individual therapy. Neither are optimal options.

Gottman-RED couples therapy is a new therapy for relationships in which one or both partners has an eating disorder, has an eating disorder history, or struggles with weight, compulsive exercise, or body image issues. Although Gottman-RED couples therapy evolved from traditional Gottman method couples therapy, the interventions can be easily incorporated into or augment other couples therapy modalities. The therapy is versatile. When treatment planning for eating disorder recovery, it can stand alone, enhance individual outpatient therapy, or be integrated into a residential, inpatient, or outpatient program. When helping a couple adapt to a chronic eating disorder with recovery unlikely or distant, it can be the treatment of choice. When a couple with binge eating disorder needs to navigate weight loss for health reasons, couples therapy offers a road map. When all else has failed in terms of therapies or programs, it is a good last resort. After studying the perplexing problems affecting these couples and the healing power of empathetic engagement, it would appear that without a doubt, a therapy like Gottman-RED that fosters synchronous growth in both partners is timely.

6

Enter the Couples Therapist

It is clear from the review of the literature that an effective method for treating eating disorders in adults remains elusive. As noted, individual therapy has been the gold standard; however, it appears to provide some, but not all of the answers. Some with diagnosable eating disorders enter a revolving door, spinning from one treatment program (particularly those with anorexia nervosa, bulimia nervosa, or OSFED) or one weight management program (particularly those with binge eating disorder) to another with periods of partial or full remission followed by relapse. Still others with subclinical disordered eating thoughts or behaviors suffer in secrecy and silence, feeling undeserving or too ashamed of behaviors that are not extreme enough to "qualify" for an eating disorder diagnosis, or live in a state of denial that anything about their obsessions with food, exercise, or weight lies outside of the normal curve. However, in all of these cases, the non-eating disorder partners sense that something is not right. They can feel the distance created by this ubiquitous acidic presence that eats away at the intimacy in the relationship, whether it is clearly defined or nebulous.

Sir Arthur Conan Doyle wrote a short story titled, *The Speckled Band*, in which Sherlock Holmes and Dr. Watson investigated a mysterious murder. In this story, the murderer concocted an ingenious plan employing a poisonous snake that he passed from one room to the next through a room ventilator. The snake slithered down from the ceiling on a bell pull, then landed in the bed of the innocent victim who was fast asleep. When a whistle sounded, the snake was trained to crawl back up the bell pull, slip through the ventilator grates, and return to the murderer for a reward of delectable snake food. Night after night, the snake would enter the adjacent room, drop onto the bed, and return through the ventilator at the sound of a whistle. The murderer was patient. It could take many nights before the snake would actually bite the victim, injecting its poisonous venom and killing her, but eventually it would happen. After she died, the family, mystified by the death, contacted Sherlock Holmes.

Although not a perfect analogy, there are some interesting parallels in this story that are relevant to the Gottman-RED couples therapist. I want to highlight the stealthy intermittent snakelike nature of the eating disorder thoughts and behaviors. It is these thoughts and behaviors that poison the relationship, not the person suffering from it nor the non- eating disorder partner. If the thoughts and behaviors go unchecked, they can destroy the relationship. When a relationship is suffering, the couple hires a therapist to unravel the mystery of what keeps happening that causes distance and distress in the relationship. Usually, at least one partner desperately wants the relationship to survive and be out of danger. Just like Holmes and Watson, the therapist sets out to solve the mystery by learning the history, understanding what has happened, assessing the pain, and determining how the person with the eating disorder and their partner can work collaboratively to minimize the eating disorder's impact so that their relationship can survive. I will leave it to your imagination to figure out who or what would be the murderer in this analogy.

Each of our four couples come to the therapist with different stories and different needs. *Carmen and Luciano are feeling disconnected, fighting a lot, using self-destructive behaviors, and thinking about ending the relationship. Demarcus and Quisha are committed to the relationship but are coping with problems by avoidance and distraction. Amy and John are teetering close to divorce over what is becoming an irreconcilable difference—the issue of having biological children. Abe and Ezra want their relationship to work, but both are worried that the eating disorder thoughts and behaviors will be too much for the relationship to handle.* Just like these couples, all couples experience a sense of urgency when they enter couples therapy and are looking to the therapist to figure out what is wrong and help them fix it. Some wish repairing a relationship was like repairing a car: you drop it off at the shop, mechanics work on it, you pick it up a week or so later, and it is good as new. Most people realize it is not that easy, but many underestimate the amount of effort it takes to implement new ways of interacting and managing conflict. Ironically, couples therapists may also underestimate the amount of effort and practice it takes to work effectively with couples, particularly those with eating disorders.

The Complexities of Couples Therapy: A Plus Two is Much More Than a Plus One

There is no doubt that couples therapy is challenging (Friedlander et al., 2006; Goldberg, 1985; Gottman & Gottman, 2013; Halford et al., 2016; Halford & Pepping, 2019; Oral et al., 2022). One way that couples therapy differs from individual therapy in that there is an observer to every interaction between two people. Each partner will carefully watch the interactions between the therapist and the other partner, sensitive to the potential for alliances or favoritism, while, at the same time, the therapist is watching how the two partners interact with each other (Friedlander et al., 2006).

Working with a couple puts the therapist in a group of three, ripe for triangulation, coalitions, and struggles for allegiance (Friedlander et al., 2006; Halford & Pepping, 2019). Way back in 1985, Daniel Goldberg, a professor of psychiatry and human behavior at Jefferson Medical College in Pennsylvania, wrote a pioneering chapter about therapist reactivity in which he proposed that the ideal couples therapist has the ability to take in the emotional field of each of the partners, experience what it is like to see the world from their perspective, and then detach, remaining on the periphery of the relationship without being drawn into the emotional turmoil of the couple or adding their own reactivity into the mix. This is not to say the therapist is to be robotic or like the surgeon who lacks a bedside manner. Without warmth and compassion, the like-lihood of connection is small (Oral et al., 2022). Goldberg (1985) noted that empathy is the one reaction of the couples therapist that strengthens the therapeutic alliance, so the challenge for the therapist is to be empathetic without becoming fused and overinvolved or disengaged and underinvolved. If fused, the couples therapist tends to be a pursuer (overinvolved), indicated by overfocusing on content rather than process, being too eager to help and talking too much, absorbing the emotional state of the couple, acting out sexual feelings toward one partner, taking sides, or investing way too much in saving the marriage. If disengaged, the couples therapist tends to be a distancer (underinvolved), indicated by emotionally retreating, allowing the couple to run the session by arguing endlessly or decreeing how the sessions should be conducted, feeling helplessly caught in an alliance with one partner to either side with them or avoid discussing certain issues, or emotional disconnection to the couple, evidenced by rescheduling, lateness, clockwatching, or boredom. Thus, the therapist can take the role of pursuer or distancer when working with a couple in which this dynamic is acted out between them with one partner as the pursuer and the other as the distancer. Quite the tangled web of interactions!

Interested in the impact of the couples therapist's presence, Oral et al. (2022) developed the Person of the Therapist Training Model (POTT) that stressed intentionality about use of self and heightened self-awareness on the part of the couples therapist. Three access points were identified: the wounded child, intimate relationships, and social location. The wounded child access point includes the feelings, memories, and reactions the couples therapist experienced when they were a child if they witnessed tension or conflict between their parents. The intimate relationship access point is the state of the couples therapist's current intimate relationship. Objectivity may become more difficult if one or both members of the couple they are trying to help reminds them of their own partner or if the couple sitting across from them is struggling with the same issues that the therapist has been unable to resolve in their own relationship. The social location access point refers to socioeconomic, religious, or ethnic differences. The latter requires vigilance when working with a couple if the therapist is unfamiliar with one of these areas. For example, if the couples therapist has never worked with someone of a particular religious faith, they need to be more sensitive in their work while focusing primarily on improving the quality of the relationship, not these religious differences. Access points allow couples therapists to artfully interject self-disclosure and metaphors as appropriate and to seek consultation when feeling lost in the weeds of a relationship that is not their own.

It is natural for the couples therapist to compare their own relationship to the relationship in the therapy room. They tend to react either with jealousy or gratitude, as articulated by one participant in the Oral et al. (2022) study who said, "When you see someone is worse off than you, you just thank God" (p. 235). At other times, they may feel envious when working with a couple who has successfully worked through a problem currently causing tension or conflict in their own relationship. It is quite common for a couples therapist to scratch their head in bewilderment, thinking, how did I just help that couple change a communication pattern in their relationship that I have tried for years to fix in my own without success?

The Honor of Working with Couples

In *The Wizard of Oz*, the great and powerful Oz turned out to be a man with foibles just like anyone else, but what he presented to the world was a mask of power, control, and superhuman capabilities. Most couples present an Oz-like mask to the world, even to their closest friends and family. When a couple shares their story with a couples therapist, the therapist is invited to look behind the curtain. The therapist may be the only person in the world to see the relationship when the mask is removed and the struggles facing the couple are exposed to the light. This is an honor and privilege to be held in high regard.

A couples therapist enters the private world of a couple during the first session when the couple shares the story of their relationship, revealing the hurt and pain that brought them to the point of asking for help. As mentioned previously, John and Julie Gottman

(2018) noted that couples wait an average of 6 years past the point when problems first began before contacting a therapist. One can speculate about why this is, but the bottom line is that it takes courage to reach out to a stranger and ask that person to help with your deepest, most personal, and private relationship. As aptly articulated by Friedlander et al. (2006), "When we are invited into the most intimate parts of people's lives, their stories cannot help but stir us . . . self-aware therapists who have worked on their own issues are in the best position to recognize countertransference and use it to therapeutic advantage" (p. 243). Gottman-RED couples are indeed inviting the therapist into the most intimate aspects of their lives. Not only are they choosing to talk about their issues related to very vulnerable topics like parenting, money, and sex, but they are also choosing to speak about issues related to the eating disorder. Many have had great difficulty conversing about eating disorder–related issues with each other when in the privacy of their own home, let alone in the presence of another person.

The most effective couples therapists are able to both impart knowledge and presence as well as learn from their clients, striking the delicate balance between identifying with their couples and differentiating themselves from them (Oral et al., 2022). These therapists are aware of their wounded parts and can see how a byproduct of working as a couples therapist can be healing for their own wounded child; helping others is often healing and fulfilling. One of the therapists interviewed by Oral et al. (2022) commented, "We work in the here and now; but actually we heal and cure the past. And what we did in the therapy room also heals the future" (p. 237). In the worst-case scenario, the couples therapist is caught unawares and stopped in their tracks by one of their own issues or blind spots during a couples therapy session. In the best-case scenario, the couples therapist also experiences self-healing as they guide others down the path of relationship recovery.

Therapist Reactivity

As aptly stated by John and Julie Gottman (2013) as they reflected upon their own work with couples, "Therapists, no matter how skilled, struggle with their own negative reactions to particular clients . . . because we treat couples, however, we may experience frustration, aggravation, or exasperation with a particular relationship rather than some hapless individual" (p. 91). If two of the most renowned and experienced couples therapists admit to reacting at times to the couples they are treating, we can all admit to and discuss our reactivity to the couples we treat.

This rarely discussed phenomenon of therapist reactivity merits some attention. The blessing and curse of being a human being providing couples therapy to a population as complex and vulnerable as relationships with eating disorders is that we are able to offer the empathetic and compassionate encounters that promote growth and healing while, at the same time, open ourselves up to pokes and triggers we would never experience otherwise. We cannot control which issues will surface during the therapy that will push our own buttons, but we can become better and better at managing our reactions when they do. Wolf and their colleagues (2016) made this astute observation,

> . . . successful psychotherapy relies on relational and technical interventions to alleviate psychological pain and that the therapist's experience of negative reactions to his or her clients represents a serious, perhaps the most serious, source of interference in the practice of those interventions. As such, we believe that these experiences and the ways they are dealt with during psychotherapy explain, in least in part, therapist effects—the fact that some therapists are better and, perhaps more particularly in this case, worse than others. (p. 175)

Couples therapists need to constantly be on the lookout and aware of their internal state when working with a couple. Couples therapy differs from individual therapy in that marital issues are acted out rather than talked about, thus having the potential to evoke strong reactions on the part of the couples therapist (Friedlander et al., 2006). Daniel Goldberg, as noted earlier in this chapter, was intrigued by the idea of therapist reactivity in couples therapy, so set out on a quest for literature on the topic, and just like Don

Quixote seeking the fountain of youth, found it difficult, if not impossible, to find. Almost 40 years later, the quest was picked up again by Sedef Oral and his team in Istanbul, Turkey, in 2022, with similar results; very little had been published about the person of the therapist when working with couples (Oral et al., 2022). Oral et al.'s (2022) concept of access points helps explain the phenomenon of therapist reactivity as does Karney and Bradbury's (1995) concept of enduring vulnerabilities, specifically the idea that the backgrounds and traits that spouses bring to the marriage, or in this case the therapist brings to the therapy room, from their pasts affect their adaptive processes.

The access points can be thought of as windows into the darker recesses of the couples therapist's psyche. During a couples session, the light may suddenly illuminate these shadowy corners, suddenly revealing blind spots and adding a new dimension to the potential for therapist reactivity. As mentioned previously, Oral et al. (2022) identified three aspects of the couples therapist's personality that have the potential to affect their responses to a couple. They include the wounded child who is sensitive to interactions reminiscent of their family of origin, particularly when interactions happening right in front of them result in reliving of parental interactions; the wounded partner who likewise reacts to interactions reminiscent of current or previous romantic relationships; and the hurt or bullied human for whom issues related to social location may trigger emotional wounds. When triggered, the couples therapist may appear distracted, insensitive, or shut down.

Enduring vulnerabilities are the wounds that the therapist has that predate the work with the couple. Inadvertently reopened unbeknownst to the couple, they may elicit subtle negative interpersonal reactions by the couples therapist that have the potential to skew the outcome of therapy (Karney & Bradbury, 1995; Macdonald & Muran, 2021). Staying attuned to their own immediate internal experience while simultaneously focusing on the couples interactions is no small task, but is necessary to be an effective couples therapist.

Well aware of the potential negative impact on therapy outcome of therapist reactivity, Macdonald and Muran (2021) explored the effectiveness of what they called "mindfulness-in-action" practices to help therapists self-regulate. They stressed the importance of three skills: self-awareness enhanced by self-compassion; affect regulation on the part of the therapist, so that they can remain empathic without regulating their affect through complementary hostility or avoidance; and interpersonal sensitivity, allowing for sensitive and therapeutic communication if a rupture in the therapy relationship has occurred. They noted that therapists are called to a higher standard than the average person when in the therapy room, acknowledging that the majority of people are unable to execute these skills effectively in the moment.

Therapist reactivity in couples therapy can be distinguished from countertransference in that the focus is not on the therapist–patient relationship but on the therapist's reactions to the interactions between the two partners. Sometimes, the couples therapist may align more with one partner than the other, subtly communicating dislike by avoiding eye contact or ignoring bids for attention or overtly disagreeing with or challenging one of the partners. It is easy for the couples therapist to be swept up in the need for the couple to change, or in the case of couples with eating disorders, for the partner with the eating disorder to recover.

Talking about their reactions with a couple is appropriate when the couples therapist's reaction is in actuality a result of behavior by the couple toward the therapist but not appropriate when the feelings are based on the therapist's own reactivity (Goldberg, 1985). In the latter case, the couples therapist should process these reactions with their supervisor, consultant, or therapist.

The Gottman-RED Couples Therapist Working with Eating Disorder Couples

As noted, the playing field is more complex with couples therapy than with traditional psychotherapy. It is even more complex in couples therapy for eating disorders. Whereas there are three players in the room in classic couples therapy, there are four when an eating disorder is present. As mentioned previously, the stealthy, intermittent, unpredictable presence of the eating disorder thoughts and behaviors is ubiquitous and overshadows every session in the therapy room. As we have seen in earlier chapters, there seems to be a growing wave of interest in integrating couples work into the treatment of people with eating disorders, given that the vast majority of adults with eating disorders are in a committed relationship or married. Given that the most efficacious way to include a partner in treatment is still a mystery (Kirby et al., 2016), Gottman-RED couples therapists have the opportunity to test out a new approach and add to the knowledge base in the field. Teaching couples how to work together so that the relationship becomes a protective factor that supports recovery and decreases the likelihood of relapse is essential. Halford and Pepping (2019) noted that for both alcohol use disorder and depression, individual treatment helped but did not relieve relationship distress, and ongoing relationship distress predicted relapse in those successfully treated as individuals. Thus, couples therapy was the recommended treatment of choice as it effectively and simultaneously treated the problem while enhancing relationship satisfaction. Might this also be the case for people with eating disorders?

Many of the couples approaches to date tend to focus more on the partner with the eating disorder and their eating disorder behaviors or thoughts than on the needs of the non-eating disorder partner or the quality of the relationship. Gottman-RED is different. It focuses on improving the quality of the relationship while simultaneously addressing the needs of the partner with the eating disorder and the needs of the non-eating disorder partner that are connected to the eating disorder. It is not uncommon for couples to need help with both the relationship and the eating disorder recovery process, with the eating disorder partner more motivated to work on the relationship and the non-eating disorder partner more motivated to focus on the eating disorder. Thus, this method is likely to engage both partners from the beginning. Working together in couples therapy with a skilled therapist encourages each partner to face the issues that are anxiety producing for them, whether it be those related to the relationship or those related to the eating disorder (Kirby et al., 2012).

As you learn about Gottman-RED couples therapy, I would like you to consider the perspective that for those in long-term committed relationships or marriages, a strong, healthy relationship is a prerequisite to opening the door to recovery. Thomas Lynch (2018) echoed this viewpoint when he introduced RO-DBT as a preferred therapy for people with treatment-resistant restricting anorexia nervosa. Lynch expressed concern that treatment that focused on eating disorder behaviors made these behaviors the "top treatment priority" (2018, p. 27), unwittingly reinforcing the very anorexic behaviors one wanted to eliminate. In this therapy, the clinician gently seeds, or "smuggles," the idea that the person is more than their eating disorder, believing that resolving issues related to overcontrol opens the door to recovery without making behavior change the number one goal. Mitchison and colleagues (2015) have also advocated for a shift away from symptom-focused interventions for eating disorders toward quality of life as a focus of treatment, especially for those with a severe and enduring chronic eating disorder (Haracz & Robson, 2017) as have Schmidt and Treasure (2006) who emphasized interpersonal rather than culture bound shape or weight-related maintaining factors. In a similar way, I propose that resolving issues related to a marriage or committed relationship has the potential to open the door to recovery, with behavior change being important, but not the number one goal.

Please keep in mind that opening the door to recovery does not mean that the person with the eating disorder will choose to work on recovery. What it does mean is that there is a strong, transparent, open, loving relationship characterized by synchronous growth and empathetic engagement that provides a substantive base on which to build. If the eating disorder partner achieves partial remission or full remission, that is the cherry on top of a good relationship. If not, the two people still have each other and can have a meaningful relationship and improved quality of life despite one struggling with a chronic mental disability.

The Competencies for Gottman-RED Couples Therapists

Gottman-RED can be thought of as a competency-based couples therapy. A competency can be defined as, "a cluster of related abilities, commitments, knowledge, and skills that enable individuals to act effectively" (Francisca & Gomez, 2020, p. 11). I like working with competencies because they allow for flexibility and adaptability. How one reaches a certain level of competency or how long it takes is not the focus. Achieving a minimal level of competency is what is important. In other words, there may be many roads to the same destination or more than one way to cook an egg. A competency-based approach provides an organized, integrated, and coordinated sequence of steps for the therapist and for the couple when learning a new therapy.

We will be discussing six competencies for couples therapists using Gottman-RED couples therapy in this chapter and 10 Competencies for Couples in chapters to follow. Being a Gottman-RED couples therapist is a challenging yet rewarding opportunity for couples therapists to expand their practices. Therapists desiring to work with couples in which one or both partners have an eating disorder will be most effective if they have achieved minimal competency in all of the following areas.

Competency One: Training in Couples Therapy

Although I strongly encourage couples therapists to be trained in the Gottman Method of couples therapy (minimum of Level One and Level Two), couples therapists with training in other approaches can utilize Gottman-RED couples therapy interventions. The most important requirement is that the therapist has received formal training and supervision in working with couples. As discussed in the beginning of this chapter, the couples therapist faces unique challenges that differ from those experienced by the therapist providing individual therapy. An appreciation for these challenges prepares the couples therapist for working with relationships with eating disorders. Since this population can be quite challenging, I recommend a minimum of 2 years of experience as a couples therapist before working with eating disorder couples.

Competency Two: Eating Disorder Knowledge

Gottman-RED couples therapists need enough familiarity with eating disorder symptoms, psychopathology, and language to be able to facilitate couples interactions around these topics. Treating people with eating disorders is a specialty field requiring specialized training. Gottman-RED couples therapists are *not* treating the eating disorder. It is very important to remember this. Nevertheless, they will be facilitating conversations about the eating disorder, so it is important to have a basic understanding of the etiology of an eating disorder, the behavioral manifestations, and indicators that a higher level of care is needed. Hopefully, the previous chapters provided a solid, rudimentary information base. I want to emphasize that the Gottman-RED couples therapist does not need to know how to treat an eating disorder. If they have this training, that is a plus, but not a prerequisite.

Competency Three: Ability to Build a Strong Therapeutic Alliance With Both Partners

In the outcome literature regarding psychotherapy, the relationship with the therapist is second only to patient variables in determining the likelihood that a person will continue in therapy. As in individual therapy, a strong therapeutic alliance predicts better outcomes in couples therapy (Halford et al., 2016; Halford & Pepping, 2019). It can be a little more challenging when working with couples because the effective couples therapist must maintain a neutral stance and have a positive relationship with both partners. A thorough understanding of therapist reactivity is critical, which is why it was addressed earlier in this chapter. Gottman-RED requires and emphasizes the importance of a strong therapeutic alliance, nevertheless the couples therapist must remember that the most important alliance in the room is the one between the two partners (Kirby et al., 2012).

Deliberately connecting with each partner early on in the treatment process increases the likelihood that the couple will stay engaged in the process. The partner with the eating disorder is more likely to trust a couples therapist who exhibits basic knowledge about eating disorders and their treatment whereas the non-eating disorder partner is seeking a couples therapist who demonstrates understanding of their unique challenges.

The therapist needs to show no favoritism, carefully walking the fine line of neutrality. Asking questions that reflect knowledge and insight into the complexities of an eating disorder relationship during the assessment sessions will engage the couple and engender confidence in the process.

Competency Four: Awareness and Understanding of the Levels of Care Available for People With Eating Disorders, Working as Part of an Integrated Care Team

A person with an eating disorder is referred, usually by a physician or outpatient therapist, to the program that provides the best level of care for them, often moving in and out of programs as needed based upon symptom severity and level of functioning. These levels of care include: inpatient (hospitalization), residential, partial hospitalization, intensive outpatient, and outpatient. Intensive outpatient programs can range from several evenings or days per week to every day. A strength of all of these programs, except perhaps outpatient, is that the care team is right there on site, so case consultation is easy and routine. Most use a model of integrated care.

My passion for helping people with eating disorders started early in my career. At that time, treatment was referred to as multidisciplinary. This meant that a team of professionals with different areas of expertise and training would come together and discuss cases with the hope of providing the best care possible. Our team was comprised of an internal medicine physician, nutrition therapist, psychiatrist, dentist, psychologist, and the patient. We met regularly, but the person with the eating disorder traveled to each of our offices for appointments. If they were hospitalized, the care team was in the same physical location, but when an outpatient, the person had to hop from office to office.

Soon, eating disorder treatment programs began to appear, but they were primarily inpatient. As time when on, outpatient multidisciplinary programs popped up and evolved into the multilevel system we use now, with on-site, integrated, collaborative care.

So, what does this mean for the couples therapist? Ideally, the couples therapist will be an integral part of the care team as couples therapy becomes routinely incorporated into all levels of care. Gottman-RED couples therapists may find themselves working as part of an integrated care team for the first time, routinely communicating and collaborating with physicians and nutritionists in order to provide the best care possible. However, for the outpatient couples therapist who has a solo office or is working using telehealth, this may not be the case. Asking RED (Relationship with Eating Disorder) couples to sign a release of information so that there can be open communication with the care team is important, as is regular communication if the person is in a higher level of care along with the couples therapy. In some cases, the person with the eating disorder may relapse or experience an intensification of symptoms while in couples therapy, so the Gottman-RED couples therapist needs to be familiar with the different levels of care and resources that are available so they can make an appropriate referral if necessary.

If the couple is at home together, the person in recovery is able to work on behavior change in the context in which they exist on a daily basis. If the couple is meeting while the person with the eating disorder is attending an inpatient or residential treatment program, they will learn skills to practice when they are both together again at home.

Competency Five: Awareness of One's Own Biases/Sensitivities Regarding Weight, Eating Disorder Behaviors, and Body Image Issues

The American Psychological Association has identified benchmarks for those entering the field of professional psychology.

Benchmark #4 is "Reflective Practice/Self-Assessment/Self-Care: Practice conducted with personal and professional self-awareness and reflection; with awareness of competencies; with appropriate self-care" (Campbell et al., 2012).

The challenges faced by couples therapists when working with relationships with eating disorders give couples therapists plenty of opportunity for self-awareness and reflection, not to mention the need for self-care. These include biases about weight, biases about eating disorder behaviors, feeling pulled to focus the therapy directly on the eating disorder rather than the couple dynamics, wanting to make suggestions, walking into challenging conversations about eating disorder behaviors, countertransference related to control, countertransference related to the therapist thinking they know best, and countertransference related to body image issues. In this competency, couples therapists work toward self-awareness through reflective practice and self-assessment in each of these key areas of potential bias.

BIASES ABOUT WEIGHT OR BODY IMAGE. We live in a culture in which weightism is commonplace and acceptable (Lampson, 2021). Therapists working with RED couples need to reflect upon their attitudes about weight and their own body image and be on the lookout for countertransference. These biases have the potential to affect the couple (Linville et al., 2015). Some therapists have difficulty looking at someone who is emaciated whereas others have difficulty looking at someone who is obese. When a person's weight falls outside of the normal curve, it is noticeable; Gottman-RED couples therapists need to be mentally prepared to receive all people with acceptance and lack of judgment. Gottman-RED couples therapists also need to be prepared for comments about their own weight or questions about their personal eating patterns, diet history, or exercise routines when working with eating disorder couples. Furniture in the room should be accommodating and welcoming, with a soft chair available for someone who is extremely thin and a non-constricting chair (no arms), couch, or large chair with arms available for someone who has a large body.

BIASES ABOUT EATING DISORDER BEHAVIORS. Certain eating disorder behaviors such as self-induced vomiting, extreme binge eating, food refusal when emaciated, chewing and spitting food, and laxative abuse have the potential to evoke strong negative responses, feelings of revulsion, or judgment. Being familiar with eating disorder behaviors can desensitize the Gottman-RED couples therapist to the unusual nature of these behaviors and helps them prepare to listen to conversations about them in the therapy room. Again, couples therapists working with RED couples need to be self-aware and learn enough about eating disorders to come to a neutral, if not compassionate, stance regarding these unfamiliar behaviors.

FEELING PULLED TO FOCUS THE THERAPY DIRECTLY ON THE EATING DISORDER RATHER THAN THE COUPLE DYNAMICS. When an issue arises such as the person with the eating disorder having an episode of binge eating the night before, it will be tempting for the therapist to address this directly. However, the therapist needs to direct the couple to talk to each other instead (Kirby et al., 2016). If the couples therapist is also trained as an eating disorder specialist, it can be a facile move to offer individual therapy to help the partner with the eating disorder process what happened, leaving the non-eating disorder partner on the sidelines. As frustrating as this might be, the Gottman-RED couples therapist's focus needs to remain on helping the couple talk these situations through with each other using an intervention like *The Aftermath of a Behavior* and refer the person with the eating disorder to individual therapy as needed.

WANTING TO MAKE SUGGESTIONS. When working with couples dealing with binge eating disorder or weight management issues, there may be the temptation for the couples therapist to suggest exercising more or trying a particular weight loss program or medication, especially if it has helped the therapist with weight management. However, just as this type of intervention is not helpful when a partner uses it, it is not helpful when a therapist does, either, and is outside of the scope of practice. Better outcomes follow when therapists use interventions characterized by autonomy support:

asking what might be helpful, showing empathy for the challenges, and validating efforts (Gorin et al., 2019).

WALKING INTO CHALLENGING CONVERSATIONS ABOUT EATING DIS-ORDER BEHAVIORS. Couples therapists may share the fears and discomfort of non-eating disorder partners when it comes to addressing sensitive topics related to the eating disorder. The non-eating disorder partner may feel so desperate at times that they welcome and encourage any sign that the therapist will "take their side," champion their cause, or tell the person with the eating dis-order to change. This can be tempting for the couples therapist, but it is not therapeutic. Talking to a consultant or supervisor about these potential feelings may be warranted. As alluring as it may be, it is essential that the Gottman-RED therapist does not fall into the role of individual therapist for the person in recovery or coach for the supportive partner, but instead constantly redirects the conversation so that the members of the couple learn how to have conversations and solve problems on their own.

COUNTERTRANSFERENCE RELATED TO CONTROL. It may be enticing for the therapist to become authoritarian when fears about secu-rity and trust are perceived as power struggles. This typically hap-pens when the person with the eating disorder persists in engaging in behaviors that endanger health and may require a higher level of care (Schmidt & Treasure, 2006; Woodside et al., 1993). This type of situation has the potential to become a countertransference issue if the Gottman-RED couples therapist taps into their own issues about power and control. For example, the therapist may have been raised by a very controlling mother who did not accept influence from them or listen to their ideas. If either of the part-ners seems resistant to the therapist's suggestions, strong negative feelings toward that person may arise and need to be processed in therapy or supervision.

During my internship, I worked in an inpatient treatment pro-gram for people with anorexia nervosa. In those days, tube feeding was common practice. The nurses working with that unit were not trained to work with psychiatric patients and were used to patients who did what they asked. Consequently, they became confused and frustrated with the patients who refused to follow orders and found devious ways to undermine the tube feeding process, including surreptitiously dumping their solution into the pot of a large jade plant in one of the waiting rooms. (This was only discovered when the plant began to wilt.) Although a somewhat humorous and definitely creative workaround, the care team did not find it funny, and some found it infuriating.

Many therapists steer clear of working with people with eating disorders because of the chronicity of behaviors and the lack of compliance. The Gottman-RED couples therapist who keeps the processing of behaviors within the couple, thereby avoiding potential power struggles with either member of the couple, will be the most effective.

COUNTERTRANSFERENCE RELATED TO THE THERAPIST THINKING THEY KNOW BEST. In this case, the couples therapist may think they can be a better partner to the person in recovery than the actual partner and starts taking over their role by talking more rather than helping the non-eating disorder partner develop new skills. As stated by Woodside et al. (1993), "the therapist must be aware that he or she can be neither a better wife, husband, father, or mother for either member of the couple than the one who is already in place" (p. 136).

Competency Six: Self-Care

As mentioned previously, many individual therapists view working with people with eating disorders as daunting and avoid this population, particularly those with chronic, treatment-resistant anorexia nervosa or bulimia nervosa. Although the role of the couples therapist working with RED couples is dramatically different than that of the individual therapist working with someone with an eating disorder, the couples therapist may find the process emotionally taxing at times. To avoid burnout or compassion fatigue, self-care is essential. Preserving time to debrief with colleagues, exercise, and practice mindfulness strategies as well as engaging in avocations and activities totally unrelated to the work at hand will be of immense benefit.

Concluding Thoughts

It is hoped that the couples therapists who learn and implement Gottman-RED couples therapy will become passionate about using couples therapy when helping couples where one person has an eating disorder. One of the therapists using the UCAN approach for treating anorexia nervosa commented, " . . . we can't expect the extent of change that is needed without involving one of the most influential people in the patient's life. And why should we ask a patient to engage in something as challenging as eating disorder treatment without facilitating support from the person who cares most?" (Kirby et al., 2016, p. 249). That is exactly why Gottman-RED was developed. However, this work is not for the fainthearted couples therapist.

Many therapists avoid working with couples, finding the tension and conflict distressing, particularly if the therapists grew up in emotionally volatile or argumentative homes. Many individual therapists who are well aware of the challenges of managing their own reactions to one client in the therapy room avoid moving into the couples realm. They look on from afar and wonder how couples therapists can consistently regulate their own emotionality when there are two other people in the room with them (Goldberg, 1985; Halford & Pepping, 2019). As we have seen in this chapter, sometimes couples therapists do this well and sometimes not as well. Adding on the layer of complexity of an eating disorder makes the work more challenging and more rewarding.

In summary, the most effective Gottman-RED couples therapists are cognizant of the honor and privilege of being a couples therapist, the pitfalls of reactivity, and the potential biases when working with this population. *They will be prepared when Carmen says she cannot stop throwing up if Luciano is going to be mean to her (when the therapist's father was verbally abusive), Demarcus says he overeats because Quisha is gambling too much and nags him about his food (just like the therapist's parents did), John desperately asks for ways* to make Amy eat more (when the therapist struggles with dieting), or Ezra says he will do couples therapy on the condition that he never has to gain weight and risk being bullied again (when the therapist was bullied as a kid). Empowered by this knowledge and preparation, the Gottman-RED couples therapist is now ready to assess the needs of their couples and guide them through the interventions that have the potential to transform their relationship.

7

A Road Map for Moving Forward: Assessment and Conceptualization

Carmen and Luciano are sitting on their couch facing their computer screen. Dr. Sharma, the couple's therapist, appears on the screen for the telehealth session and welcomes them. After a few pleasantries and introductory comments, Dr. Sharma begins, "I would like each of you to tell me how you decided this would be a good time in your relationship to begin couples therapy."

Luciano turns to Carmen, so she starts, "Well. We just aren't getting along. We tried couples therapy a while back and it helped a little, but we never talked about some of our bigger issues."

"Like Carmen's eating disorder," Luciano jumped in. "We didn't talk about it because she didn't want to. I think she wants to now, but neither of us knows how to do it without fighting."

Carmen, "I do want to talk about it, but that's not our only problem." Carmen's voice is a little strained. She is feeling defensive.

Luciano, "I know it isn't, but we can talk about the other ones. Every time I try to talk to you about this one it never goes well."

Carmen, "That's because you don't understand." Luciano rolls his eyes, shrugs, then looks at the therapist, "See? That's why we're here!"

For couples like Carmen and Luciano, their inability to calmly discuss the nuances of the eating disorder and the impact of the associated thoughts and behaviors on each partner and the relationship is a major source of tension and distance. The foundational competencies in Gottman-RED couples therapy that assist couples with taking breaks when needed, listening, validating, and showing empathy are dedicated to alleviating this problem.

As mentioned in Chapter 6, Gottman-RED can be described as a competency-based couples therapy that provides an organized, integrated, and coordinated sequence of steps for the therapist and for the couple. Thus, the role of the Gottman-RED couples therapist is to guide the couple through a series of competencies with the hope that, over time, the couple will achieve a level of mastery that will allow for a healthy, stable relationship and improved quality of life.

This chapter highlights assessment, communication of the results of the assessment to the couple via a feedback report, and integration of the framework of the Gottman Sound Relationship House as a structure and guide for the therapy.

Assessment

Assessment is as important for the couples therapist couples therapy as a physical evaluation is to a surgeon or an oral exam is to an oral surgeon. Suppose you were referred to an oral surgeon for a tooth to be extracted. You arrive at the office and sit in the chair. The surgeon enters and says, "Well, I think I will just start with this tooth here and if the pain does not go away, we can try pulling another one." No history taking, no x-rays, no examining your mouth, no probing. Would you stay? Not likely. I think you would be leaving that office as fast as you could.

When people go for couples therapy, they often seem surprised that there is a rather thorough assessment process. Many expect the therapist to jump right in and start working on the first problem that is presented without trying to identify the deeper issues in the relationship first. This is a mistake. If the therapist does start without an assessment, the therapy may provide a Band-Aid fix, without addressing significant problems in the relationship, and the couple will continue to struggle.

In Gottman-RED couples therapy, the assessment tools include questions about food, weight, exercise, and body image that most likely have never been discussed by the couple. The responses aid the couples therapist when determining treatment goals.

Assessment for RED couples has a threefold purpose: (1) assessing the health of the relationship, (2) assessing the impact of the eating disorder on the relationship, and (3) assessing the extent to which both partners understand the eating disorder in the same way.

Relationship Assessment

GOTTMAN CONNECT. The Gottman Relationship Assessment measures the health of the relationship in terms of The Sound Relationship House. It is recommended that both partners take the online assessment or something equivalent. These assessments can be found at http://gottmanconnect.com/.

Eating Disorder–Related Assessments

These assessments should be completed by both partners. The answers will be discussed and compared during the feedback session and may also open conversations in subsequent sessions.

OWL CONVERSATIONS (WISE CONVERSATIONS ORCHESTRATED WITH LOVE). (SEE APPENDIX I.) This assessment tool will open the door for RED couples to have conversations about topics related to the eating disorder including recovery, how to talk about sensitive issues, the partner experience, the experience of the person with the eating disorder, treatment, practical issues of living together, and ways to build trust and create safety.

EDE-Q: THE EATING DISORDERS EXAMINATION QUESTIONNAIRE (HTTPS://WWW.CBTE.CO/FOR-PROFESSIONALS/MEASURES/). The EDE-Q should be filled out by both, with the person with the eating disorder in mind when answering the questions. The answers provided give the couples therapist (1) understanding of the extent of involvement in eating disorder thoughts and behaviors by the partner identified as having an eating disorder history and (2) knowledge of the level of awareness the non-eating disorder partner has of the other's food or weight-related thoughts or behaviors.

DTBT-Q: ARE YOU DYING TO BE THIN? QUESTIONNAIRE. (SEE APPENDIX 2.) The DTBT-Q should be filled out by both partners about their OWN thoughts, behaviors, and attitudes toward food and weight. This tool aids the couples therapist in understanding if one or both partners have issues in these areas.

AESED: ACCOMMODATION AND ENABLING SCALE FOR EATING DIS-ORDERS (DOI.ORG/10.1037/T57448-000). The AESED measures behaviors by the non-eating disorder partner and indicates responses that need improvement. It is to be filled out by both partners, with the non-eating disorder partner in mind so that the couples therapist can evaluate both the kind of responses extended by the non-eating disorder partner and the degree of awareness the person with the eating disorder has of the impact of their behaviors on their partner (Sepulveda et al., 2009).

Assessment Sessions #1 & #2: Relationship History

I recommend using the standard Gottman Oral History Interview or a structured interview of your choice and adding the following questions.

1. **Eating disorder history.** When did you first talk with each other about the eating disorder? How was it disclosed? Did the eating disorder start before the relationship or during the relationship? How much do you talk about it now?
2. **Family history with food.** "Can you tell me a little about how food, eating, and weight were handled in your family? Did anyone have an eating disorder? Was dieting commonplace? Did you family eat meals together? If so, what was conversation at the dinner table like? Was it calm? Were there fights?"

In the Gottman Method, couples are observed during a conflict discussion. I recommend doing this with RED couples using the following prompt. (If in person, ask the couple to wear a pulse oximeter with an alarm setting on one finger, set at 100 bpm—85 bpm if very athletic—and 95% oxygen saturation. The pulse oximeter beeps when a person is in a more agitated state or is flooded.)

> *Choose a topic related to the eating disorder that is difficult to discuss and is unresolved. On a scale of 0–10 where 0 is something you can easily discuss for an hour without fighting, and 10 is something you cannot talk about for 10 seconds without getting into conflict, choose a topic that is a 7–8. I am going to observe you having a conversation about this topic for 10 minutes. I will say nothing during this time and not intervene, but I will be observing and taking notes.*

Assessment Sessions #3 & #4: Individual Sessions

I recommend using the standard Gottman individual interview or a structured interview of your choice and add the following questions:

1.   **Relevant family eating disorder history**

   -   Did anybody have an eating disorder?
   -   How was weight talked about in your family? Are there any specific comments that stuck in your mind?
   -   Did either of your parents diet? How often?
   -   How did your parents feel about their body image?
   -   Did your parents make disparaging comments related to weight or body size of anyone in or outside of the family?

2.   **Weight loss dieting history**

   -   Did you ever go on a weight loss diet as a child?
   -   If yes, why did you go on the diet? At what age was your first diet?
   -   What was the diet?
   -   How much weight did you lose? Did you gain the weight back?

- What other weight loss diets have you tried over your lifetime? What happened?
- Eating disorder partner: Do you believe this diet is related to your current eating-related issues?
- Non-eating disorder partner: Do you believe your experiences with dieting affect how you react to your partner's eating disorder behaviors?

3. **History of prior relationships.** Please tell me about any romantic relationships you have had prior to the relationship with your current partner.

   - Eating disorder partner: Did you have your eating disorder when in any of these relationships?

     - If so, how was the eating disorder handled in this relationship?
     - Do you believe the eating disorder had anything to do with the end of the relationship?

   - Non-eating disorder partner: Have you ever been in a relationship with another person who had an eating disorder? What happened in that relationship?

4. **Eating disorder history.**

   - Eating disorder partner: How long have you had an eating disorder? Which eating disorder (s) do you have now? How did it begin? Why do you think you are still struggling with it at this time in your life?

   - Non-eating disorder partner: How long has your partner had an eating disorder? Which eating disorder (s) do they have now? How did it begin? Why do you think your partner is still struggling with it at this time in their life?

   - Eating disorder partner: Please tell me about the therapy or treatment you have had so far for your eating disorder. Are you in individual therapy or treatment now?

- Non-eating disorder partner: Please tell me what you know about the therapy or treatment your partner has received so far for the eating disorder.

Feedback Session #5

The feedback session is the culmination of the assessment process. It is during this session that the couples therapist summarizes what they have learned about the couple and distills the information down to the most important elements to address in the work together. During the feedback session, the therapist will present the couple with a written summary of the results of all of the assessments. The feedback report will integrate the results from the relationship assessment, eating disorder questionnaires, and the interviews. The information will be synthesized by the couples therapist, who will generate a list of treatment goals to discuss with the couple that will guide their work together. These treatment goals comprise the treatment plan and serve as a road map for the couples therapy, giving direction and a means to evaluate progress. I recommend revisiting the treatment goals every 3 to 6 months, checking off those that have been accomplished and structuring the ongoing work around those that remain.

Gottman-RED Couples Therapy in Context: The Sound Relationship House

John and Julie Gottman (Gottman & Gottman, 2013) developed The Sound Relationship House theory to conceptualize and graphically depict the essential elements of a happy, stable relationship. Gottman-RED couples therapy embraces then builds on this theory with supplemental competencies specific to the unique challenges faced by eating disorder couples.

The Gottmans referred to couples with happy, stable, "good enough" relationships as the Masters of relationships and couples with unhappy and/or unstable relationships as the Disasters of relationships (Gottman & Gottman, 2013). The Gottman Method of couples therapy (GMCT) was developed to assist the Disasters so they, over time, with consistent use of the interventions they were learning and the help of the couples therapist, would become Masters. The Gottmans identified eight predictors of divorce or misery in couples relationships:

1. More negativity than positivity during conflict
2. Escalation of negative affect during conflict conversations
3. Turning away from bids for emotional connection
4. Turning against during conflict and everyday interactions: irritability, emotional disengagement, and withdrawal
5. Failure of repair attempts after the inevitability of conflict
6. Negative sentiment override, meaning neutral or positive messages are seen as negative and there is a tendency to highlight the errors of one's partner and see them as character flaws
7. Diffuse physiological arousal and flooding during conflict
8. Failure of men to accept influence from their wives (heterosexual couples)

Although awareness of these characteristics was noteworthy and important, John and Julie Gottman found that being able to predict divorce or misery in relationships had limited value. While knowing what to avoid was helpful, what therapists and couples alike really wanted to know was how couples could develop more satisfying relationships.

The Sound Relationship House

As introduced earlier in this chapter, The Sound Relationship House is a visual representation of the key building blocks of a healthy, stable, long-term relationship (Gottman & Gottman, 2013; Gottman et al., 2017). In this chapter, we expose the weaknesses and problems in each level of The Sound Relationship House that are a direct consequence of the eating disorder–related thoughts and behaviors. In the next chapter, we discuss how to fix them.

The Foundation of Friendship

The first three levels of The Sound Relationship House work together to form a foundation of friendship. This foundation increases the likelihood of more effective conflict management by fostering the expression of humor or affection during conflict and encouraging repair during or after conflict. A good friendship and improved conflict management establish a firm footing for romance, passion, and mutually satisfying sexual intimacy. To put it simply, people feel closer, are more likely to be intimate, and manage conflict more effectively when they are friends.

> *In RED Couples, the eating disorder is a third party living in the house. It impacts the relationship either by creating distance or conjuring the illusion of connection around behaviors/recovery, or a combination of the two. Regardless, this "guest" staying in the house moves the relationship from a dyad to a triad, potentially inhibiting the development of a healthy, strong emotional connection. As many of us may remember from childhood, groups of three friends are the most difficult to manage, with alliances constantly shifting and one of the three frequently perceiving that they are, in imagination or reality, excluded by the other two*
>
> *It is essential that the eating disorder becomes the "friend" who is excluded. Both partners must work on strengthening the bond between them, enjoying time together, and developing strategies that prevent the eating disorder from becoming a wedge that splits them apart.*

BUILD LOVE MAPS. A love map is a road map of your partner's inner psychological world and is the most foundational level of friendship in a relationship. Partners learn about love maps by asking open-ended questions and retaining the answers so they can build a mental picture of their partner's inner world. This kind of question— "What are some of your worries right now?"—opens the heart and leads to dialogue because it cannot be answered with a simple "yes" or "no." Love maps include:

- Your partner's current interests, opinions, and views
- Your partner's current worries and stresses
- Your partner's current hopes and aspirations
- Your partner's current dreams, values, and goals
- Your partner's mission statement

Love maps also include favorite foods, vacation ideas, and ideas for fun during free time.

> *In RED couples, love maps are incomplete due to secrecy and/or shame blocking conversations regarding eating-, weight-, exercise-, or body image–related issues, leaving uncharted territories and gaps in each partner's knowledge of the other's inner world.*

- *Secrecy shrouds eating disorder behaviors.*
- *Non-eating disorder partners avoid talking about how they think or feel about the eating disorder.*
- *Planning for the future (dreams, hopes, aspirations) is complicated by uncertainty about recovery. Will it happen? How long will it take?*
- *There is a tendency to walk on eggshells when discussing topics related to food, weight, exercise, or body image.*
- *Other dreams, worries, and stresses take a back seat to the eating disorder, particularly during the most acute phases.*

NURTURE FONDNESS AND ADMIRATION. Fondness and admiration are built by actively incorporating affection and respect into the relationship. This can be done verbally or nonverbally. It involves developing the habit of watching for things that your partner says or does that you appreciate, admire, or feel proud of and then communicating to them that you feel that way, not just thinking warm thoughts and hoping your partner will telepathically understand.

- Develop a positive habit of mind that identifies things to admire and be proud of about your partner. The opposite of this is a critical habit of mind that looks for shortcomings, flaws, and mistakes.

- Verbalize the appreciation or admiration as close to the moment it has occurred as possible. Catch your partner in the act of doing something you really like.

In RED couples, nurturing fondness and admiration may be complicated.

- *People with eating disorders tend to be highly self-critical and perfectionistic, holding themselves and their partners to unrealistic standards. This increases the likelihood of criticism entering the relationship.*

- *Close connection may be challenging for both partners. Focusing on the eating disorder (using behaviors by the partner with the eating issues or thinking about the partner's behaviors for the non-eating disorder partner) can create a sense of distance that may be more comfortable for one or both partners.*

- *When the person with the eating disorder goes through a relapse or particularly difficult time with their food, weight, or exercise behaviors, they may become so absorbed with these behaviors that they stop expressing fondness and admiration for their partner. The non-eating disorder partner may feel abandoned or unloved, misinterpreting the situation.*

- *When the partner with food, weight, or body image issues is "feeling fat" or has in reality gained weight, physical touch or sexual intimacy is avoided because the person does not want their partner touching or seeing their body. This can also happen when a person with anorexia loses weight. This aversion has nothing to do with the partner but can be experienced by the partner as rejection.*

- *If the non-eating disorder partner has been rebuffed for comments related to behavior change or appearance (e.g., "You look like you have gained some weight and look so much healthier!" [AN]; or "Of course you do not look fat in those pants" [BN]; or "You look great. Have you lost weight?" [BED]), the non-eating disorder partner may become gun-shy about saying anything at all to their partner.*

TURN TOWARD RATHER THAN AWAY. Turning Toward involves responding positively as often as possible to spontaneous bids for emotional connection that occur when people are spending time together. Bids for connection can range from something superficial like sharing a social media post to something deeper such as wanting empathy after a painful interaction with someone external to the relationship. Recognizing bids for connection requires practice and intention as some cues are more subtle than others.

> *If the eating disorder partner extends a bid for connection to their partner during recovery attempts and their partner turns toward and supports them, a very positive emotional connection develops. Suppose the partner with the eating disorder is in the habit of turning away when engaging in eating disorder behaviors or when suffering the physical discomfort or mental anguish that can occur during the aftermath of food-, weight-, exercise-, or body image-related thoughts or behaviors and the non-eating disorder partner notices, and so extends a bid for connection. More often than not, the bid will fail.*
>
> - *In RED couples, bids for connection from the non-eating disorder partner are most likely to fail when the partner with the eating disorder is engaging in behaviors. Because some behaviors are thoughts and others are acted upon but kept hidden, the non-eating disorder partner may not understand what is happening (e.g., the partner with bulimia nervosa is planning to binge because the non-eating disorder partner is planning to go out, but the non-eating disorder partner then changes plans and wants to stay home and watch a movie together).*
> - *In RED couples, there is the potential for complications if Rituals of Connection have been developed around food- or weight-related behaviors that need to change in order for the person with the eating disorder to recover.*

The Positive Perspective

The fourth level has to do with the perspective and is about noticing sentiment overrides. Sentiment override can be positive or negative. It functions as an indicator of how well the friendship and conflict management systems are functioning—one can think of it as a small, flashing light. When things are going well, a couple will be in positive sentiment override and the light is off. When the friendship is failing and conflict is poorly managed, a couple will be in negative sentiment override and the light flashes.

- **Positive Sentiment Override.** The positive sentiments about the relationship and your partner override the negative. You believe your partner likes you; you give your partner the benefit of the doubt and do not take negativity personally, but see it as an indication that your partner is stressed.

- **Negative Sentiment Override.** The negative sentiments about your partner and the relationship override anything positive. You may think your partner does not like you, be more critical of your partner, scan the environment for distance (thus creating shortcomings), and take negativity as personal criticism. You are likely to overlook the positive attributes of your partner that objective observers can see. You may expect criticism from your partner and be overly sensitive.

Manage Conflict

Conflict is natural and has functional, positive aspects. The Gottmans emphasized that conflict can actually help couples learn how to better love and understand each other, deal with change, and renew courtship (Gottman & Gottman, 2024).

Masters of relationships are gentle during conflict and are able to move out of negative exchanges without escalation. They use softened start-ups, employ preemptive repair, accept influence, engage in self-soothing, repair after fights or regrettable incidents, de-escalate when flooded, and compromise. However, the Disasters of relationships (unhappy yet stable or unstable relationships) become ensnared in negative exchanges, unable to extricate themselves from painful, negative spirals that they hate in which neither trusts that the other has their best interest at heart (Gottman et al., 2017).

Many of the issues couples fight about are rooted in fundamental differences in personality or needs of each partner and are not resolvable. As noted in Chapter 5 but worth repeating, the Gottmans identified the startling fact that in every couple, 69% of all conflict discussions were connected to these perpetual problems. If couples understand and acknowledge this, thereby recognizing what is happening when one of these issues surfaces, there is the potential for calmer conversations that do not escalate to fighting.

If the couple is unable to dialogue about one of these perpetual issues, it becomes gridlocked and creates distance. Gridlocked issues are tied to core beliefs, needs, dreams, history, or personality. Learning how to talk about these issues gently and calmly is very important.

> *RED couples have the same struggles with conflict management as non-RED couples due to variables such as poor modeling in their families of origin, attachment wounds, trauma from previous relationships, and lack of education about healthy conflict management strategies. These couples need additional help learning how to talk about perpetual issues related to food, weight, exercise, or body image thoughts and behaviors.*

Make Life Dreams Come True

Each partner has their own life dreams, values, convictions, and aspirations. It is important that the relationship support the pursuit of these. Partners need to prioritize talking about life dreams and, most importantly, remembering the dreams of the other person.

> *For RED couples, coping with the eating disorder tends to overshadow the pursuit of individual life dreams and can modify the*

trajectory for both partners, particularly if the cost of treatment is a financial burden for the couple. Regardless, both partners deserve the opportunity to purse their individual life dreams and aspirations if at all possible. Some issues that may be affected by the eating disorder include:

- **Having children.** *Sometimes, eating disorder behaviors affect fertility or affect health (weight too low or too high) such that becoming pregnant is not advisable. This may be a life dream that is on hold or thwarted by eating disorder behaviors.*

- **Career of the partner with the eating disorder.** *When eating disorder behaviors are severe, the person may not be able to work due to health issues. Sometimes, treatment is extensive, particularly if it is residential or inpatient, so a person may have to quit their job.*

- **Education for the partner with an eating disorder.** *When eating disorder behaviors are severe, the mental energy required to attend undergraduate or graduate school is seriously compromised, so the partner with the eating disorder may need to withdraw from school or take a leave of absence. This may also be a life dream that is on hold or thwarted by eating disorder behaviors.*

- **Career or education for the non-eating disorder partner.** *When eating disorder behaviors are acute, the non-eating disorder partner may need to put career or education goals on hold in order to manage the household during periods of intensive treatment, particularly if the couple has children. Finances may affect the timing as well given that treatment is expensive.*

Create Shared Meaning

The uppermost level of The Sound Relationship House is about creating a life together with shared purpose and meaning. To develop shared meaning, partners need to develop love maps at the deepest level, working hard to understand each other's most meaningful dreams and goals, life missions, traditions, and rituals of connection; out of this understanding emerges a shared, mutually meaningful vision of the future.

RED couples have difficulty planning for the future while the status of recovery is uncertain. Will the future together consist of a series of treatment episodes? Will the future involve chronic eating disorder behaviors? Will recovery or remission be partial or full? In essence, the couple is asking will the "guest" move out or maintain permanent residence? The answers to these questions have implications for career, family planning, travel, and rituals of connection.

Trust

Trust is considered to be of utmost importance to couples and the driving force behind the decision to marry, choice of partner, and relationship satisfaction (Gottman et al., 2017). In this context, the element of trust that involves the belief that one's partner has one's best interest at heart is the essential element. Trust is so important that it is one of the two support pillars for the house. Trust includes attuning to each other's emotions and needs and typically has two components, but there are three for RED couples:

- *Support and loyalty.* Does your partner have your back? Do you know that your partner will catch you if you start to fall? If your partner asks, "Will you be there for me?" can you say yes?

- *Fidelity.* Has there been infidelity, an affair, betrayals?

- *Transparency about the eating disorder and its impact on both partners.* Has there been honesty about eating disorder–related issues?

In RED couples, infidelity and betrayals are addressed in the same way as non-RED couples. Support and Loyalty and Transparency about the eating disorder are interrelated. Trust builds

*with consistency over time in attunement and honesty demon-
strated by both partners.*

- *The non-eating disorder partner needs to be consistent in creating
a safe refuge where the eating disorder partner can talk openly
about "secrets" related to eating disorder thoughts and behaviors
without fear of judgment. The eating disorder partner needs to be
willing to self-disclose without criticism or contempt. The non-
eating disorder partner must work on listening nondefensively.*

- *The eating disorder partner needs to be consistent in creating a safe refuge where the non-eating disorder partner can
talk openly about their feelings and reactions to eating disorder thoughts, behaviors, and the emotional toll of the recovery
process without fear of judgment. The non-eating disorder partner needs to be willing to self-disclose without criticism or contempt. The eating disorder partner must work on
listening nondefensively.*

Commitment

Commitment is the second support pillar and means that both
partners have two feet in the relationship. They choose to focus on
what is positive about their partner and the relationship, cherish the
relationship, and protect what they have. When all of the following
elements are present, the relationship becomes a safe refuge.

- Negative comparisons are avoided and there is a high
fence around the relationship that protects it from
alternative relationships.

- When things do not go well, the partners talk about it with
each other rather than withdrawing, building resentment, or
talking to others about the situation.

- Both partners are willing to sacrifice for the relationship.

*RED couples need to work hard to maintain commitment despite
the challenges presented by eating disorder behaviors and the pro-*

cess of recovery. For most adults, recovery takes a minimum of 3–5 years, so the couple needs to be committed to walking this road for a long time.

- *Guarding against negative comparisons is essential for both partners. The eating disorder partners may hear stories from others in treatment and start wishing their partner was more like another person's partner. The non-eating disorder partner may look at a friend who is married to someone who does not have an eating disorder and become envious.*

- *When things do not go well, or in the case of relapse, it is important that the partners come together as a team, keeping the eating disorder as the problem, not the person who has the eating disorder. Even though the conversations may be difficult, the partners need to turn toward each other at these critical times.*

- *Both partners need to sacrifice. The partner with the eating disorder does not have the luxury that a single person would of engaging in behaviors with abandon or postponing therapy. If in a committed relationship, the eating disorder partner will need to do whatever it takes to become equipped to sacrifice and/or modify their eating disorder thoughts and behaviors. The non-eating disorder partner will need to sacrifice time. This partner needs to take the time to learn about the eating disorder, attend therapy sessions, introspect, and change their ways of interacting such that they do not undermine recovery and do not accommodate to unhealthy patterns and do learn how to support recovery.*

Concluding Thoughts

The assessment tools used in Gottman-RED couples therapy provide a deep pool of information for you to use in treatment planning when designing an individualized treatment plan for each couple. Understanding the complexity of working on issues in terms of The Sound Relationship House theory affords a backdrop for conceptualizing the work going forward. Now it is time to review the foundational competencies and introduce each couple to the relevant Gottman-RED couples therapy interventions based upon their needs. In Chapter 8, you will learn about the new innovative strategies developed specifically for relationships with eating disorders.

8

The Gottman-RED
Interventions

There are 14 interventions that align with the 10 Gottman-RED competencies. These interventions have been designed specifically for RED couples. In this chapter, you will be introduced to each of them. Some of the actual exercises that you will work through with your couples can be found at wwnorton.com/therapyrelationships. Training in using these and the remaining interventions, as well as certification in Gottman-RED couples therapy, are offered at www.relationshipswitheatingdisorders.com.

One of the reasons couples therapy is challenging when helping people with eating disorders is that many people who have eating disorders are ambivalent about giving up their behaviors. In the early stages of the disorder, people with anorexia nervosa or bulimia nervosa may be reluctant to relinquish or even talk about behaviors that enable them to accomplish their thin ideal. As time goes on, the benefits of the behaviors necessary to maintain the low body weight begin to be outweighed by the liabilities; however, the fear of gaining weight, irrational though it may appear to the non-eating disorder partner, remains a driving force (Reiff & Reiff, 1999).

Some with anorexia nervosa find the function of their starved appearance to be interpersonal, eliciting special attention, extra care or gentler treatment from others, thus fear the loss of this attention implicit with recovery (Schmidt & Treasure, 2006). The behaviors associated with bulimia nervosa rarely elicit the same kind of attention from others as does the starved appearance characteristic of anorexia nervosa, but they do provide a numbing and calming effect for the person using them. Those with binge eating disorder may find refuge and safety in maintaining a higher weight and larger body size, thus the thought of stopping binge eating, losing the comfort of food, and potentially changing body size may be barriers to change. Often people are unaware of these deeper reasons for resisting behavior change. Once they are aware, they find their ambivalence difficult to articulate and sharing their secret fears leaves them in an extremely vulnerable place emotionally.

For this reason, most of the Gottman-RED interventions begin with the couples therapist guiding the couple through a psychoeducational component related to the skills they will be practicing, the work they will be doing, or the questions they will be asking each other as they work through an exercise during a couples therapy session. This knowledge empowers the couple by offering the potential for insight and understanding along with behavior change as they apply what they are learning to their unique relationship needs. The interventions are long and can be thought of as advanced skills for couples. To complete each intervention typically requires several sessions. Before practicing an intervention on their own, it is recommended that the couple moves through each exercise all the way to the end with the couples therapist at least once.

The interventions do not need to be done in order, nor does the couples therapist need to do every exercise with every couple. As the therapist becomes more familiar with Gottman-RED, they can decide how and when to introduce relevant exercises to each couple.

The 10 Competencies of Gottman-RED Couples Therapy

In the Gottman-RED therapy, there are 10 competencies for couples. Because the therapy evolved from the Gottman Method of couples therapy (GMCT), GMCT interventions are recommended to achieve the desired outcome in three of the four foundational competencies: Competencies Two, Three, and Four. However, if you are trained in another method of couples therapy, you will be able to use your preferred interventions with your couples. With your guidance, each couple will progress at their own pace from basic knowledge to effective and appropriate implementation of skills for each competency.

In competency-based learning, the intent is to steer away from simply learning something (head knowledge) to effectively applying what has been learned (Campbell et al., 2012). Many couples learn an intervention but do not practice it between sessions, so never achieve mastery in that particular skill. In a true competency-based approach, the therapist would not teach a new skill until the first has been mastered, but that is not pragmatic in the real world of therapy. It will be up to each couples therapist to decide how to orchestrate the skill-building process, recognizing that without the basic skills, it will be harder for the couple to move on to the higher level skills. After working on the four foundational competencies, the couple will be ready to move forward. The remaining six competencies are specific to Gottman-RED couples therapy and were developed for relationships with eating disorders or significant food, weight, exercise, or body image issues. Let us take a look at each competency in more depth.

Competency One: Eating Disorder Knowledge

This first of the Gottman-RED competencies underscores the importance of a shared rudimentary understanding of the etiology of an eating disorder, the function of the behaviors, the role of the non-eating disorder partner, and the challenges of recovery. The Gottman-RED couples therapist will take the couple through The Helicopter Story intervention that was included in Chapter 2 and *The Two Hands of the Behaviors* intervention and introduce *The 14 Rules for Partners of a Person Recovering from an Eating Disorder*. The latter includes suggested reading materials that both partners may find helpful. Having a common language when practicing the Basic Communication, Friendship, and Conflict Management skills described below to discuss eating disorder–related issues is necessary and fundamental: understanding underlies behavior change.

Competency Two: Basic Communications Skills and Empathetic Engagement

In this foundational competency, couples learn to attune to each other, to effectively summarize what the other has said, to ask deepening and open-ended questions, to validate each other's thoughts and feelings, and to express empathy. Mastery in this competency results in calmer, slower, more respectful conversations, characterized by listening carefully to what the other is saying. I teach the *Gottman-Rapoport* and *Dreams Within Conflict* interventions from the GMCT to help couples practice these skills. The Gottman booklet *How to Be a Great Listener* and the free *Gottman Card Deck* app are useful tools to enhance the practice of these communication and friendship-strengthening skills.

Competency Three: Conflict Management Skills

Like the Gottman Method, Gottman-RED couples therapy focuses on managing rather than resolving conflict. It seems inevitable that people will do or say hurtful things during times of stress, exhaustion, hunger, hormonal shifts, or other circumstances that impact emotional responsiveness. We all make mistakes. This foundational competency involves reviewing flooding, using gentle start-ups, determining when to take breaks, and developing a plan for repair after a fight has occurred. Mastery in this competency involves being able to accept influence from each other as well as negotiate conflict while minimizing the *Gottman Four Horsemen* (criticism, contempt, defensiveness, and stonewalling) and eliminating verbal or physical abuse. I work with couples using the following GMCT concepts and interventions: the *Four Horsemen*, the *Gentle Start-Up*, the *Repair Checklist*, the *Aftermath of a Fight or Regrettable Incident*, *Accepting Influence*, *Turning Toward*, and the *Art of Compromise*.

Competency Four: Time Together

In GMCT, it is recommended that couples spend a minimum of 6 hours per week focused on the relationship. Unfortunately, people are so busy and focused on activities, work, or children that take time away from each other that they find the thought of adding another part-time job (working on the relationship) to be overwhelming. However, without mastery in this area, the relationship will suffer. This fourth foundational competency includes adding loving gestures like expressions of appreciation, communications of fondness and admiration, greetings when coming and going, and touching base briefly in the morning and at night before going to sleep. Interactions requiring more time are necessary and include weekly meetings to assess the relationship, weekly dates, rituals of connection, and daily conversations that allow for venting or relieving stress such as *The Stress Reducing Conversation*. Oddly enough, this is one of the hardest of the competencies for couples to master. The Gottman *6 Hours Per Week to a Better Relationship* diagram clearly outlines the minimum requirements for time together for a healthy relationship. The *Rituals of Connection* Card Deck is efficacious if couples lack regular activities they enjoy together.

Competency Five: Friendship for RED Couples

Most couples therapies include techniques intended to assist couples with enriching their friendship. The Gottman Method employs card decks (*Open-Ended Question, Rituals of Connection, Love Maps, Date Night Questions*); exercises in the book, *Eight Dates,* or the pamphlet, *The 7-Week Guide for Creating Fondness and Admiration*; and in-session activities like *The Adjective Checklist*.

In Competency Five, Gottman-RED couples therapy builds on the four foundational competencies by adding the following three new interventions that not only strengthen the friendship but bolster a spirit of collaboration and teamwork.

Becoming a Good Enough Couple I: Overcoming Perfectionism Together

The first of the three interventions is called *Becoming a Good Enough Couple I: Overcoming Perfectionism Together*. The exercise begins with the therapist initiating a discussion of perfectionism and how perfectionistic thinking can negatively impact a relationship. The couple is introduced to three types of perfectionism and how each can impact intimacy: self-oriented perfectionism, other-oriented perfectionism, and socially prescribed perfectionism. In the next steps, the therapist guides each partner as they identify and share Blunders and Food Flubs related to the relationship that each are willing to work to overcome with intention and persistence. The Blunders are behaviors that partners keep doing that hurt the relationship and the Food Flubs are those mistakes made around food, weight, exercise, or body image issues. These slipups continue to occur even though both partners are in couples therapy and trying to change. Applying principles that foster compassion and encouragement, the couples work with the therapist to address these issues in a supportive and nonjudgmental way with the realistic expectation of becoming "good enough." A blunder and food flub check-in at the start of each session initiated by the therapist is an effective way to encourage couples to stay focused on practicing the skills they are learning.*

The Recipe for Connection: A Fondness and Admiration and Turning Toward Exercise for Couples

The second of the interventions is *The Recipe for Connection: A Fondness and Admiration and Turning Toward Exercise for Couples*. The purpose of this exercise is to encourage couples to form new ways of expressing fondness and admiration to each other and develop different rituals of connection that support recovery and

---

* Inspirational Resources: Brown, 2010; Egan et al., 2022; Fairburn, 2008; Haring et al. 2003; Hewitt & Flett, 2003; Kim et al., 2011; Robinson & Wade, 2021; Shafran et al., 2018; Schmit & Bell, 2017; Shafran et al., 2018; Winter, 2005.

health. Food-Based Rituals of Connection are predictable, regular, pleasurable, conjoint activities that involve food-, exercise-, or weight-related thoughts or behaviors that are connected to the eating disorder, disordered eating, or related behaviors (past or present) of one or both partners. The exercise begins with the couples therapist educating the couple about resistance to change and how food can become a language of love. The exercise itself has five steps beginning with discussions of family history related to food and weight; losses due to the eating disorder; and parenting around food-, weight-, and body image-related issues. The fourth step involves sorting out behaviors and identifying those that need to change to support recovery and health. The last step is about changing behaviors that are not helpful.*

The Loving Filter: Minding, Noticing, and Savoring the Positive in Your Partner and Your Relationship

The third intervention is *The Loving Filter: Minding, Noticing, and Savoring the Positive in Your Partner and Your Relationship.* This exercise is about infusing loving thoughts, warm feelings, and affirmations into the relationship through minding, noticing, and savoring. It helps each partner look for, see, capture, and embrace positivity about the other and is particularly effective for those prone to criticism, contempt, and/or a negative perspective. This exercise begins with the therapist introducing the concepts of positive psychology followed by three exercises—beginning, intermediate, and advanced levels—in which partners work on bringing positivity into the relationship and assuming positive intent. The exercise then moves into a discussion of savoring that is also followed by three exercises—beginning, intermediate, and advanced levels—in which couples learn about savoring through reminiscing, humor, and synchronous storytelling with strategic chapter breaks.†

---

* Inspirational Resources: Chapman, 2015; DeLuise, 1988; Gottman & Gottman, 2017; Roth, 1991; Theiss et al., 2016.
† Inspirational Resources: Adler et al., 2013; Adler er al., 2015: Brown, 2018; Bryant & Veroff, 2007; Dunlop et al., 2021; Gibbon, 2020; Gottman & Gottman, 2017; Land, 2000; McAdams et al., 2006; Seligman & Csikszentmihalyi, 2000.

Competency Six: Transparency and Trust—Open Conversations About Eating Disorder–Related Issues

Competency Six is about transparency, trust, and open conversations, particularly around eating disorder issues. There are three interventions in Gottman-RED couples therapy intended to help couples talk about sensitive topics related to the behaviors in an eating disorder. Although the issues RED couples face are definitely not all about food, some of the worst fights and misunderstandings do have to do with food, weight, exercise, or body image. All three of the interventions encourage more risk taking and openness in conversations while fostering increased vulnerability.

OWL Checklist (Wise Conversations Orchestrated With Love)

The first intervention is the *OWL Checklist (Wise Conversations Orchestrated with Love)* that was completed as part of the assessment process. There are two versions of the *OWL Conversations Checklist*: one for therapists and the other for couples. This checklist is primarily to help the therapist and the couple identify and address potentially avoided topics important to one or both of the partners. The couple will have already seen the results of this assessment during the feedback session, but now is the time to return to the conversations earmarked by each partner. The couples therapist will guide them through the conversations using the indicated GMCT intervention suggested in the therapist version or an intervention of their own choosing.

The Vulnerability Leap: A Trust-Building Exercise

The second intervention is *The Vulnerability Leap: A Trust-Building Exercise*. This exercise is intended to facilitate deeper conversations between partners about topics that may be challenging by slowly building safety and trust for this level of sharing. *The Vulnerability Leap* is the emotional equivalent of the trust leap or the trust fall. It involves taking a risk, but rather than a physical risk, an emotional risk. Just as there is a moment of suspense when running across the room and leaping, there is a moment of uncertainty when revealing something very personal. If you share something and open yourself up and your partner does not catch you emotionally, you may feel hurt or rejection. If you share nothing, you are guaranteed to not feel hurt or rejection but are unlikely to deepen connection. However, if you share something and open yourself up and your partner does catch you emotionally, the odds are that you will feel closer, more connected, and safer and be likely to risk this type of sharing again.

In this exercise, both partners choose topics that push the envelope a little in terms of comfort as it encourages them to share personal stories that they have not shared with each other before. These can be stories of incidents that took place both prior to and during their relationship. The topics extend beyond eating disorder behaviors and thus remove the person with the eating disorder from center stage. In preparation for sharing, each person is asked to think about a subject in more depth, thus the topics are referred to as "Think Abouts." The exercise can be done by reading from a list of Think Abouts or by using a card deck. Examples include, "Think about a meaningful conversation with one of your parents. Tell the story." or "(eating disorder partner) Think about the hardest thing for you about having an eating disorder. Explain this to your partner as best as you can." Practicing in a structured way is intended to encourage open dialogue in the future.*

The Aftermath of a Behavior: A Recovery Exercise for Couples

The third intervention, *The Aftermath of a Behavior: A Recovery Exercise for Couples,* allows for processing what happened after an eating disorder behavior, with the hope that it will be less likely to occur in the future. This intervention facilitates vulnerable sharing in a way that supports recovery and the relationship. In this exercise, it would seem as though the spotlight is on the person with the eating disorder history because they have the role of speaker, however, the non-eating disorder partner's role as supportive listener is

---

* Inspirational Resources: Brown, 2010; Hempel et al., 2018.

extremely important. The person with the eating disorder initiates the conversation after using an eating disorder behavior, processing what happened with their partner to decrease the likelihood of subsequent occurrence, with the ultimate goal being to reach for their partner *before* using a behavior the next time they feel the urge or temptation to cope using their eating disorder. Learning to turn toward their partner for support after a behavior has occurred is a very powerful and potentially life-changing intervention for the person with the eating disorder.

The exercise has six steps for the speaker that include identifying feelings before and after the behavior, telling the story of what happened, looking for triggers, behavior analysis, forgiving and showing compassion for oneself, and thinking about how to do things differently in the future. It also has five steps for the listener that involve showing empathy and support and asking key questions.*

Competency Seven: Commitment to Synchronous Growth

Gottman-RED couples therapy harnesses the power of the couple to promote healing and growth in both partners. Based on the idea that more can be accomplished if the partners are working together and are aligned than if either is trying to move ahead on their own, synchronous growth is the process by which couples help each other shine light on blind spots, increase self-awareness, and grow together. In order for this to happen, both need to be open to learning, changing, and transforming by nondefensively examining areas of woundedness. The three exercises in this competency emphasize teamwork and assume both partners are going to grow through participating in this therapy, not just the person with the eating disorder. In all three, the partners will support each other as they work together to overcome the identified challenges. It is very healing for the person with the eating disorder to leave the "hot seat" behind for a while. Three areas of particu-

---

* Inspirational Resource: Briggs, D. C. (1986). *Celebrate yourself: Enhancing your self-esteem*. Main Street Books.

lar relevance for RED couples are emotion regulation, self-worth, and perfectionism.

The first intervention, *TOES*, the letters in the acronym standing for *Tolerating Others' Emotional Storms,* is about emotional co-regulation and helping couples stay present without matching the emotional intensity of their partner when the partner is expressing strong feelings.

The couples therapist's work with the couple on emotional storm tolerance begins with psychoeducation:

- First, the therapist will guide the couple through the section on parenting styles and emotional storms, then instruct them to answer the questions in *Action Item One* during the session.

- Second, the therapist will guide the couple through the section on relationships and emotional storms, then instruct them to answer the questions in *Action Item Two* during the session.

- Third, the therapist will walk the couple through the *TOES at Home* activity, giving them the opportunity to discuss and ask questions.

The TOES exercise is best used *in the moment* when one partner is experiencing strong feeling; consequently it cannot be scheduled. If the opportunity presents itself during a session, use TOES with your couple in the therapy room.

Alternatively, you can guide the couple to practice TOES using the *Gottman Meta-Emotions Interview* or a similar intervention that encourages dialogue that focuses on emotions during a session. Instead of you, the therapist, being the interviewer, ask the couple to interview each other, going back and forth with each question, and moving down the list of emotions that includes sadness, anger, affection, and pride. Do this as long as you as the therapist think it is useful for the couple. Sometimes strong emotions surface during this exercise, but not always. When they do, this exercise allows each partner to practice listening to intense feelings expressed by their partner. If the listener becomes emotionally aroused or flooded, help the couple take a break and self-soothe, and then try again when the listener feels ready to begin again.

You will also teach the couple how to use *TOES at Home* so that they can practice on their own at the exact moment when one partner is experiencing strong emotions at home.

There is a version of TOES called *TOES for the Couples Therapist* that you will find at the end of this chapter. Couples therapists who were exposed to a significant amount of fighting in their family of origin or have been or currently are in a conflictual relationship may find that the idea of being in a small room with two people fighting evokes a visceral negative response, emotionally and in their bodies. Being able to tolerate the emotional storms of the couple is an essential skill when doing this type of work. This intervention helps therapists practice staying present in very challenging, emotionally charged sessions.*

Supporting Each Other's Dreams: Building Self-Worth Together

The second intervention is *Supporting Each Other's Dreams: Building Self-Worth Together*. People with higher self-esteem have better quality relationships. The goal of this exercise is to work on building self-esteem together. The couples therapist helps the couple to support their partner in building self-acceptance and finding a foundation of worth in who you are on the inside rather than who you present to the outside world through appearance, achievements, or accomplishments. The *Gottman Adjective Checklist* and *The Loving Filter* (Advanced Minding and Noticing) are used to identify inner qualities in each partner. All in all, it appears that building self-worth in both partners in a RED relationship may not only have a positive impact on eating disorder recovery but may result in a better quality of relationship. As noted by Fairburn (2013), lower self-esteem is one of the maintaining factors in an eating disorder. This observation underscores the importance of working on this issue.

---

* Inspirational Resources: Fischer et al., 2017; Gottman, 1997; Gottman & Gottman, 2013; Weber et al., 2019.

The image of a flower is used to illustrate the self-esteem-building process. The therapist guides the couple in working through the three stages of the flower and then dialoguing about how to affirm each other's worth and value for inner rather than outer qualities.*

Becoming a Good Enough Couple II: Having Fun While Learning Something New

The third intervention is the second in the series on perfectionism, *Becoming a Good Enough Couple II: Having Fun While Learning Something New.* Many couples come into therapy saying that they no longer have fun together and/or have very few interests in common. The therapist will guide the couple as they ask each other four groups of questions related to previous experiences from their background or childhood history that relate to perfectionism and then help the couple select a new ritual of connection that includes a fun activity that neither partner has done before that is intended to bring fun and closeness to their relationship. The therapist will encourage them to practice extending patience, compassion, and acceptance toward each other while learning this activity. It is hoped that any tendency toward perfectionistic attitudes or competitiveness when learning something new will fade into the background. There is a twofold purpose to this exercise: to infuse more fun into the relationship and to help both relinquish perfectionistic thoughts or attitudes.

Competency Eight: Sexual Intimacy

RED in Bed is an intervention designed to open communication about eating-disorder-specific issues that can impact sexual intimacy. There are many resources already available for enriching conversations about technique, frequency, initiating and refusing, enhancing satisfaction, and increasing pleasure, including the *Gottsex Toolkit*. *RED in Bed* is not about any of these things.

* Inspirational resources: Boyes et al., 2007; Brown, 2010; Cortes & Wood, 2018; Woodward et al., 2019; Zamani Sani et al., 2021.

Instead, it facilitates conversation about eating disorder–related changes in sexual desire and the impact on sexual intimacy of variables such as body image, weight, weight changes, binge eating, and body sensitivities.

In this intervention, the couples therapist facilitates open and transparent conversations about sexual intimacy and intimate touch. People with a history of eating disorders or related behaviors often have complex feelings and thoughts about sex for a variety of reasons, with discomfort concerning their bodies being touched or viewed during sexual intimacy as a persistent theme. The focus of this exercise is mostly on issues unique to relationships with eating disorders, but some topics are universal. Using a series of structured exercises, the couples therapist helps the couple talk about thoughts concerning the meaning of intimate touch and sex, intimate touch and body image, changes in weight, sexual trauma history, and body sensitivities. *RED in Bed* ends by introducing the concept of sexual empathy, a special type of savoring that brings closeness in relationships.*

Competency Nine: Future Planning

Although no couple has a crystal ball allowing them to see what the future holds, people in relationships where one or both partners have significant issues related to food, weight, body image, or exercise often live one day at a time because the future is truly unpredictable, making it very difficult, if not impossible, to plan ahead. There can be full remission, partial remission, relapse, or stagnation. The course can be an upward climb toward recovery, a downward plunge deeper into behaviors, or a chronic state of semi-recovery. These variables make discussing the future challenging and increase the potential for avoidance of conversations of this kind. There are three exercises to help RED couples as they think about how to move forward.

* Inspirational resources: Bass & Davis, 2008; Castellini et al., 2020; Calogero et al., 2009; Fairburn, 2013; Gottman et al., 2016; Gottman et al., 2020; Kluck et al., 2018; Nagoski, 2015; Moulding, 2015.

Faithing Forward: A Search for Shared Meaning

The first is *Faithing Forward: A Search for Shared Meaning*. This intervention is about walking into the future together with openness about spirituality, transparency about beliefs, and respect for differences. Some couples do not consider discussion of spirituality to be important. If this is the case, the couples therapist may bypass this exercise. However, other couples are very interested and still others have never taken time to explore this area of their relationship but would like to. Sarah Skellern assembled a team of international researchers (2021) who focused on assessing perceived importance of religion in couple relationships in Christians, Muslims, Buddhists, and the nonreligious. They were surprised by the fact that couple relationship standards have not included standards held about religion given that in many cultures religion is very important, particularly Pakistan (85%), Malaysia (57%), and America (41%), although less so in Australia (15%) and China (3%). Consequently, they developed an assessment tool to facilitate conversation about religion that could be used by couples therapists.

If faith has been an integral part of one or both of the partner's lives, this exercise will be relevant. Sometimes one partner believes spirituality to be very important and the other does not. In these cases, it is worth doing this exercise even if one partner has little to say. If neither partner values faith nor spirituality, it makes sense to skip these exercises.

Since spiritual beliefs are dynamic and the way a couple shares or does not share in religious practices can change over time, it is important to open the channels of communication. Updating Love Maps in all areas including spirituality is important for a healthy relationship. What one partner believed about God/higher power or both shared when they first met may be very different from what they believe in the present. Open conversations can strengthen this aspect of the relationship.

Faithing Forward opens conversations about how the couple thinks about God, spirituality, and faith as they walk into the uncertainties of the future. Each couple will decide if they want spirituality or religious practices to be an element of how they move forward in general and with regard to the eating disorder in specific. Asking open-ended questions and doing the following exercises about spirituality and faith are ways to begin the dialogue.

The couples therapist will guide the couple though a faith journey writing exercise, a drawing exercise, discussions of spiritual coping styles, the position of God/higher power in their relationship, faith-based rituals of connection, and spiritual beliefs about the eating disorder, and the development of a plan for "faithing forward."*

Co-Constructing the Eating Disorder Narrative: A Shared Meaning Exercise

The second intervention, *Co-Constructing the Eating Disorder Narrative: A Shared Meaning Exercise*, provides couples with the opportunity to identify and discuss expectations, hopes, and dreams related to eating disorder recovery. The onset of a long-term mental illness like an eating disorder interrupts the expected natural course of events of someone's life; in other words, almost no one plans on developing an eating disorder when dreaming about their future. Even after the onset of the eating disorder, most people do not expect it to last for as long as it typically does or for recovery to be such an arduous process. The future is very uncertain as there can be full remission, partial remission, relapse, or stagnation.

When someone in relationship has an eating disorder, it is impossible for it to not affect the relationship. Conversations about recovery are inevitable, with expectations about what recovery means and when it will occur either overtly or covertly imbedded into the discussions. Each partner will have a spoken or unspoken narrative for the future of the relationship and the role of the eating disorder.

The RED couple will use this exercise to talk about each partner's perspective, then co-construct a narrative that works for the future of their relationship. Three potential narratives are explained: *The Restitution Narrative, The Chaos (or Wreckage) Narrative, and The Quest Narrative*. The couples therapist will ask each partner to sep-

---

* Inspirational resources: Buser et al., 2015; Richards et al., 2018; Rizkallah et al., 2019; Skellern et al., 2022.

arately write their future narrative then share what they have written in a session. This intervention meshes well with the GMCT *Mission and Legacy* exercise that guides the couple through a conversation about the future and what they want their legacy to be as individuals and as a couple. Doing them together is recommended. The therapist will then guide the couple in co-constructing a narrative that will hopefully work for both partners. Couples therapists need to be aware that doing this work has the potential to elicit strong feelings and difficult conversations.*

Becoming a Good Enough Couple III: Defining Our "Good Enough" Relationship

The third intervention is the third in the series on perfectionism, *Becoming a Good Enough Couple III: Defining Our "Good Enough" Relationship*. In this exercise, the couple outlines realistic, "good enough" expectations for their relationship that foster acceptance of the perpetual problems that are woven into the fabric of their relationship while allowing for change as they move into the future. It is the final in the series of exercises designed to help couples be less perfectionistic.

Just as there may be a honeymoon stage in a relationship, there can be a honeymoon stage when a couple starts couples therapy. Often, people enter couples therapy with the hope that their partner will make a remarkable transformation. As time goes on, the couples therapist helps the couple develop pragmatic expectations, guides the couple to focus on what they can change (themselves) and encourages acceptance of the other person and of the reoccurring problems in their relationship.

The couples therapist assists the couple in drawing Venn diagrams to help them identify common values and behaviors that will equate to "good enough" for their relationship. One set of Venn diagrams is for non-eating-disorder-related issues and behaviors

---

* Inspirational resources: Dunlop et al., 2021; McAdams, 2015; Papathomas et al., 2015; Vendantam, 2023.

and the other set is for those directly related to unhealthy eating, weight, food, or exercise behaviors.*

Competency Ten: Monitoring Relationship Health

This final competency is about developing the habit of regularly evaluating progress and the health of the relationship. In GMCT, this is done with the *State of the Union Meeting*, the *Poop Detector*, and the *Relapse Questionnaire*. These tools are all very useful and you may have others that you like to use in your practice.

Monitoring relationship health is very important. It is disillusioning and disheartening when a couple invests a significant amount of time and money in couples therapy only to find their relationship back at square one after the couples therapy ends. In my experience, this is most likely to happen when couples do not practice learned skills or protocols outside of the sessions. The Gottmans recommend phasing out couples therapy slowly to minimize the likelihood of this occurrence, but a couple cannot do couples therapy forever. Consequently, self-monitoring by the couple is essential.

The last Gottman-RED couples therapy exercise is a monthly check-in called *The Garden* that is intended to monitor and maintain the health of the relationship. Weekly check-ins like the Gottman Method *State of the Union Meeting* are recommended as well. *The Garden* is a little more extensive, so occurs less often.

The exercise is called *The Garden* because, in many ways, a relationship is like a garden. With care and love, it will stay healthy and strong. If neglected, it will become overgrown with weeds and, in the worst-case scenario, it could wither or die. In a real garden, it does not take long for the garden to show signs of neglect. It is interesting that the newest plants are the first to suffer, but the ones that have been around for a long time rarely die. Behaviors in a relationship are like that too. The ones that are ingrained are hard to uproot, but the new ones need lots of care and nurturing. The couple will gauge the health of their relationship through

---

* Inspirational resource: Gottman & Gottman, 2023.

structured conversations by applying concepts related to planting, watering, fertilizing, pulling weeds, dealing with pests, pruning, and harvesting to their relationship.

The couples therapist will explain *The Garden* to the couple, then walk with them through it during a session. In this exercise, the couple will thoroughly assess their relationship—celebrating the good and the progress and identifying strategies to improve areas where they are struggling. They will notice what is flourishing in their relationship, what is positive about their partner, what progress has been made on each of the Gottman-RED couples therapy interventions, and what eating disorder related issues still need to be discussed. The couple then chooses areas of growth for the coming month.

After practicing it in session, the couples therapist will request that the couple set a date to repeat the exercise on their own and then report back regarding the outcome during a subsequent session.

Summary

The couples therapist will need to become familiar with the 14 Gottman-RED interventions before presenting them to their couples. With the guidance of their therapist, it is hoped that each RED couple will become "good enough" in each competency area covered by these interventions: friendship, transparency and trust, synchronous growth, sexual intimacy, future planning, and monitoring relationship health.

TOES for Couples Therapists

As promised earlier, the *TOES for Couples Therapists* exercise is now presented for you as a couples therapist to practice on your own if you like; however, it is more fun in a group and learning is optimized when group role plays are incorporated to enhance the experience.

TOES (Tolerating Others' Emotional Storms) for Couples Therapists

You will be guiding your couples through the TOES exercise designed for couples. In this exercise, you will begin by helping couples understand how parenting styles from childhood can affect adult relationships, then teach them how to increase their tolerance of emotional storms. This particular exercise is unique because it not only has application to the couple's relationship but also the therapy relationship. For this reason, you will benefit from working through the *TOES for Couples Therapists* exercise first before introducing TOES to your couples.

Couples therapists who were exposed to a significant amount of fighting in their family of origin or have been or currently are in a conflictual relationship may find that the idea of being in a small room with two people fighting evokes a visceral negative response, emotionally and in their bodies. Developing the capacity to stay internally calm while listening to the emotional storms of a couple is a listening skill at the highest level and is very hard to do. Very few people learned this skill in childhood and most of us are not very good at it. If fact, many grew up listening to their parents fight with no one to tell them how to cope with the tension. They coped in the best way they could as a child by hiding under the bed, staying in their room, developing physical symptoms, acting out, escaping into video games or books, staying with friends as much as possible, comforting or siding with one parent or the other, trying to stop the fight, yelling, or dissociating. As adults, they may have a tendency to do the same thing that worked back then.

A reactive therapist is vulnerable to co-regulation, the bidirectional linkage of emotions. Co-regulation in couples therapy means that the therapist matches the couple's level of emotional arousal, which drastically decreases the likelihood that the session will go well. As the couple becomes more upset, so does the therapist. As the couple becomes more distressed, there is increased likelihood of the therapist accommodating by doing whatever they need to for the couple to calm down—perhaps more to reduce their own distress than that of the couple. The unspoken message to the couple is that it is not safe to express strong emotions in the therapy session because they will upset the therapist.

The one time when this coupling of emotions is useful in a couples therapy session is when it allows for empathy that helps strengthens the therapeutic alliance.

Emotion regulation can be enhanced or foiled by a therapist. Emotion regulation enhancers work to listen without becoming emotionally aroused or emotionally shut down themselves.

Emotion regulation foilers become reactive and act in ways that distract from or derail the couple's attempt to manage their distress such as rescuing, problem solving, interrupting, trying to control due to your own anxiety, and talking too much.

The reactive couples therapist can be a pursuer (overinvolved), indicated by overfocusing on content rather than process; being too eager to help and talking too much; absorbing the emotional state of the couple; acting out sexual feelings toward one partner; taking sides; or investing way too much in saving the marriage. The couples therapist can be a distancer (underinvolved), indicated by emotionally retreating; allowing the couple to run the session by arguing endlessly or decreeing how the sessions should be conducted; feeling helplessly caught in an alliance with one partner to either side with them or avoid discussing certain issues; or emotionally disconnecting to the couple, evidenced by rescheduling, lateness, clockwatching, or boredom.

In summary, emotion regulation foilers work to relieve distress in the moment, which *is not* helpful in the long term, whereas emotion regulation enhancers encourage partners to learn how to live through and manage the emotions, which *is* helpful.

As a couples therapist, your role is twofold: (1) to manage your own emotions to reduce therapist reactivity and allow you to tolerate emotional intensity in your couple and (2) to help your couple increase their tolerance of emotional storms in each other. To do this, you cannot be reactive, as that will draw the attention away from the couple. In order to not be reactive, you must increase your tolerance of emotional storms.

When allowing emotional storms, the therapist must monitor them so that they never become abusive expressions of feeling. They involve intense emotions, but verbal or physical abuse is not allowed, nor is the presence of the Gottman Four Horsemen: criticism, defensiveness, contempt, or stonewalling. As the therapist, you need to be focused and to stay present so you can coach the couple and keep them on track, knowing when it would be best to have them stop and take a break.

You may find yourself reacting to emotional intensity that triggers your own past or current relationship issues. Here are some examples that may be challenging for a couples therapist: a partner is upset about the other's drinking, a partner is devastated because of an affair or betrayal, a partner is sad because the other is distant, a partner is angry because the other partner is controlling, a partner is lonely in the relationship, a partner feels rejected because their partner does not want sexual intimacy, a non-eating disorder partner is depleted by the effects of an eating disorder, or a partner feels powerless because the other refuses to forgive or repair and holds grudges.

The goal of this exercise is twofold: (1) to identify tendencies to be reactive and (2) to become an emotion regulation enhancer. To do this means practicing tolerating increasing levels of intensity of the emotional storms of your couple without trying to relieve their distress or becoming reactive. You will continually monitor your own level of emotional arousal and work to stay calm.

Introduction to TOES

Everyone has emotional storms. Some people are more vulnerable to them than others. When experiencing a storm, the speaker may have some control over the intensity, but sometimes has minimal control depending upon the nature of the storm. Some people shut down completely when experiencing an emotional storm. This scale is only applicable to people who are verbal when experiencing intense emotions.

The TOES Intensity Scale: The 10 Levels of Emotional Storms

INTENSITY LEVEL		POSSIBLE BEHAVIORS
10	*Hurricane*	May include loud voice, swearing, sobbing, shaking, facial expression matching emotions, and/or body tension.
9	*Tornado*	
8	*Thunderstorm*	
7	*Downpour/Hail*	
6	*Heavy Rain*	May include quivering voice, tears welling, crying, face showing emotional distress, furrowed brow, and/or scowl.
5	*Light Rain*	
4	*Shower*	
3	*Sprinkle*	
2	*Cloudy*	
1	*Sunshine*	Calm, relaxed, smiling, happy face

Sometimes emotional storms are about the listener and sometimes not. The storm may be due to something upsetting at work or with an extended family member or a child. The storm could be a fear of a pet dying or a family member dying. Storms may be rational or irrational. Sometimes storms are hormonally driven and other times fueled by alcohol or drugs.

The hardest storms to weather are those that have to do with the listener's behavior or words. We all hurt each other in couples relationships. We all cause pain, usually unintentionally. We all say things we regret. We need to be willing to stand strong and tolerate the emotional consequences of these things even though they may be very difficult to hear. Tolerating these storms requires practice and intentionality.

Tolerance of Emotional Storms is like building muscles. The more you flex and lift, the greater your ability. This takes intentionality and practice. It takes thought, self-awareness, and self-challenge. TOES can be practiced with children, adult children, siblings, parents, coworkers, employees, and friends. Family and romantic relationships are always the most challenging.

TOES FOR COUPLES THERAPISTS

Step One: Thinking About TOES

If doing this exercise in a workshop, pick a partner. If alone, write out your answer so you can put your thoughts on paper and minimize rumination.

Action Item One: Reflecting On TOES

Part One. Think of a recent couples session when you reacted to the emotional storm in the therapy room by having difficulty staying focused or present, intervened when it would have been better to stay silent, found your mind wandering, or could feel yourself becoming inwardly upset. Write or talk about what happened. Include thoughts about what was triggered in you by this interaction. What level of emotional storm were you experiencing on the TOES intensity scale?

Part Two. Occasionally, an emotional storm will be about the therapist. Although unusual in couples therapy, it does happen that one or both partners will experience strong emotions that are directed at the therapist. Think of a recent couples session when this occurred. Write or talk about what happened. Include thoughts about what was triggered in you by this interaction. What level of emotional storm were you experiencing on the TOES intensity scale?

Part Three. Discussion Questions:

1. What should you, the couples therapist, do if the emotional storm or the issue it represents is so triggering for you that you are unable to stay focused or neutral during the session?

2. Suppose you do react during a couples session, should you address this with the couple during the next session? If so, what could you say?

3. What will you write in your notes about this situation?

Step Two: TOES Role Plays

In these role plays, the couples therapist has the opportunity to think about their presence in the session when emotional storms are potentially triggering or are directed toward the therapist. It may be useful to review the Therapist Preparation for an Intense Session that follows first.

Action Item Two: The Role Plays

The role plays work best in a group of three but can also work with four where one person is a consultant. Ideally, each person will have the opportunity to be the couples therapist. There are three role plays.

Role Play One. Role play a couples session in which one partner is expressing strong feelings about an issue exterior to their relationship (e.g., interaction with a family member, upsetting news from the doctor, car accident, political issue or event). Switch roles.

Role Play Two. Role play a couples session in which one or both partners are expressing intense negative emotions toward the therapist (e.g., therapist was late, feels therapy not going well, feels therapist sided with one against the other). Switch roles.

Role Play Three. Role play of your choice. The couples therapist can create the scenario that will allow the couple to practice what is most challenging for them with respect to TOES.

Therapist Preparation for an Intense Session Using Knowledge of TOES

Sometimes you know in advance that the session will be intense. Other times, you will have no advance warning. If you know in advance, you can mentally prepare in advance. If you become aware during the session, try to remember these steps in the moment.

Step One: **PREPARE yourself for the session.** Take time to meditate, pray, or take calming breaths.

Step Two: **Be an emotion regulation enhancer.** This means LISTENing without:

- rescuing one partner or the other
- problem solving
- distracting
- interrupting
- trying to control due to your own anxiety
- making a joke, using humor
- or changing the subject

Step Three: **INTERVENE only if you hear the Four Horsemen or verbal abuse.**

Step Four: **ENCOURAGE THE COUPLE TO TAKE A BREAK IF NEEDED.** Only intervene in this way if they need a time out, not if you do.

Step Five: **HELP THE COUPLE.** Help the couple to stay on track with the TOES exercise or other intervention until the storm has passed.

Step Six: **PROCESS YOUR FEELINGS LATER.** Talk to a colleague or supervisor to process the feelings that came up for you during the session.

9

Gottman-RED in the Therapy Room

Author's Note: The reader will benefit from downloading *The After-math of a Behavior, The Recipe For Connection, RED in Bed, and The Loving Filter* from wwnorton.com/therapyrelationships before reading this chapter and then following along as Dr. Sharma leads each couple through the respective exercise.

Dr. Sharma was looking forward to the session with Ezra and Abe. It was the third session after the feedback session. Dr. Sharma began every session with appreciations—each person was asked to say two things they appreciated since the last session that they believed their partner did that helped their relationship. Appreciations are not to be edited or commented on, simply responded to with "thank you" or "you're welcome."

Ezra jumped in first. "Thank you for your encouragement about the job interview yesterday and thank you for picking up my clothes from the cleaners."

Abe replied, "You're welcome. Thank you for cooking dinner for us last night and for buying my favorite ice cream for the party."

Dr. Sharma's ears perked up but she said nothing.

Ezra replied, "You are welcome."

Dr. Sharma asked, "Is there anything you would like to focus on today?"

Abe hesitated, then responded, "Well, I noticed that Ezra has been spending more and more time at the gym." Ezra tensed. Abe noticed but went on, "I mentioned it to him and he just said, 'I don't want to talk about it.' So, I stopped, but I want to talk about it. I am concerned about him. Four hours a day seems excessive and cuts into our time together."

"It's not 4 hours, Abe. You always exaggerate!" Ezra was defensive.

"OK. Well, let's talk about it now, then. How many hours is it?"

"I don't want to talk about it!" Ezra snapped, heating up. Feeling exposed, he was putting up walls.

Abe's tone was changing. There was desperation in his voice when he added, "This is what always happens. You will not talk to me about anything related to food, weight, or exercise! I am so frustrated because you are clearly eating less and losing weight and now, to top it off, want to exercise more!"

Dr. Sharma said, "I am going to interrupt for a moment. I would like to make this easier for both of you. I know that food, weight, and exercise are sensitive topics. I will introduce you to some exercises that will make it easier for you to talk about these things."

There are 14 interventions in Gottman-RED that are intended to help couples talk about sensitive topics, most of which are directly related to the behaviors in an eating disorder. Although the issues RED couples face are definitely not all about food, some of the worst fights and misunderstandings do have to do with food, weight, exercise, or body image. All of the interventions encourage more risk taking and openness in conversations while fostering increased vulnerability.

One of the reasons couples therapy is challenging when helping people with eating disorders is that many people with eating disorders are ambivalent about giving up their behaviors, whereas the ideal dream for their partners is that they become behavior free.

Some with anorexia nervosa find the function of their starved appearance to be interpersonal, eliciting care or gentler treatment from others, thus fear the loss of this attention implicit with recovery (Schmidt & Treasure, 2006). Those with bulimia nervosa tend to not receive the same kind of attention from others for their behaviors but benefit from the numbing and calming effect of binge eating followed by purging. Those with binge eating disorder may find refuge and safety in maintaining a higher weight and larger body size, thus the thought of stopping binge eating, losing the comfort of food, and potentially altering body size may be barriers. Often people are unaware of these deeper reasons for resisting behavior change. Once they are aware, they find their ambivalence confusing at best, but often shameful, thus difficult to articulate to their partner. Sharing the magnetic pull of their eating disorder as well as their secret fears about behavior change leaves them in an extremely vulnerable place emotionally. Gottman-RED couples therapy offers strategies for the couples therapist intended to bring hope for the couple by facilitating conversations involving both partners. For many, the support that emerges from understanding may become a springboard for recovery.

In this chapter, we are a fly on the wall in the office of Divya Sharma, a Gottman-RED couples therapist, as she meets with our four couples. In each session, she will guide the couple through a different intervention, thereby introducing us to four of the Gottman-RED interventions: *The Recipe for Connection*, *The Aftermath of a Behavior*, *RED in Bed*, and *The Loving Filter*.

Doing the Work

Dr. Sharma had a full day ahead. Her first appointment was with Quisha and Demarcus. This was their 10th session and, based on their conversation last session when they were talking about how their relationship revolved around food and only food, Dr. Sharma decided it was time to introduce *The Recipe for Connection* exercise.

Dr. Sharma began the session as usual, asking Quisha and Demarcus to each share two appreciations from the past week. They were quite practiced at this now and shared meaningfully.

Quisha turned to Demarcus and said, "I appreciate the text that you sent to me last night telling me that you loved me and I appreciate that you initiated the State of the Union meeting last week."

Demarcus smiled, "Thank you. I appreciate that you called me for support before stopping at the casino on Tuesday and I appreciate that you supported me by making dinner rather than ordering in my favorite, not so healthy meal last night."

Quisha replied, "You are welcome!"

Dr. Sharma began, "As we discussed last session, we are going to do *The Recipe for Connection* exercise today unless something urgent has come up since I saw you last. How does that sound?"

"Sounds good to me," Quisha said.

"Nothing urgent this week—for a change!" Demarcus laughed.

"OK, then, I will email it to you" This was a telehealth session. Dr. Sharma preferred to email documents rather than screen sharing so that she could see her couples clearly during the sessions. "As soon as you receive the email, open it and look at the list of food-based rituals of connection and food-based expressions."

Quisha and Demarcus agreed that the items checked below applied to their relationship and admitted that they both enjoyed them, so knew they would be hard to change.

Examples of Food-Based Rituals of Connection

☑ Ordering in food and eating it together. For one partner, it is just a meal, but for the other, it is a binge food.

☑ Eating out at a particular restaurant. For one, it is just a meal, but for the other partner, it is a binge or a way to feel safe and in control when eating away from home.

☐ Exercising together. For one, it is a workout to be healthy. For the other, it is compulsive exercise that is an eating disorder behavior.

☐ Cooking together. For one, it is an enjoyable activity. For the eating disorder partner, it is a way to control the food that is made and is an eating disorder ritual.

☐ Watching a particular show on the cooking channel. For one, it is just a fun show to watch. For the other partner, it fuels their obsession with food or allows vicarious eating of "forbidden" foods that are restricted or denied.

☐ Following a diet together (e.g., paleo, plant-based, vegan). For one, it is health promoting. For the other, it is an eating disorder behavior to prevent weight gain.

☑ Going to the movies and "binge eating" popcorn and candy. For one, it is fun and a splurge. For the other partner, it is a binge followed by either purging or eating more later, and, often, feelings of regret, guilt, or self-hatred.

☑ Eating special snack foods together while watching TV. For one, it is relaxing and enjoyable. For the other, it is stressful, potentially triggering a binge or inducing guilt if a dietary rule is broken.

☐ Other:

_____

_____

They also realized that they used food to express love to each other and checked almost all of the boxes in the next list.

Examples of Food-Based Expressions of Love, Fondness, or Appreciation

☑ Ordering or making a favorite dessert for your partner.

☑ Making special foods for each other.

☑ Bringing comfort food to your partner when they feel sick or depressed.

☑ Having food-based traditions to celebrate birthdays, anniversaries, and holidays where one partner makes or buys this special food for the other.

☑ Buying a favorite food for each other as a surprise.

☑ Giving a favorite food as a reward after a major accomplishment.

☑ Going out late at night to buy binge food or an acceptable food at the person's request.

☐ Going out to a restaurant that serves acceptable foods for the eating disorder partner.

☐ Other:

_____

_____,

Dr. Sharma then instructed Quisha and Demarcus to ask each other the questions in *Action Item One* about their family history with food.

Quisha started, "We went to this really cool ice cream place every Saturday and got double-dip ice cream cones. I always brought my best friend. It was the best ice cream I have ever had. We would also buy scones at the fair every year—it was the first thing we would do after walking through the gate. My family celebrated everything with food, especially holidays and birthdays."

Demarcus chimed in, "That was the same for us. We would go to Dairy Queen and get our favorites every Wednesday after church. My Momma made the best birthday cakes—she would not let a mix box in the house—always from scratch. I remember licking the beaters! They were so good. There was so much food on holidays that we could never eat it all, so had leftovers for a week!"

Quisha asked Demarcus, "Did people talk about weight in your family?"

Demarcus thought a minute then said, "Not very much. My sister was pretty skinny and got teased about that. My dad gained weight as he got older, but no one said anything about it. I was really muscular from sports, so no one gave me a hard time even though I tipped the scales at a pretty high number. How about you?"

Quisha said, "My mom was always worried about weight and going on a diet. She didn't want us girls to be skinny, but she didn't want us to be fat either. She never put us on a diet, though. I remember sneaking diet pills in high school with my best friend.

Now, I really don't know why because I didn't need to lose weight. It was just a thing we all did. Did your parents like their bodies?"

Demarcus replied, "I have no idea. It was never talked about." Quisha added, "Same here. I just know my mom tried to lose weight a few times, so she must have thought she would look better if she did, but she never talked about it."

Dr. Sharma then asked about losses due to eating disorder behaviors. Both indicated they really had not experienced changes related to the eating disorder that felt like losses. They anticipated more of those in the future if they gave up some food-based rituals or expressions of love. They then moved onto *Action Item Three* and started talking about their kids.

Quisha began, "I really want our kids to be healthy. I worry about Tyler because he seems to be gaining weight lately and I have seen him eat way too many snacks at night. I don't think we have been very good examples for him or Kalisha. I have tried to cook healthier things in the past few years but didn't do so well when they were younger. We ate way too much fast food!"

Demarcus added, "Yeah, I worry about Tyler too. I know I set a bad example for him. I tell him not to eat chips out of the bag, but then he sees me do it, so he does it, too. He never says anything about my weight, but I wonder if he feels embarrassed of me around his friends. I definitely show love through food and really enjoy making a good prime rib or lasagna for everyone."

Quisha added, "Yeah, we have to do better. How can we help them not develop an eating disorder?"

Demarcus answered, "I don't know. I guess by teaching them to talk about their feelings rather than eating them. No one ever taught me how to talk about what I was feeling when I was growing up. No one asked me how I felt. I don't even know if I knew what a feeling was!"

Dr. Sharma mentioned a few things. "I think you can teach them what you have learned about expressing and listening to feelings. What we work on in couples therapy works for relationships with kids too. Now, let's see if we can come up with a new ritual of connection that does not involve food. That will be another way you can model a different way of connecting for your kids." They had made a card deck so she asked them to sort the cards during the session.

Dr. Sharma suggested, "Since we are getting close to the end of our time today, let's focus on the "Need to change to support recovery/health" cards today and we can talk about the others next time. What do you have in that pile?"

Demarcus began, "Well, we have 'Going out late at night to buy binge food or an acceptable food at the other's request.' Remember that time right after I lost my job and you went out at midnight to the grocery store and bought peanut butter chocolate chip ice cream for me? I love it when Quish does that for me, but I know she shouldn't. Also, 'Making special foods for each other.' She makes this amazing chocolate cheesecake—it is my favorite, but I can't stop eating it. I know it has to stop. And then 'Ordering special coffee drinks in the morning.' That doesn't sound so bad, but I like a venti double chocolate mocha with extra whip. That one will be really hard to give up. There are some others, but those are the top three."

Dr. Sharma validated that the change would be difficult, then asked, "What new rituals do you want to add?"

Quisha started, "We would really like to eat healthy meals together. I want to make better choices when I go shopping. I don't do all of the cooking, but when it is my turn, I will do that. What about you, Demarcus?"

Demarcus laughed, "This is hard for me, Quish. I love cooking certain things, but I need to turn a new leaf. I want to be healthier. I have to be healthier. We also identified that we want to still have coffee together in the morning but will make coffee at home and add creamer or milk."

Dr. Sharma said, "Those sound like realistic goals. Write them down so you both remember and check in on these when you do *The Garden* exercise. Last thing, what can you each do to express love to the other this week that does not involve food?"

Quisha replied, "I will give Demarcus a back rub!" Demarcus smiled.

Demarcus offered, "I will take you out to the beach to watch the sunset." Quisha also smiled.

Dr. Sharma responded, "Write these down as well. I have made a note of them so I will follow up next time! See you next week!"

———

Dr. Sharma took a short break. Her next session was in person with Ezra and Abe. All set to begin the session with appreciations, Dr. Sharma could feel the tension in the room, so decided to change course and check in with the couple first.

She opened by saying, "Hello, Ezra and Abe. It is good to see you. You both look very upset. Is everything OK?"

Abe looked at Ezra who nodded then looked down at the floor. Abe cleared his throat then spoke, his voice thick with emotion, "Ezra passed out at the gym today. I had to go pick him up. It turns out he had not eaten anything all day."

Ezra added, "I was so embarrassed."

Abe sounded stressed and angry, "You promised me that you would not go to the gym unless you had a good meal first. Do you just say things like that because you think it is what I want to hear?"

Dr. Sharma jumped in, "Before this conversation becomes a fight, I am going to make a suggestion. Let's try *The Aftermath of a Behavior* exercise."

She paused and looked at Abe, then added, "Abe. I can tell you are upset. Do you need a few minutes to calm and take some deep breaths or do you feel ready to work through an exercise with Ezra that might help?"

Abe thought for a moment, then replied, " Give me just a minute to take a few breaths and then I will be OK."

When he indicated he was ready, Dr. Sharma continued. "I have wanted to introduce *The Aftermath of a Behavior* exercise to you for a while now and today seems like the perfect opportunity. Ezra, you may not think of restriction as a behavior, but it definitely is."

Ezra nodded.

Dr. Sharma handed a copy of *The Aftermath of a Behavior* to each of them and introduced the exercise.

Dr. Sharma explained, "We are going to go over this exercise together. In this exercise, there is a speaker role and a listener role and both are very important. It is called a recovery exercise because it is intended to help the person with the eating disorder history analyze their behaviors with the hope that through understanding and insight and the support of their partner, it will be possible to decrease frequency. This exercise is a little different in that only Ezra has a turn as speaker and Ezra will always be the speaker. Abe will always be the listener."

Dr. Sharma continued by explaining *The Toilet Training Analogy* to help Ezra and Abe understand that behavior change is not like flipping a light switch, but takes place over time in a two steps forward, one step back fashion.

Dr. Sharma turned to Abe and said, "Abe, please focus on the section describing the listener's job. Let's read the introduction jointly. I will briefly mention the steps you will follow now, but go over them in more depth when it is your turn. Do you have any questions?"

Abe replied, "Just one question. If I think Ezra left out something, can I mention it?"

Dr. Sharma said, "No. Ezra is in charge of what he shares. Your job is to listen and show support."

Abe nodded.

Dr. Sharma turned to Ezra, "Ezra, if you are willing, we will talk about the restriction today."

Ezra indicated, "Sure, I can do that."

Dr. Sharma continued, "Let's look at your job, Ezra. As it says on the paper, when you are the Speaker, you are to talk honestly about your experience. Avoid the Four Horsemen as you recount what has happened. Be especially careful to sidestep criticism and contempt especially if you are talking about a situation that involves the Listener, Abe. This exercise works best if I take you through the steps one by one. Let's start with Step One. This step has two lists of feelings: one is for explaining what you felt before using the behavior and the second is for explaining how you felt after using the behavior. Please read each list and name off the feelings that you experienced, no explanations and no discussion right now."

Ezra responded, "OK. In Part One, I felt hurt, sad, fat, worthless, insecure, unattractive, self-hate, and hopeless. In Part Two, I felt safe, better, thin, powerful, and emotionless."

Dr. Sharma said, "Thank you, Ezra. Now let's go to Step Two. This is where you tell the story of what happened to the best of your ability."

Ezra said, "OK. I was feeling fine yesterday, I ate dinner and then after dinner, Abe and I were talking and Abe said . . . "

Dr. Sharma said, "I am going to interrupt Ezra, Please tell Abe and not me and be sure to put I before you when recounting something Abe did by saying something like, 'I remember that you . . . ,' 'I think that you . . . ,' 'It seems like you . . .' "

Ezra turned toward Abe and continued. "We were talking and I heard you say, 'Are you depressed about something *again*?' Then I said, 'I know I have been really quiet and I didn't want to talk about it because I feel like a broken record, but I am really worried that my face is looking fat and, to make it worse, I think I am losing my hair so that makes it look even fatter. It totally stresses me out.' So after I told you about it, which was really hard for me, I remember you saying something like, 'Just stop looking in the mirror. Why do you have to do that? Just ignore how you look like I do.' And then I got upset and said something like, 'I thought you would be more understanding and not tell me what to do.' Then, you left the room and I went upstairs and started planning how I could eat as little as possible the next day."

Abe interrupted. "I didn't say that!"

Dr. Sharma said, "Abe, I know you want to tell your side of the story, but this is actually not about what happened between you and Ezra. This is about understanding what triggers Ezra into using eating disorder behaviors. If it is important to you to talk about what you experienced last night, we can use another exercise to do that later." She turned to Ezra. "Thank you, Ezra. Now, let's do Step Three. This is the Behavior Analysis. Look at the list of triggers for behaviors and tell us which apply."

"Hmm," Ezra paused. "I think emotions, negative thoughts, and a relationship pattern seem to apply."

Dr. Sharma acknowledged what he said, "So helpful, Ezra. Now, how about past triggers? Read the description for Step 5 and see if anything comes to mind."

Ezra thought for a few minutes. "Yes, this does remind me of something. When I was being bullied, I would come home and tell my parents about it, and they would tell me to just ignore those kids or walk a different way so that I didn't see them. I know they felt bad for me, but they were also really frustrated that I kept getting upset about the same thing over and over again. I know that Abe has a lot more patience and compassion for me than they did, but comments like the one he made last night remind me so much of how they treated me. It's funny, but I actually felt like I was that young boy again."

Dr. Sharma said, "What you shared is really important, Ezra, and is an example of the enduring vulnerabilities that we have talked about. It sounds like what you experienced growing up was so painful that anything that triggers those memories brings up a lot of feelings for you. Thank you for telling us about that. Because Abe really cares about your feelings, he can learn to be more sensitive in situations like this. Now, look at Step Five."

Ezra grunted. "Ugh, this is a tough one for me. I have a hard time forgiving myself."

Dr. Sharma said, "Just do the best that you can. I will help you."

Ezra said, "Well, I regret looking in the mirror. I just have such a hard time not doing that. There is this huge mirror right over the sink in the bathroom, but anyway, I kind of regret not eating before going to the gym, but not so much. I do regret fainting at the gym, so I know I need to eat. Ugh." He paused.

Dr. Sharma encouraged Ezra to continue. "Can you extend some self-forgiveness and some self-compassion? Look at the words on the page and see if you can fill in the blank."

Ezra stumbled over his words a little, "I know this should not be so hard for me . . . OK. . . . I forgive myself for fainting at the gym. And I feel badly for myself because I think such awful things when I look in the mirror, so I will be kind to myself by not looking in the mirror today. How is that?"

Dr. Sharma answered, "That was great!"

Abe, who had been holding his tongue, could not do it any longer and blurted, "But shouldn't he be regretting not eating and forgive himself for that?"

Ezra said defensively, "See—I can never do it right for him!"

Dr. Sharma commented, "Abe. I see that you have some strong opinions about Ezra restricting intake, but your job is to be the listener and to support Ezra's process."

Abe sighed. "Got it! Sometimes, that is really hard. It's just that Ezra is so important to me that I don't want anything to happen to him. I just want him to be over this!"

Dr. Sharma replied, "I understand, but supporting him while doing this exercise *is* a way to help him recover."

Abe nodded.

Dr. Sharma said, "Ezra, that was great. Let's move on to Step Six. This is where you think about what you can do differently in the future to decrease the likelihood of turning to eating disorder behaviors as a solution when you are upset and one thing Abe can do to be supportive of you."

Ezra thought for a moment. "I think, as much as I hate to admit it . . . " he said as he glanced at Abe and smiled, "It would be better for me to not look in the mirror so much. I could use the other bathroom that has a small mirror so it would be less of a temptation and then, I could do some writing if I was getting upset. I think it would really help me if Abe . . . "

Dr Sharma interrupted. "Ezra, I would like you tell Abe and not me."

Ezra nodded and looked at Abe. "Abe, it would really help me if you would just say something like, 'That sounds really hard. Is there anything I can do to help you right now?'"

Dr. Sharma looked at Abe. "Does that sound realistic for you, Abe?"

Abe said, "Yes, I can do that. I just need to think before I speak." He laughed.

The mood in the room was noticeably lighter than when the session began.

Dr. Sharma said, "Abe, take a moment to look at the Instructions for the Listener. Please start with Steps One and Two."

Abe read the steps, then began, "Thank you for sharing about your behaviors with me, Ezra. I really appreciated it. I had no idea how hard this was for you. It sounds really rough and I am here for you. I want to learn how to support you."

Ezra smiled, then said, "Thanks, Abe."

Dr. Sharma said, "That was really good, Abe. Now, move onto Step Three."

Abe asked, "Would you like me to summarize what I heard you say?"

Ezra thought for a minute, then responded, "I don't think so. Hearing myself recount what happened was enough for me for now."

Dr. Sharma explained, "Sometimes Ezra may want you to summarize and other times like today, not. Either way is OK. Now move on to Step Four, Abe."

Abe turned to Ezra and asked, "How can I best support you right now? Would it help to have physical touch?"

Ezra said, "A hug would be nice."

Abe then asked, "Would you like some advice or to do something together?"

Ezra replied, "I don't think I need advice right now, but I would like it if we could go out for coffee after this session."

Abe liked that idea and said, "Sure. That sounds good. There is that coffee shop we both enjoy that is right near here."

Dr. Sharma said, "Now, the final step is to reassure Ezra that you are available to talk about this more later if he wants to."

Abe cleared his throat, then said, "Ezra, I think you already know this, but I want to be here for you whenever you want to talk. I know that sometimes I say the wrong thing, but I am committed to learning what is helpful to you and what is not."

Ezra was still smiling. He acknowledged Abe by saying, "Thanks, Abe. I know you are there."

Dr. Sharma commented, "Now that we have done this exercise together one time, I would like you to try it on your own. When you practice, Abe will ask Ezra the questions when Ezra is speaker and then respond by following the steps for the listener."

Ezra remarked, "I like this exercise, Dr. Sharma. I think it will really help me. Thanks for teaching it to us!"

Dr. Sharma's next appointment was a telehealth session with Amy and John. Both seemed in fairly good spirits. The session began with appreciations, and then Dr. Sharma explained the activity.

"We ended last time with the plan to do the *RED in Bed* exercise this week. Do you still want to do that?" Dr. Sharma asked.

"I can't say that I want to, but I think it is a good idea," Amy replied.

Amy and John continued to have difficulties in the area of intimate touch and sexual intimacy. When at a low weight, Amy had very little interest in sex and John felt less attracted to her when she was extremely thin. Consequently, they had not been intimate for several months. John mentioned this at the last session and said it was especially important to him because he knew it would help him feel closer to her and he knew this part of the relationship needed to improve if they ever hoped to have a child together.

Dr. Sharma had emailed the exercise to them after the last session with instructions to do Action Item One at home prior to this session, so checked in to see how that went. "Were you able to do *Action Item One* as we discussed?"

John replied, "Yes, we were. The activity was very helpful and I think we both have a better understanding of how we learned about sex and how we think about it now."

"I am happy to hear that it went well," she responded, then added, "I am going to read the introduction to you as a review and then we will start with Step Two. During the exercise, you will be asking each other a set of questions. Answer them as honestly as you can. If there is a question you do not want to answer, you can say so. Look at the top of the page and read along with me, please.

"'This exercise is a guide to help you and your partner have conversations about sex and intimate touch. Sex can be defined as 'any intimate touch between people with the mutual intent to share connection and pleasure . . . the body, mind, heart, and soul are engaged, not just the genitals.' *RED in Bed* is intended to open discussions characterized by transparency and vulnerability. It is not about technique or enhancing sexual pleasure. The focus is mostly on issues unique to relationships with eating disorders, but some topics are universal."

"Do you have any questions before we begin?"

Both said no, so Dr. Sharma moved on with the exercise. "Step Two is about body image and intimate touch. You each need a piece of paper and a pen, pencil, markers, crayons, or colored pencils." They indicated they were ready.

Dr. Sharma instructed them, "Remembering that this exercise has nothing to do with artistic ability, I would like you to draw two pictures. One is of your body in a swimsuit as you see it when looking in the mirror or a photo and the second is of your body in a swimsuit as you believe your partner sees it. When you are finished, we will share the drawings and discuss them."

John laughed nervously and said, "I am definitely not an artist. This should be interesting."

After about 5 minutes, both indicated that they were finished. Amy showed John her drawings and also held them up for Dr. Sharma to see. She described them like this, "In the first one, my legs and arms are pretty small, but my stomach is big. I look kind of like a snowman. I really focus on my stomach and do not like it. No matter what I do or what I weigh, it is never flat. I hate for John to touch that part of my body. I like my eyes and my feet. When you look at me, John, I think you see that I am too thin so I drew my body as a big blur, because I think you block it out of your mind when we are intimate and pretend it is different than it is."

"That is totally not true!" John said immediately.

Dr. Sharma jumped in to say, "John, right now I just want you to listen to Amy and think about what she has said. Try to take it in without presenting your perspective. Tell Amy about your drawings."

John showed Amy and Dr. Sharma his drawings, then said, "I see myself as tall, kind of flabby around the middle with muscular arms and legs and a decent backside for a man. I really don't feel uncomfortable with Amy touching any part of my body. In fact, I wish she would touch me more. I think she thinks of me as the sexiest man alive. Just kidding. I think she sees me pretty much like I do. I also think she would prefer that I work out a little more, but I have never really thought much about it."

Dr. Sharma commented, "Good work. Now let's move on to the questions. Please take turns asking each other the questions on the list."

John, "Amy, how do you feel when I make a positive comment about your appearance?"

Amy, "I don't like it. It makes me feel like I have to make sure that part of me never changes. It feels like pressure. How about you?"

John responded, "Well, that is too bad you feel that way. Would you prefer I not make positive comments?"

Amy answered, "Yes, that would help me."

John paused, then said, "I actually like it when you say positive things about my body, but I can't remember the last time that you did."

Amy said nothing.

John asked, "How do you feel if I make a critical comment about your appearance?"

Amy responded, "Like when you tell me I look too thin or that you can feel my bones and don't like it? Well, the eating disorder part of me lives for those comments, but the healthier part of me really does not like them."

John asked with surprise, "So the eating disorder part actually takes the criticisms as a compliment?"

Amy said, "Yup!"

John continued, "Hmmm. I didn't know that. Well, I don't like it if you criticize my body. I remember one time when you told me my stomach was getting big and I should work out more and I really didn't like it."

Amy agreed, "You're right. I shouldn't have said that, but you shouldn't tell me I am too thin, either."

John said, "Probably true, but they seem different somehow. Like yours relates to your eating disorder so I feel like I should say something."

Amy noted, "It only makes things worse, John."

Dr. Sharma interjected, "It sounds like you are moving on to the next question."

Amy said, "You are right. I would really appreciate if John did not comment on my appearance."

John indicated that he would stop and asked that she do the same.

Dr. Sharma instructed, "Now, ask question four."

John started, "Amy, do you monitor your body or engage in body checking?"

Amy replied, "Yes, all the time. I am always looking in the mirror and noting how my clothes fit. If they are too tight, I feel fat and think I need to eat less. I really don't know how much of my mental energy goes to this, but it is always in the back of my mind."

John responded, "That is so interesting because I never do that. I barely look in the mirror at myself except when I am shaving. If a pair of pants is tight, I just assume they shrunk and put on another pair. I don't ever think I might have gained weight."

Amy commented, "Well, I wish I thought about it like you did, John. It would make my life so much easier."

John then asked Amy, "Do you ever avoid having sex with me because of body shame or appearance anxiety?"

Amy looked down, then answered, "Almost all the time. I don't want you to see me without my clothes on or to touch certain parts of my body. How about you?"

John replied, "Never."

Dr. Sharma asked, "So how would you like to move forward?"

John answered, "Well, I think we should stop making comments about each other's bodies, but I don't know what to do about how Amy feels about me seeing her body during sex."

Amy said, "I don't know either, but it would help me if there were no comments made and if I knew you would not touch my stomach."

John responded, "I can agree to that."

Dr. Sharma instructed them to write this down as a plan they would try for a while and evaluate after a month or so. She then suggested moving on to Step Three, which is talking about weight changes and intimate touch. She explained how weight loss or gain has the potential to affect how a person feels about their body and about intimate touch. She asked them to ask each other the questions in *Action Item Three* just as they did for *Action Item Two*.

John started and asked Amy, "How do you feel about your body after changes in your body weight?"

Amy thought for a moment, then replied, "I feel good if I lose weight and I hate my body if I gain weight. Even if I know I need to gain weight, I do not like to see the changes and really don't like how it feels to gain weight. Seeing the numbers go up on the scale also stresses me out. I get scared I will start gaining weight and never stop. How about you, John?"

John also thought for a moment, "Well, my weight doesn't change very much, but I have gained a few pounds as I have gotten older. It really doesn't bother me. I think I would look a little better if I lost a few pounds, but it just isn't important enough for me to do anything about it. I know I should work out more, but I would rather do other things."

Amy reacted, "I just can't imagine thinking like you do, but I wish I did. I have friends who don't care much about their weight, but I do care and I know I care way too much." She glanced at question two and added, "If you notice that I have gained weight even if I need to, it makes me want to lose it again. I feel embarrassed and like a failure."

John replied, "I had no idea you felt that way. That sounds awful. If you comment on me losing or gaining weight, I might feel irritated or like it is none of your business, but I don't feel bad about myself."

Dr. Sharma mentioned, "Let's answer the next two questions together since they are closely related."

John asked Amy, "How do changes in your body weight affect your desire to be sexually intimate with me and do changes in my body weight affect your desire to be sexually intimate with me? If so, how?"

Amy replied, "Well, when I gain weight, I don't want to have sex. When I lose weight, I don't want to have sex either because I am afraid you will notice I lost weight and say something critical. Since we decided not to make those comments, that might change. If you gain or lose weight, it does not change things for me, but, to be totally honest, if you got really fat, I don't think I could have sex with you. I feel awful for saying that, but I don't think I could."

John responded, "Thanks for being honest. I am not surprised by anything you said. There is not much that will make me not want to have sex." John laughed, then went on, "My body weight has no effect on whether I want to have sex or not. The only thing that does affect me is if you get super thin. It wouldn't change my desire to have sex with you if you were fat, but I know for sure that I don't like making love to a skeleton."

Dr. Sharma pounced on this comment, "John, I am hearing a horseman here, so I would like you to say that differently." Amy who was fighting back tears, looked relieved that Dr. Sharma corrected John.

John had a guilty look on his face, "You are right. I am sorry, Amy. That was unkind. Let me try again. I will delete that last sentence and just say that I am not as attracted to you when you are super thin."

Amy said, "Thanks, John. I appreciate you saying that. I was having a hard time with the skeleton comment. So as I look at question five, I think one thing that makes it hard for me is that I know how you feel when I am super skinny, so I get uncomfortable and avoid intimate touch with you. I don't like being criticized or rejected, so I keep my distance. Do you actually want to have sex with me when I am really thin?"

John answered, "Even though I feel less attraction, I think it is important because it helps me feel connected to you. So, I guess that is a roundabout way of saying yes, I do."

"Can you promise to stop making comments?"

John reassured her, "Yes."

Dr. Sharma led them to the next step, "The next step may not apply directly to both of you since neither of you have a history of sexual trauma. However, you may find some of the questions are still relevant. Look them over and see if there are any you would like to ask each other."

John began, "I think we have a good understanding of what we are both comfortable with doing during sex, but, Amy, I would like to know if you ever avoid things like hugging because you are worried it will lead to more?"

Amy answered slowly, "Yes, actually I do. I like being close to you and cuddling and hugging but I don't want it to always lead to something else and it seems like it does, so I just avoid touching all together. Sometimes, I even wait until I know you are asleep before I come to bed because I don't want snuggling in bed to lead to more."

John looked surprised, "Wow! I didn't realize that. I know it is hard for me to be close to you without getting aroused especially when we have not had sex for a while, but I don't want that to mean we can't hug or cuddle. Can you just be direct with me and say you want to cuddle, but don't want more?"

Amy replied, "I can try that, but will it really work? What if you get aroused?"

John answered, "If I do, I do. That doesn't mean we have to have sex. So moving on to the next questions, how often would you like to have sex with me?"

Amy sighed, then said, "John, I don't want to hurt your feelings. I find you very attractive, but when I am at a low weight, I am not very interested, so once every couple weeks is enough for me. When I am healthier, I like it more often like once or twice a week. How about you?"

John smiled, "Well, I am sure it will come as no surprise, but every day would be great. Realistically, two or three times a week. It would really bother me if we never had sex again. If we couldn't because something happened to one of us, I would adapt, but it would be really hard. How about you?"

Amy responded, "I would be sad and would miss it if we never had sex again, but I think it would be easier for me to adjust to it than it would be for you. What about planning sex versus it being spontaneous?"

John answered, "I really like spontaneous sex and I love it when you initiate."

Amy smiled, "No surprise! I would rather plan it. I never feel ready when initiation is spontaneous. Usually, I need to mentally prepare especially with all my body image issues and sometimes, I feel fat because I have eaten too much or planned to exercise and don't want anything to get in the way. If we plan it, it is more likely to happen. I'm not sure about who I prefer to initiate. I will have to think about that."

John said, "That's fair. When will you get back to me?"

Amy replied, "How about we bring it up at the *State of the Union* or *The Garden*?"

John said, "Deal."

Dr. Sharma had been listening intently, then added, "I am very impressed with how you talked through these sensitive topics. Let's move on to Step 5, which is talking about body sensitivities during intimate touch. Then at the end I will ask each of you to summarize what you learned from the other during this activity. I am going to read the introduction to this step with you.

" 'Most people with eating disorders struggle with body image issues and often have a distorted image of their body or body dysmorphia and a tendency to compare themselves to unrealistic standards of thinness or muscularity. Even people who are behaviorally recovered may still struggle with unresolved feelings about their physical appearance. When sexually intimate and naked, these issues are highlighted.'

"In Step Two, we opened up this area a little. Now we will go into more depth. Amy, I know you already told John that your stomach is a very sensitive area for you and John agreed to not touch you there, so let's move to question three. Amy, would you like to ask John first?"

Amy agreed. "John, does lighting in the room affect how you feel about being touched? What is ideal for you in terms of lighting?"

John thought for a minute, then replied, "I like low lighting at night, but not dark and I also like bright sunlight on a summer day, but, frankly, I am fine with any lighting. How about you?"

Amy hesitated, then said, "Well, I prefer the dark. I just don't like to be seen. Second best would be low lighting, but I feel too exposed with lights on or in bright sunlight, so we are definitely different here."

John stated, "Well, we are, but we both like low lighting so maybe we can just do that."

Amy said, "That is true. Hmm, this next question might be a little rough. The one about what do you like to wear?" She started laughing. "I would love to wear all my clothes but know that is silly. I am OK wearing my underwear, I guess. I like it when you wear shorts and a tee shirt when we start."

John's turn to hesitate, "You know I like lingerie and we have had some fights about this, so this might be a topic we need to revisit at some point."

Dr. Sharma interjected, "Sometimes, when you are doing this exercise, you do identify topics that you want to talk about later using an exercise like *Gottman-Rapoport* or *Dreams Within Conflict*. I recommend you make a note of this one so you can discuss it more later."

Amy said, "OK. This is a hard topic for us."

Dr. Sharma continued, "How about the last question? Amy, is there anything John can say that would help you feel more comfortable with him seeing or touching sensitive areas of your body?"

Amy replied, "You know, we didn't talk about that one question at the start of this action item about asking to stop and I actually think if I knew that I could ask John to stop if he touched those areas, particularly my stomach, that would really help."

Dr. Sharma said, "Amy, can you look at John and ask him about this?"

Amy answered, "Yes. John, would it work for you if I asked you to stop if you were touching a part of my body and I felt fat or uncomfortable?"

John, "Yes, definitely."

Dr. Sharma led them to the next step, saying, "Here is where you synthesize and summarize what you have heard your partner say about intimate touch and sexual intimacy during this exercise. When you have finished summarizing, ask your partner if they feel heard and if there is anything they would like to clarify or add. Who would like to go first?"

Amy said, "I will. John feels comfortable in his body and has no areas of sensitivity for intimate touch."

Dr. Sharma redirected Amy, "Please tell John."

Amy turned toward John, "You like it when I make positive comments about your appearance but not criticisms. You feel more connected to me when we have sex and would like it often. You are flexible with lighting, dress, and initiation, but prefer it be spontaneous and with me initiating more. When I am really thin, you are less attracted to me, but still enjoy having sex with me, but maybe not as often. You are willing to listen if I ask you to stop touching a particular area of my body and agree to stop commenting on my body, positive or negative. Did I get everything?"

John replied, "Yes, I feel understood."

Dr. Sharma prompted, "Now, it is your turn, John."

John started, "Amy, you are particularly sensitive about your stomach and do not like me to touch it or look at it, but you are also sensitive about me seeing your whole body especially if you are feeling fat or have lost weight. When you gain weight, you do not want to have sex. You prefer I not make any comments about your body, positive or negative. If you want me to stop doing something, just let me know and I will. You are not a fan of spontaneous sex and prefer to have time to mentally prepare. When at a low weight, your desire drops really low, like maybe twice a month, but when you are healthier you prefer once or twice a week. Did I miss anything?

Amy responded, "That was really good, John. There is one part I think you missed. The part about cuddling and, oh, the part about light and lingerie too."

John answered, "Right. You said you have avoided hugging or cuddling at times because you were worried it would lead to more so we talked about how we could agree in advance that we would not go any further. You also said you prefer dim light or dark and we agreed we both like dim light and that we table the lingerie talk for the future. How's that?"

Amy smiled, "That was great!"

Dr. Sharma noted, "It is clear that you were both listening carefully to each other. Well done! Now there is one last step. Number Seven." She read the introduction to them and then added, "Showing sexual empathy is something you will do on your own after a time of sexual intimacy or intimate touch. It involves noticing something positive about the experience and communicating that to each other, savoring each intimate encounter."

Amy noted, "I really don't do that. John is a lot better at that than I am, but I can see how it would be a really good thing. I can definitely work on that!"

Dr. Sharma again commented on how well they discussed this sensitive topic. Noting that the time for the day was gone, she concluded the session with a reminder to review all that was talked about and to plan a time for the follow-up discussion regarding lingerie.

———

Dr. Sharma had one more session that day. It was with Carmen and Luciano. They had been fighting often. Dr. Sharma was worried about their relationship. She let out a long sigh. That sigh expressed how deeply she cared about her couples and how hard the work was when a couple was experiencing a significant amount of pain. "It is time to introduce *The Loving Filter*," she reflected. When she noted that Carmen and Luciano had logged into the waiting room for the telehealth session, she exhaled deeply, then clicked and the session began. It was clear that they were still struggling, but they were able to give some heartfelt appreciations. However, before Dr. Sharma could vocalize, Carmen dove into talking about what happened last night.

"Last night was awful. We just returned home after a trip to the grocery store. Luciano was unpacking the groceries and saw a package of chocolate chip cookies from the bakery. He knows that I binge and purge cookies so he got all fired up. He waved the bag of cookies at me and yelled, 'What are these? I don't remember buying any cookies. I thought you were going to stop that disgusting behavior!'

"So, I got defensive and started explaining, 'I bought them for my dad who is coming to visit this week. They are his favorites. Why do you always think everything has to do with my eating disorder?'"

"Of course, he thought I was lying, so he threw the package of cookies on the counter and rolled his eyes, then stormed out of the room. I heard him shout, "Because everything does!" I started crying and cried myself to sleep. He slept in the other room. We didn't talk at all after that until now."

Dr. Sharma's thoughts were racing, but her voice was calm when she responded, "It sounds like you had a really hard night. I am grateful that you both came today. Rather than do *The Aftermath of a Fight*, which we have done many times, I would like to try something different. Let's do *The Loving Filter* exercise with the hope of infusing some positivity into the relationship."

Carmen replied, "That sounds like a great idea, Dr. Sharma. We have been fighting so much that something positive would be a nice change."

Luciano agreed, "Yes, let's give it a try!"

Dr. Sharma introduced the exercise and explained how the Gottmans' research indicated that couples who sunk into negativity quicksand and could not extricate themselves from it were likely to divorce. She noted that these couples no longer liked spending time together, or looked forward to reunions at the end of the day, or felt any closeness. After this, she explained how Martin Seligman and Mihaly Csikszentmihalyi (2000) introduced the concept of positive psychology with the focus on basic human strengths rather than weaknesses and how two researchers, Fred Bryant and Joseph Veroff (2007), put forth the idea that savoring the positive enhanced relationships.

After this, Dr. Sharma said, "Let's read the first paragraph together."

" 'This exercise is about bringing loving thoughts, warm feelings, and affirmation into your relationship through minding, noticing, and savoring. It will help you look for, see, capture, and embrace positivity about your partner.' "

"There are three levels of Minding and Noticing and three levels of Savoring. Beginning, Intermediate, and Advanced. It may take a few sessions to get through all of them, so we will start with Beginning today. Are you with me so far?"

They nodded.

Dr. Sharma continued, "The beginning level of Minding and Noticing is *Noticing the Positive*. Luciano, would you be willing to read the instructions for the Beginning Level?"

Luciano, "Sure. 'Developing the habit of minding requires intentionality and a conscious decision to attend. Begin by noticing **one thing per day** that is positive about your partner, make a note of it, and communicate what you noticed to your partner either verbally or in writing. This also requires choosing to look past the eating disorder. When minding, just thinking something positive about your partner is not enough. It must be communicated.' "

Dr. Sharma thanked him, then went on, "Look at the examples. You can see what is good to say and what is not helpful. Sometimes, people slip in a little jab or meta-message when noticing the positive, like saying 'I noticed that you got off the couch and got around to making dinner for me. I have only been asking you to do this for about 5 years,' rather than saying 'I noticed that you made my favorite dinner last night.' Can you see the difference?"

Carmen responded, "Yeah. I definitely can. I know I have said things like, 'Luciano. Looks like you finally got around to taking down the Christmas tree. It's only February!' Rather than just saying something like, 'I noticed you took down the Christmas tree. Thank you!'

Dr. Sharma affirmed what she said, "That is exactly what I mean, Carmen. What I would like each of you to do now is to practice noticing something positive about your partner. Share two things that you have noticed over the past week or so."

Luciano looked at Carmen and started, "I noticed that you took Fluffer for an extra walk even thought it was raining and that was really nice. And I noticed that you have a nice laugh."

Carmen replied, "Thank you, Luciano. I actually didn't know that you liked my laugh. OK, now my turn. Luciano, I noticed that you did the dishes last night after I went to bed and that was a great surprise when I woke up. I also noticed that you spent a lot of time playing with Luna yesterday morning and she seemed really happy."

Dr. Sharma commented, "Both of you demonstrated good understanding of minding and noticing. I would like you to set the intention of being mindful and telling each other one positive thing that you notice every day. Let's look at Beginning Savoring. Savoring is similar to noticing, but a little different. In this first level, the focus is on reminiscing. Bryant and Veroff found that people who savor the past are happier in the present. Sometimes, people embellish a little when they remember past events, so they end up sounding better than they actually were. That is OK and is called rosy retrospection. The other thing that can happen is that one person will remember an event from the past and the other person will say, 'I don't remember that. Are you sure that happened?' If that occurs, just go with it rather than question the memory and enjoy the story. So, let's practice a little. I would like each of you to tell the story of one good memory from the past."

Luciano volunteered, "I'll go first. I remember when we went skiing at Mount Baker and it started snowing really hard—so hard we could hardly see coming down the mountain. We went into the lodge and had huge mugs of hot chocolate while sitting by the fire. There were tons of people there, but that didn't matter because we were having so much fun being together."

Carmen chimed in, "Yes! I remember that. And my toes were so cold and you rubbed my feet. That was so sweet!"

Carmen added her memory, "I remember when we got all dressed up to go out to dinner at that fancy restaurant in Seattle for our anniversary and when we got there, we found out our reservation was for the next night. They had no tables open for 3 hours, so we just said forget it and went to the Taco Time down the street in our fancy clothes and everyone was looking at us like we were crazy."

Luciano, "I forgot about that time. That was so funny. I got really mad at the maître d' because he wouldn't give us a table. Why did we go to Taco Time?"

Carmen answered, "Because we were going to go back the next night and didn't want to spend a ton of money two nights in a row!"

Luciano said, "That's right!"

They both laughed.

Dr. Sharma made an observation. "See how the reminiscing feels good? In this exercise, you set aside time to reminisce. Ideally, once a week."

Carmen commented, "I like these exercises. They do feel good!"

Dr. Sharma added, "I think you are ready to try the intermediate levels as well." Let's look at Intermediate Minding and Noticing. In this level, you are *Assuming Positive Intent*. Brené Brown has written about this. She found that people who assumed positive intent have a better quality of life, but some found it difficult to assume positive intent, especially if they had perfectionistic tendencies. The assumption of best intent requires the core belief that people are doing the best they can in the moment with what they have and are not being lazy, rude, or inconsiderate on purpose. So, I want you to think about a situation where you may have assumed negative intent and then check it out with each other."

Luciano paused, then said, "Well, I guess the argument we had last night is an example of me assuming negative intent on Carmen's part. I assumed she was going to binge on those cookies when in reality she bought them for her dad. It is hard not to do that because she has lied to me in situations like that in the past, but I can work on it."

Carmen smiled smugly.

Dr. Sharma said, "That is great example, Luciano. I am glad that you brought that up How about you, Carmen. Do you ever assume negative intent about Luciano?"

Carmen replied, "I think the time I do that the most is when he wants to give me a hug. I think that means he wants sex and then he gets mad at me when I push him away and accuse him of only hugging me because he wants more. He tells me sometimes a hug is just a hug and he wants to hug me because he loves me, but I have a hard time believing him. I can try."

Luciano added, "Yeah, sometimes I just want a hug. Since you never want sex anyway, why would I be trying?"

Dr. Sharma jumped in, "Luciano, I hear a horseman coming into the room. Let's stay positive right now."

Luciano said, "Sorry, doc. She just hit a nerve."

Dr. Sharma said, "Thanks, Luciano. Assuming positive intent is something you work on individually. Try to be mindful of when you are assuming the worst or something negative about your partner's motivations. There are steps to follow that will help you process. The most important of them is checking with each other to see if your assumptions are accurate. Since our time is getting short, let's look quickly at Intermediate Savoring. This is about adding more humor into the relationship and finding ways to laugh together. When people laugh together, they have a nice, warm connection. When you notice your partner making a bid for connection with you through humor, be receptive and respond positively. Avoid comments like, 'That was a stupid joke,' 'I don't get your humor,' or 'Stop being silly.' As you may recall, we have also talked about how the Gottmans found that the Masters of relationships were able to add humor to their conflict discussions in a way that kept things from escalating. How are you both feeling about the amount of humor in your relationship now?"

Carmen sighed, "Well, we used to laugh all the time. We would make jokes and puns and tease each other, and it was really fun. But now, everything seems so serious."

Luciano said, "Yeah, I try to be funny, but she never laughs at my jokes anymore. I miss laughing with her. Like I said earlier, she has a great laugh."

Dr. Sharma said, "This is an area of your relationship that you can bring back to life. Look over the suggestions or come up with some of your own."

Luciano said, "I would really like that!"

Dr. Sharma said, "There are two levels left: Advanced Noticing and Minding and Advanced Savoring. We will save those for next time. The Advanced Noticing and Minding has to do with identifying and observing basic human strengths in each other and it feels really good. The Advanced Savoring is about collaboration characterized by synchronous moments. This is a form of savoring that strengthens a relationship. Synchronous storytelling is one way to practice this skill. It is a way of telling a story such that you take turns building on what the other has said without correcting or interrupting each other. We will practice these at our next session."

Luciano mentioned, "It is really nice to do something during our session that is lighter. It seems like our conversations are always so intense. This exercise gives me some ideas of ways to reach out to Carmen and get closer to her. I like it."

Dr. Sharma closed the session by summarizing what they could work on before the next session.

———

As Dr. Sharma shut down her computer and packed up her things, she reflected on her day. She thought about *The Loving Filter* exercise. In the advanced level of this exercise, the couples therapist teaches the couple about the difference between the Relationship Condemnation Story, where their narrative moves from good to bad, and the Relationship Redemption Story, where their narrative moves from bad to good. At the start of couples therapy, most of her couples recounted a Relationship Condemnation Story. They would tell her how they used to be so happy and in love but now were on the verge of divorce with the eating disorder ruining their relationship and they needed help. She knew that her job as a couples therapist was to work with the couple for months, teaching, correcting, and listening with the hope and belief that the couple could and would change their narrative from the Relationship Condemnation Story to a Relationship Redemption Story. It is her hope that the couples that have struggled during challenging times, will, through couples therapy, learn valuable tools, navigate difficult conversations, and, like the phoenix rising from the ashes, emerge stronger and more resilient. Dr. Sharma sat for a moment on the same couch where her couples sat and reflected on the amazing opportunity she has to walk with couples on this most intimate journey. This was why she chose to be a couples therapist. She smiled, turned off the light, and went home. Now, it is your turn.

Epilogue

The four couples continued in couples therapy with Dr. Sharma for various lengths of time.

Quisha and Demarcus repaired their relationship. Quisha learned how to support Demarcus and he learned how to reach for her rather than food when he was upset. They frequently used *The Aftermath of a Behavior* and found it very helpful. In addition to having special times at home, they started playing pickle ball together and found they liked it so much that they have joined a couples league. Their lives no longer revolve around food. Demarcus stopped binge eating, began to exercise more, and became much healthier, but still occasionally makes his famous prime rib and lasagna. Quisha found better ways to cope than gambling. Checking in regularly with *The Garden*, they keep moving forward. Their two children, Tyler and Kalisha, noticed the difference and told their parents they are really proud of the work they have done to help the family.

Ezra and Abe continued their relationship. Their communication improved and they were able to find workable compromises for their differences. The exercises about perfectionism made a huge difference. Abe accomplished his goal of learning how to be supportive and that helped Ezra maintain a low but healthy weight and exercise less, although he still feared gaining weight and becoming fat. Ezra became less rigid about his food choices and that made it possible for the couple to do more with friends and eat out together without tension. Ezra is still struggling with eating disorder thoughts and behaviors, but Abe is accepting of that since they can now talk openly about their feelings.

Carmen and Luciano were able to talk honestly about hard issues, but, unfortunately, as a result of these candid, direct conversations, they decided to get divorced. As they talked about their respective eating disorder narratives, it was apparent that they saw the future very differently. Carmen determined that she was not ready to give up her eating disorder and Luciano was unwilling to stay in the relationship unless she did. Because of the tools they had learned, the divorce was amicable, and they remained friends and effective coparents for Luna.

Amy and John benefited from their open discussions. Amy was able to stabilize her behaviors with John's support without having to go back into treatment. They found the *Building Self-Esteem Together* exercise very helpful as well as the ones that addressed perfectionism, opening the door for them to talk about their blunders and "food flubs" without criticizing each other. Once John learned what to do to help her, he dedicated himself to being the most supportive partner he could, and it made a huge difference. Amy's health improved and she was able to get pregnant and they are expecting a baby in a few months. They continue to see Dr. Sharma for support as they approach this important life transition.

Dr. Sharma has a full practice using Gottman-RED couples therapy interventions with her couples. She is also a clinical supervisor and wants to ensure that when she passes the baton, the next generation of couples therapists will have learned how to effectively help couples in relationships with eating disorders.

Appendix 1

The OWL Conversations Checklist

Wise Conversations Orchestrated with Love (OWL)

Developed by Kim Lampson, PhD

INSTRUCTIONS FOR THE THERAPIST

The *OWL Conversations Checklist* is an assessment tool. It tells you, the therapist, the food, weight, exercise, or body image issues that are important to your couple and it reveals to the couple which issues are significant to one or both of them.

Begin by explaining to the couple that the *OWL Conversations Checklist* is intended to open the door for them to have conversations about potentially sensitive topics related to food, weight, exercise, or body image. Often partners are hesitant to bring up a potentially sensitive subject even though they really want to address this particular issue. Some conversations will be fairly easy, but others may be difficult and emotional.

Mention that these conversations are called *OWL Conversations* for two reasons. First, they are *Orchestrated With Love* meaning that their foundation is built upon the love the two partners have for each other. The dialogues are intended to strengthen their relationship, increase transparency, and build trust. Second, they are based on the premise that it is wise to have conversations like these. Avoiding discussion of sensitive topics will create distance in a relationship. Emphasize to your couple that you will help them have these conversations in a way that is productive, respectful, and emotionally safe.

Give a copy of the couples version of the *OWL Conversations Checklist* to the couple or email it to them after the first session to complete before the individual sessions. Instruct them to read the list and check all the topics that they would like to discuss during the couples therapy. If one partner indicates a desire to discuss the topic, it should be discussed even if the other partner has not checked the box. During individual sessions, ask questions if you think clarification would be helpful in your work with the couple.

Compile a composite list. Give a copy of the combined list to the couple during the feedback session.

Optional activity during the feedback session. It will be up to the therapist's discretion whether or not to do this activity. Ask each partner to read the items that they checked out loud. Explain that there will be no explanation or discussion at this time.

While teaching communication skills such as the Gottman Rapoport (GR), Dreams Within Conflict (DWC), and Art of Compromise (AC), use this list to identify topics the couple will address. With each topic, Gottman interventions that might facilitate the conversation are suggested in parentheses, but the therapist and couple together decide which approach is best. These suggestions are present on the therapist version, but not on the version you will give to your couples. There may be other interventions you find helpful, and you can use your clinical judgment regarding the timing for substituting those when facilitating conversations. The *OWL Checklist* follows.

The OWL Conversations Checklist

Wise Conversations Orchestrated with Love (OWL)

INSTRUCTIONS FOR THE COUPLE

Check every topic that you would like to discuss with your partner during couples therapy even if the topic is something you have been hesitant to bring up in conversation. Some topics may be sensitive, but talking about them during couples therapy will help you learn how to talk about delicate or potentially volatile issues in a constructive way.

Conversations Regarding Eating Disorder Recovery

☐ What does it mean for us to work together as a team to overcome the eating disorder? (DWC)

☐ What does recovery mean to you? (DWC)

☐ Miracle Question: How would the relationship change if we woke up tomorrow and the eating disorder was gone? (Speaker/Listener Dialogue)

☐ Relapses and Lapses: How do we think about them? What do we do if they happen? (DWC and AC)

Conversations Regarding Interactions

☐ *Bidirectionality of Eating Disorder Behaviors.* There is some evidence that the more stable a relationship is, the fewer eating disorder symptoms there are, and the less stable a relationship is, the more eating disorder symptoms there are. Is that true for us? Do we have any vicious cycles? (GC or DWC)

☐ *Accommodating.* Sometimes efforts to help such as providing reassurance when a partner is anxious, buying binge foods, supporting a partner in restriction, only going to acceptable restaurants, keeping binge foods out of the house, or adapting schedules to accommodate excessive exercise can reinforce behaviors that decrease distress in the moment, postponing resolution of issues that must be confronted in order that the person recovers and/or the relationship grows. Does this happen in our relationship? (GR or DWC)

Conversations About Issues

☐ *Timing of Disclosure.* This is a conversation about when the non-eating disorder partner found out about the eating disorder and how that affected the relationship. (GR or DWC)

☐ *Timing of Onset.* This is a conversation about when the eating disorder started: Did it predate the relationship or start after the couple was together? How do you both think about this? (GR or DWC)

☐ *Cost of Treatment.* This is a conversation about the financial impact of the eating disorder treatment and behaviors on the relationship. Cost of treatment includes time taken off work by either partner as well as health professional services expenses. Cost of behaviors includes items such as binge foods, specialty foods, exercise equipment, gym memberships, diet program fees. (GR and/or AC)

☐ *Satisfaction with Appearance.* This is a conversation in which both partners share their thoughts about this topic. (GR)

☐ *Body Ideals and Beliefs about Weight/Health/Aging.* This is a conversation in which both partners share their thoughts about this topic. (DWC)

☐ *Meaning of Sex.* This is an amazing conversation for couples in which both partners talk about how and what they learned about sex and what it means to them now. It is a conversation in which both partners share their thoughts about this topic. (DWC)

☐ *Sex and Body Image.* This conversation is about how feelings regarding body image impact sexual intimacy and physical touch and can include topics such as the effect of weight gain or loss, the impact of a binge, or the impact of stepping on the scale. It is important that both partners share how they feel about their own body image and how or if that impacts their desire for sexual intimacy. (GR or RED in Bed)

☐ *Secrecy.* Secrecy limits recovery and empowers the eating disorder. It also has the potential to damage a relationship because of the deception, potential for manipulation, and the withholding of information from the partner. This topic is also addressed in The Vulnerability Leap exercise. This conversation may uncover some regrettable incidents. This is a conversation in which both partners share their thoughts about this topic. (DWC and GR)

☐ *What Do We Tell the Children?* How do you explain eating disorder related issues to children? Relevant issues include time away for treatment, dietary changes, weight fluctuations, rigidity regarding mealtimes and food, and excessive exercising. These are all issues that can affect day-to-day living to varying degrees depending on the age of the children. (GR and/or AC)

Conversations Regarding the Non-Eating Disorder Partner Experience

☐ *Subjective Burden.* Subjective Burden refers to the extent to which the partner feels like they are carrying a heavy load. There is a sense that the person in recovery is very dependent on them and cannot cope well on their own. (GR)

☐ *Objective Burden.* Objective Burden refers to the disruption in the carer's life due to the patient's condition (e.g. hiding food, buying particular foods, limited choices for eating out, not eating meals together, having to prepare separate menus, rigid rituals around eating and food preparation interfering with plans, excessive or obsessive exercise, concerns related to body image, and lost opportunities for socializing with others). (GR)

☐ *Concerns of Both Partners Regarding the Non-Eating Disorder Partner's Emotional and Physical Health.* This is a conversation in which both partners share their thoughts about this topic. (GR)

☐ *Level of Involvement of the Non-Eating Disorder Partner in Treatment.* This is a conversation in which both partners share their thoughts about this topic. The conversation may lead to an agreement regarding how to move forward that is a win-win and works for both partners. (DWC, GR, AC)

☐ *What Happens if the Non-Eating Disorder Partner Wants to Lose Weight, Go on a Diet, or Start an Exercise Program?* This is a conversation in which both partners share their thoughts about this topic. (GR and/or AC)

Conversations Regarding the Eating Disorder Experience for the Person with an Eating Disorder

☐ *Eating Disorder History.* (Person with the eating disorder is speaker, non-eating disorder partner is listener)

☐ *Experiences with Treatment.* (Person with the eating disorder is speaker, non-eating disorder partner is listener)

Conversations Regarding Practical Issues of Living Together that Relate to the Eating Disorder

(Conversations about these topics can use GR, DWC, AC or a combination of these interventions)

☐ Body image and full-length mirrors: Should we have them?

☐ Comparing to others when it affects socializing

☐ Eating together

☐ Involvement in regulating eating behavior of each other

☐ Socializing with family and friends

☐ Grocery shopping: Who does it?

☐ Hiding food

☐ Sharing food

☐ Dieting

☐ Exercise: What and how much?

☐ Having or not having a scale

☐ Expenses related to food

☐ Meal preparation: Who does it? Do we eat the same thing or different things?

☐ Shared meal schedule: How do we decide when to eat?

Conversations That Will Build Trust and Create Safety

☐ *What Will Help Me?* Both partners express what they need at the moment with regard to coping with the eating disorder. (GR)

☐ *Boundaries.* How much to discuss the eating disorder with family and friends. There is a balance between need for privacy and need for support that is important to discuss. (GR and/or AC)

☐ *Secrecy and Shame.* This involves a conversation about honesty and fear of judgment or ridicule. (DWC)

Appendix 2

Are You Dying to be Thin?

The following questionnaire will tell you whether or not you think or behave in a way that indicates that you have tendencies toward anorexia nervosa or bulimia nervosa.

Answer the questions below honestly. Respond as you are now, not the way you used to be or the way you would like to be. Add up your answers. Do not leave any questions blank unless instructed to do so.

1. I have eating habits that are different from those of my family and friends.	1=Often 2=Sometimes 3=Rarely 4=Never
2. I find myself panicking if I cannot exercise as I planned, because I am afraid that I will gain weight if I don't.	1=Often 2=Sometimes 3=Rarely 4=Never
3. My friends tell me that I am thin, but I don't believe them because I feel fat.	1=Often 2=Sometimes 3=Rarely 4=Never
4. (females only) My menstrual period has stopped or become irregular due to no known medical reasons.	1=True 2=False

5. I have become obsessed with food to the point that I cannot go through a day without worrying about what I will or will not eat.	1=Almost always 2=Sometimes 3=Rarely 4=Never
6. I have lost more than 15% of what is considered to be a healthy weight for my height and body	1=True 2=False
7. I would panic if I got on the scale tomorrow and found that I had gained two pounds.	1=Often 2=Sometimes 3=Rarely 4=Never
8. I find that I prefer to eat alone or when I am sure that no one will see me, and thus make excuses so that I can eat less and less often with friends or family.	1=Often 2=Sometimes 3=Rarely 4=Never
9. I find myself going on uncontrollable eating binges during which I consume large amounts of food to the point that I feel sick and make myself vomit.	1=Never 2=Less than one time per week 3=One to six times per week 4=One or more times per day
10. (NOTE: Answer only if your answer to #9 is "1" Otherwise leave blank.) I find myself compulsively eating more than I want to while feeling out of control and/or unaware of what I am doing.	1=Never 2=Less than one time per week 3=One to six times per week 4=One or more times per day
11. I use laxatives or diuretics as a means of weight control.	1=Never 2=Rarely 3=Sometimes 4=On a regular basis
12. I find myself playing games with food (e.g., cutting it up in tiny pieces, hiding food so people will think I ate it, chewing it and spitting it out without swallowing it, keeping hidden stashes of food).	1=Often 2=Sometimes 3=Rarely 4=Never

13. People around me have become very interested in what I eat and I find myself getting angry at them for pushing me to eat more.	1=Often 2=Sometimes 3=Rarely 4=Never
14. I have felt more depressed and irritable recently than is typical for me and/or have been spending and increasing amount of time alone.	1=True 2=False
15. I keep a lot of my fears about food and eating to myself because I am afraid no one would understand.	1=Often 2=Sometimes 3=Rarely 4=Never
16. I enjoy making gourmet and/or high calorie foods for others as long as I don't have to eat any myself.	1=Often 2=Sometimes 3=Rarely 4=Never
17. The most powerful fear in my life is the fear of gaining weight or becoming fat.	1=Often 2=Sometimes 3=Rarely 4=Never
18. I exercise a lot (more than 4 times per week and/or more than 4 hours per week) as a means of weight control.	1=True 2=False
19. I find myself totally absorbed when reading, watching videos, or viewing social media posts about dieting, exercising, fitness, or calorie counting to the point that I can spend hours studying them.	1=Often 2=Sometimes 3=Rarely 4=Never
20. I tend to be a perfectionist and am not satisfied with myself unless I do things perfectly.	1=Almost always 2=Sometimes 3=Rarely 4=Never
21. I go through long periods of time without eating (fasting) or eating very little as a means of weight control.	1=Often 2=Sometimes 3=Rarely 4=Never

22. It is important for me to try to be thinner than all of my friends.

1=Almost always
2=Sometimes
3=Rarely
4=Never

SCORING

Step 1: Add your responses to find your total score.

Step 2: Compare your score with the chart below.

38 or less	Strong tendencies toward anorexia nervosa If you scored 38 or below, it would be wise for you to: 1. Seek more information about anorexia nervosa and bulimia nervosa. 2. Contact a counselor, pastor, teacher, or physician in order to find out if you have an eating disorder and, if you do, how to get some help.
39–50	Strong tendencies toward bulimia nervosa If you scored 50 or below, it would be wise for you to: 1. Seek more information about anorexia nervosa and bulimia nervosa. 2. Contact a counselor, pastor, teacher, or physician in order to find out if you have an eating disorder and, if you do, how to get some help.
50–60	Weight conscious. It is unclear if you have tendencies toward an eating disorder, but you appear to very focused on food, weight, exercise, or body image. You are not likely to have anorexia or bulimia nervosa, but you may have tendencies toward OSFED* (other specified feeding or eating disorder), binge eating disorder, obesity, orthorexia, overeating, or another significant pattern of disordered eating. If you scored between 50 and 60, it is highly recommended that you to talk to a counselor, pastor, teacher, or physician in order to determine if you would benefit from some help from a health care provider who understands disordered eating issues.

Over 60   It is extremely unlikely that you have anorexia nervosa
               or bulimia nervosa, however, you may have binge
               eating disorder, OSFED*, or another significant pattern
               of disordered eating.

               Scoring over 60 does not rule out tendencies toward
               a pattern of overeating, orthorexia, a subclinical eating
               disorder, or obesity.

               If you scored over 60, and have questions and
               concerns about the way you eat and/or your weight,
               it would be a good idea for you to talk to a counselor,
               pastor, teacher, or physician in order to determine if
               you would benefit from some help from a health care
               provider who understands disordered eating issues.

*OSED includes people whose quality of life is significantly negatively impacted but food-or weight-related behaviors but do not meet the full criteria for diagnosis of any other eating disorder.

Note: Eating disorders are potentially life-threatening disorders which can be overcome with the proper information, support, treatment, and therapy. The earlier you seek help the better, although it is never too late to begin the road to recovery.

* Copyright Kim Lampson, Revised 1995, 2023, 2024. All rights reserved. Please contact Dr. Lampson at drkimlampson@gmail.com for permission to copy.

References

American Psychiatric Association. (2022). *Diagnostic and statistical manual of mental disorders* (5th ed., text rev.) (DSM-5-TR). https://doi.org/10.1176/appi.books.9780890425787

Arcelus, J., Yates, A., & Whiteley, R. (2012). Romantic relationships, clinical and sub-clinical eating disorders: A review of the literature. *Sexual and Relationship Therapy, 27*(2), 147–161. https://doi.org/10.1080/14681994.2012.696095

Associated Press (November 3, 2020). CDC *Says More Americans on Diets Compared to a Decade Ago*. https://www.nbcnews.com/health/health-news/cdc-says-more-americans-diets-compared-decade-ago-n1246017

Austin, S. B., Ziyadeh, N. J., Forman, S., Prokop, L. A., Keliher, A., & Jacobs, D. (2008). Screening high school students for eating disorders: Results of a national initiative. *Preventing Chronic Disease, 5*(4): A114. Epub 2008 Sep 15.

Azmy, S. (2019). *The eating disordered couple*. Routledge.

Bailey, L., Markey, C. N., Markey, P. M., August, K. J., & Nave, C. S. (2015). Understanding same-sex male and female partners' restrained eating in the context of their relationships. *Journal of Health Psychology, 20*(6), 816–827. https://doi.org/10.1177/1359105315573431

Baucom, D. H., Kirby, J. S., Fischer, M. S., Baucom, B. R., Hamer, R., & Bulik, C. M. (2017). Findings from a couple-based open trial for adult anorexia nervosa. *Journal of Family Psychology, 31*(5), 584–591. https://doi.org/10.1037/fam0000273

Blok, S. L. (2002). Eating disordered women's descriptions of issues leading to conflict and the communication strategies used to manage conflict in their family and romantic relationships: A qualitative study [ProQuest Information & Learning]. In *Dissertation Abstracts International Section A: Humanities and Social Sciences* (Vol. 63, Issue 3–A, p. 816).

Bomben, R., Robertson, N., & Allan, S. (2022). Barriers to help-seeking for eating disorders in men: A mixed-methods systematic review. *Psychology of Men & Masculinities, 23*(2), 183–196. https://doi.org/10.1037/men0000382.supp (Supplemental)

Boyes, A. D., Fletcher, G. J. O., & Latner, J. D. (2007). Male and female body image and dieting in the context of intimate relationships. *Journal of Family Psychology, 21*(4), 764–768. https://doi.org/10.1037/0893-3200.21.4.764

Breland, J. Y., Donalson, R., Li, Y., Hebenstreit, C. L., Goldstein, L. A., & Maguen, S. (2018). Military sexual trauma is associated with eating disorders, while combat exposure is not. *Psychological Trauma: Theory, Research, Practice, and Policy, 10*(3), 276–281. https://doi.org/10.1037/tra0000276

Briggs, D. C. (1986). *Celebrate yourself: Enhancing your self-esteem.* Main Street Books.

Brown, B. (2010). *The gifts of imperfection: Letting go of who you think you're supposed to be and embrace who you are.* Hazeldon.

Brown, B. (2018). *Dare to lead.* Random House.

Brown, T. A., & Keel, P. K. (2015). Relationship status predicts lower restrictive eating pathology for bisexual and gay men across 10-year follow-up. *International Journal of Eating Disorders, 48*(6), 700–707. https://doi.org/10.1002/eat.22433

Bruch, H. (1978). *The golden cage: The enigma of anorexia nervosa.* Harvard University Press.

Bryant, F., & Veroff, J. (2007). *Savoring: A new model of positive experience.* Lawrence Erlbaum Associates.

Bulik, C. M., Baucom, D. H., & Kirby, J.S. (2012). Treating anorexia nervosa in the couple context. *Journal of Cognitive Psychotherapy, 26*(1), 19–33.

Buser, J. K., Kearney, A., & Buser, T. J. (2015). Family, friends, and romantic partners of eating disorder sufferers: The use of spiritual/religious coping strategies. *The Family Journal, 23*(4), 320–329. https://doi.org/10.1177/1066480715601132

Bussolotti, D., Fernández-Aranda, F., Solano, R., Jiménez-Murcia, S., Turón, V., & Vallejo, J. (2002). Marital status and eating disorders: An analysis of its relevance. *Journal of Psychosomatic Research, 53*(6), 1139–1145. https://doi.org/10.1016/S0022-3999(02)00336-7

Calogero, R. M., Herbozo, S., & Thompson, J. K. (2009). Complimentary weightism: The potential costs of appearance-related commentary for women's self-objectification. *Psychology of Women Quarterly, 33*(1), 120–132. https://doi.org/10.1111/j.1471-6402.2008.01479.x

Campbell, L., Fouad, N., Grus, C., Hatcher, R., Leahy, K., & McCutcheon, S. (2012). *Guidebook for competency benchmarks.* American Psychological Association. https://www.apa.org/ed/graduate/guide-benchmarks.pdf

Castellini, G., Rossi, E., & Ricca, V. (2020). The relationship between eating disorder psychopathology and sexuality: Etiological factors and implications for treatment. *Current Opinion in Psychiatry, 33*(6), 554–561. https://doi.org/10.1097/YCO.0000000000000646

Chen, E. Y., & Kaye, W. H. (2018). We are only at the tip of the iceberg: A commentary on higher levels of care for anorexia nervosa. *Clinical Psychology: Science and Practice, 25*(1). https://doi.org/10.1037/h0101750.supp (Supplemental)

Chen, Y., Kawachi, I., Berkman, L. F., Trudel-Fitzgerald, C., & Kubzansky, L.

D. (2018). A prospective study of marital quality and body weight in mid-life. *Health Psychology, 37*(3), 247–256. https://doi.org/10.1037/hea0000589 .supp (Supplemental)

Coffino, J. A., Udo, T., & Grilo, C. M. (2019). Rates of help-seeking in US adults with lifetime DSM-5 eating disorders: Prevalence across diagnoses and differences by sex and ethnicity/race. *Mayo Clinic Proceedings, 94*(8), 1415–1426. https://doi.org/10.1016/j.mayocp.2019.02.030

Collisson, B., Howell, J. L., Rusbasan, D., & Rosenfeld, E. (2017). "Date some-one your own size": Prejudice and discrimination toward mixed-weight rela-tionships. *Journal of Social and Personal Relationships, 34*(4), 510–540. https://doi.org/10.1177/0265407516644067

Cornelius, T., Gettens, K., Lenz, E., Wojtanowski, A. C., Foster, G. D., & Gorin, A. A. (2018). How prescriptive support affects weight loss in weight-loss intervention participants and their untreated spouses. *Health Psychology, 37*(8), 775–781. https://doi.org/10.1037/hea0000630

Cortes, K., & Wood, J. V. (2018). Is it really "all in their heads"? How self-es-teem predicts partner responsiveness. *Journal of Personality, 86*(6), 990–1002. https://doi.org/10.1111/jopy.12370

Croll, M. S., Neumark-Sztainer, C., Story, M., & Ireland, M. (2002). Preva-lence and risk and protective factors related to disordered eating behaviors among adolescents: Relationship to gender and ethnicity. *Journal of Adoles-cent Health, 31*(2), 166–175. https://doi.org/10.1016/S1054-139X(02)00368-3

Dobrescu, S. R., Dinkler, L., Gillberg, C., Råstam, M., Gillberg, C., & Wentz, E. (2020). Anorexia nervosa: 30-year outcome. *The British Journal of Psychi-atry :The Journal of Mental Science, 216*(2), 97–104. https://doi.org/10.1192/bjp.2019.113

Dick, C. H., Renes, S. L., Morotti, A., & Strange, A. T. (2013). Understanding and assisting couples affected by an eating disorder. *American Journal of Fam-ily Therapy, 41*(3), 232–244. https://doi.org/10.1080/01926187.2012.677728

Dunlop, W. L., Bühler, J. L., Maghsoodi, A., Harake, N., Wilkinson, D., & McAd-ams, D. P. (2021). The stories couples live by. *Journal of Social and Personal Relationships, 38*(2), 690–710. https://doi.org/10.1177/0265407520969900

Egan, S. J., Shafran, R., & Wade, T. D. (2022). A clinician's quick guide to evidence-based approaches: Perfectionism. *Clinical Psychologist, 26*(3), 351–353. https://doi.org/10.1080/13284207.2022.2108315

Fairburn, C. (2008). *Cognitive behavior therapy and eating disorders*. Guilford.

Fairburn, C. (2013). *Overcoming binge eating*. Guilford.

Fischer, M. S., Baucom, D. H., Baucom, B. R., Abramowitz, J. S., Kirby, J. S., & Bulik, C. M. (2017). Disorder-specific patterns of emotion coregulation in couples: Comparing obsessive compulsive disorder and anorexia ner-vosa. *Journal of Family Psychology, 31*(3), 304–315. https://doi.org/10.1037/fam0000251

Francisca, C. J., & Gómez, J. R. (2020). Profile of durable and successful mar-riages: A new competency-based marital education program. *Revista Latino-*

americana de Psicología, 52. https://doi.org/10.14349/rlp.2020.v52.2

Frankl, V., Winslade, W., & Kushner, H. (2006). *Man's Search for Meaning.* Beacon Press.

Friedlander, M. L., Escudero, V., & Heatherington, L. (2006). *Therapeutic alliances in couple and family therapy: An empirically informed guide to practice.* American Psychological Association. https://doi.org/10.1037/11410-000

Gibbon, P. (2020). Martin Seligman and the rise of positive psychology. *Humanities, 41*(3) https://www.neh.gov/article/martin-seligman-and-rise-positive-psychology

Goldberg, D. (1985) *Contemporary marriage: Special issues in couples therapy.* Dorsey Press.

Gorin, A. A., Le Grange, D., & Stone, A. A. (2003). Effectiveness of spouse involvement in cognitive behavioral therapy for binge eating disorder. *International Journal of Eating Disorders, 33*(4), 421–433. https://doi.org/10.1002/eat.10152

Gorin, A. A., Powers, T. A., Gettens, K., Cornelius, T., Koestner, R., Mobley, A. R., Pescatello, L. S., & Huedo-Medina, T. B. (2017). Project TEAMS (Talking about eating, activity, and mutual support): A randomized controlled trial of a theory-based weight loss program for couples. *Public Health, 17*, 1–10. https://doi.org/10.1186/s12889-017-4732-7

Gorin, A. A., Powers, T. A., Gettens, K., Cornelius, T., Koestner, R., Mobley, A. R., Pescatello, L. S., & Huedo-Medina, T. B. (2019). A randomized controlled trial of a theory-based weight-loss program for couples. *Health Psychology, 39*(2), 137–146. https://doi.org/10.1037/hea0000808

Gottman, J. (January 9, 2023). The truth about expectations in relationships. [Blog]. Retrieved from https://www.gottman.com/blog/truth-expectations-relationships/

Gottman, J. M., and Gottman, J. S. (2000). *Level 2 clinical training Gottman method couples therapy: Assessment, intervention, and co-morbidities.* The Gottman Institute.

Gottman, J. M., & Gottman, J. S. (2013). Difficulties with clients in Gottman method couples therapy. In A. W. Wolf, M. R. Goldfried, & J. C. Muran (Eds.), *Transforming negative reactions to clients: From frustration to compassion.* (pp. 91–112). American Psychological Association. https://doi.org/10.1037/13940-004

Gottman, J. M., & Gottman, J. S. (2017). The natural principles of love. *Journal of Family Theory & Review 9*(7), 7–26. https://doi.org/10.1111/jftr.12182

Gottman, J., Gottman, J., & McNulty, M. A. (2017). The role of trust and commitment in love relationships. In J. Fitzgerald (Ed.), *Foundations for couples' therapy: Research for the real world* (pp. 438–452). Routledge/Taylor & Francis Group. https://doi.org/10.4324/9781315678610-43

Gottman, J. M., & Gottman, J. S. (2018). *The science of couples and family therapy: Behind the scenes at the love lab.* Norton.

Gottman, J., Gottman, J. S., Abrams, D., & Abrams, R. C. (2019). *Eight Dates:*

Essential Conversations for a Lifetime of Love. Workman.

Gottman, J. M., Gottman, J. S., Abrams, D., Abrams, R. C., & Hardin, L. L. (2016). *The man's guide to women: Scientifically proven secrets from the "Love Lab" about what women really want.* Rodale.

Gottman, J. S. & Gottman, J. (2024). *Fight right: How successful couples turn conflict into connection.* Harmony.

Halford, W. K., Pepping, C. A., & Petch, J. (2016). The gap between couple therapy research efficacy and practice effectiveness. *Journal of Marriage and Family Therapy, 42,* 32–44. https://doi.org/10.1111/jmft.12120

Halford, W. K., & Pepping, C. A. (2019). What every therapist needs to know about couple therapy. *Behavior Change, 36,* 121–142. https://doi:10.1017/bec .2019.12.

Haracz, K., & Robson, E. (2017). A bidirectional relationship between eating disorder symptoms and quality of life supports a recovery focused approach to treatment. *Australian Occupational Therapy Journal, 64*(4), 345–347. https:// doi.org/10.1111/1440-1630.12413

Haring, M., Hewitt, P. L., & Flett, G. L. (2003). Perfectionism, coping, and quality of intimate relationships. *Journal of Marriage and Family, 65*(1), 143–158. https://doi.org/10.1111/j.1741-3737.2003.00143

Harron, D. (2019). *Loving someone with an eating disorder.* New Harbinger.

Hempel, R., Vanderbleek, E., & Lynch, T. (2018). Radically open DBT: Targeting emotional loneliness in Anorexia Nervosa. *Eating Disorders, 26*(1), 92–104.

Hewitt, P. L., & Flett, G. L. (1991). Perfectionism in the self and social contexts: Conceptualization, assessment, and association with psychopathology. *Journal of Personality and Social Psychology, 60*(3), 456–470. https://doi.org/10 .1037/0022-3514.60.3.456

Hibbs, R., Rhind, C., Sallis H., Goddard, E., Raenker, S., Ayton, A., Bamford, B., Arcelus, J., Boughton, N., Coan, F., Goss, K., Lazlo, B., Morgan, J., Moore, K., Robdertson, d., Schreiber-Kounine, C., Sharma, S., Whitehead, L., Lacey, H., Scmidt, U., & Treasure, J. (2014). Confirmatory factor analysis for two questionnaires of caregiving in eating disorders, *Health Psychology and Behavioral Medicine, 2*(1), 322-334, https://doi.org/10.1080/21642850 .2014.894889

Highet, N., Thompson, M., & King, R. M. (2005). The experience of living with a person with an eating disorder: The impact on the carers. *Eating Disorders: The Journal of Treatment & Prevention, 13*(4), 327–344. https://doi.org/10 .1080/10640260591005227

Holmes, S. C., Johnson, N. L., & Johnson, D. M. (2019). Understanding the relationship between interpersonal trauma and disordered eating: An extension of the model of psychological adaptation. *Psychological Trauma: Theory, Research, Practice, and Policy.* https://doi.org/10.1037/tra0000533 .supp (Supplemental)

Huke, K., & Slade, P. (2006). An exploratory investigation of the experiences of partners living with people who have bulimia nervosa. *European Eating Dis-*

orders Review, 14(6), 436–447. https://doi.org/10.1002/erv.744

Johnson, S. (2008). *Hold me tight: Seven conversations for a lifetime of love.* Little, Brown Spark.

Karney, B. R., & Bradbury, T. N. (1995). The longitudinal course of marital quality and stability: A review of theory, methods, and research. Psychological Bulletin, *118*(1), 3–34.

Keys, A., Brozek, J., Henschel, A., Mickelson, O., Taylor, H. L., Simonson, E., Skinner, A. S., Wells, S. M., Drummond, J. C., Wilder, R. M., King, C. G., & Williams, R. R. (1950). *The Biology of Human Starvation: Volume I.* University of Minnesota Press. https://doi.org/10.5749/j.ctv9b2tqv

Kim, L. M., Johnson, J. L., & Ripley, J. (2011). A "perfect" storm: Perfectionism, forgiveness, and marital satisfaction. *Individual Differences Research, 9*(4), 199–209.

Kirby, J. S., Fischer, M. S., Raney, T. J., Baucom, D. H., & Bulik, C. M. (2016). Couple-based interventions in the treatment of adult anorexia nervosa: A brief case example of UCAN. *Psychotherapy, 53*(2), 241–250. https://doi .org/10.1037/pst0000053

Kluck, A. S., Garos, S., & Shaw, L. (2018). Sexual functioning and disordered eating: A new perspective. *Bulletin of the Menninger Clinic, 82*(1), 71–91. https:// doi.org/10.1521/bumc_2017_81_12

Knobloch, L. K., Nichols, L. O., & Martindale-Adams, J. (2020). Applying relational turbulence theory to adult caregiving relationships. *The Gerontologist, 60*(4), 598–606. https://doi.org/10.1093/geront/gnz090

Lally, P., van Jaarsveld, C. H. M., Potts, H. W. W., & Wardle, J. (2010). How are habits formed: Modelling habit formation in the real world. *European Journal of Social Psychology, 40*(6), 998–1009. https://doi.org/10.1002/ejsp.674

Lampson, K. (1983). Perseverance overcomes. *The Hopeline, 2*(24), 2.

Lampson, K. (2021). We have weighted long enough: It is time! *APTC Bulletin.*

Levine, M. P. (2012). Loneliness and eating disorders. *The Journal of Psychology: Interdisciplinary and Applied, 146*(1–2), 243–257. https://doi.org/10 .1080/00223980.2011.606435

Levinson, C. A., Cash, E., Welch, K., Epskamp, S., Hunt, R. A., Williams, B. M., Keshishian, A. C., & Spoor, S. P. (2020). Personalized networks of eating disorder symptoms predicting eating disorder outcomes and remission. *International Journal of Eating Disorders, 53*(12), 2086–2094. https://doi .org/10.1002/eat.23398

Linardon, J. (2018). Rates of abstinence following psychological or behavioral treatments for binge-eating disorder: Meta-analysis. *International Journal of Eating Disorders, 51*(8), 785–797. https://doi.org/10.1002/eat.22897

Linehan, M. (1993). *Skills training manual for treating borderline personality disorder.* Guilford.

Linville, D., Cobb, E., Shen, F., & Stadelman, S. (2015). Reciprocal influence of couple dynamics and eating disorders. *Journal of Marital and Family Therapy 42*(2), 326–340. https://doi.org.10.1111/jmft.12133

Linville, D., & Oleksak, N. (2013). Integrated eating disorder treatment for couples. *Journal of Couple & Relationship Therapy*, *12*(3), 255–269. https://doi.org/ 10.1080/15332691.2013.806709

Lock, J. & LeGrange, D. (2015). *Treatment manual for anorexia nervosa: A family-based approach (2nd ed.)*. Guilford.

Lynch, T. (2018). *The skills training manual for radically open dialectical behavior therapy: A clinician's guide for treating disorders of overcontrol*. Context Press.

Macdonald, J., & Muran, C. J. (2021). The reactive therapist: The problem of interpersonal reactivity in psychological therapy and the potential for a mindfulness-based program focused on "mindfulness-in-relationship" skills for therapists. *Journal of Psychotherapy Integration*, *31*(4), 452–467. https://doi.org/10.1037/int0000200

Maier, C. A. (2015). Feminist-informed emotionally focused couples therapy as treatment for eating disorders. *American Journal of Family Therapy*, *43*(2), 151–162. https://doi.org/10.1080/01926187.2014.956620

Malova, E., & Dunleavy, V. (2021). Men have eating disorders too: An analysis of online narratives posted by men with eating disorders on YouTube. *Eating Disorders: The Journal of Treatment & Prevention*, *30*(4), 437–452. https://doi.org/10.1080/10640266.2021.1930338

Markey, C. N., Gomel, J. N., & Markey, P. M. (2008). Romantic relationships and eating regulation: An investigation of partners' attempts to control each others' eating behaviors. *Journal of Health Psychology*, *13*(3), 422–432. https://doi.org/10.1177/1359105307088145

McAdams, D. P. (2015). The redemptive self: Generativity and the stories Americans live by. In K. M. Roy (Ed.), *Second Chances as Transformative Stories Rhd V3 2&3* (pp. 81–100). Psychology Press.

Micali, N., Martini, M. G., Thomas, J. J., Eddy, K. T., Kothari, R., Russell, E., Bulik, C. M., Treasure, J. (2017). Lifetime and 12-month prevalence of eating disorders amongst women in mid-life: A population-based study of diagnoses and risk factors. *BMC Medicine*, *15*(12), 1-10. https://doi:10.1186/s12916-016-0766-4

Miller, R., Hilsenroth, M. J., & Hewitt, P. L. (2017). Perfectionism and therapeutic alliance: A review of the clinical research. *Research in Psychotherapy (Milano)*, *20*(1), 264. https://doi.org/10.4081/ripppo.2017.264

Mitchison, D., Bussey, K., Touyz, S., Gonzalez-Chica, D., Musker, M., Stocks, N., Licinio, J., & Hay, P. (2019). Shared associations between histories of victimization among people with eating disorder symptoms and higher weight. *Australian and New Zealand Journal of Psychiatry*, *53*(6), 540–549. https://doi.org/10.1177/0004867418814961

Morrison, K. R., Doss, B. D., & Perez, M. (2009). Body image and disordered eating in romantic relationships. *Journal of Social and Clinical Psychology*, *28*(3), 281–306. https://doi.org/10.1521/jscp.2009.28.3.281

Moulding, N. (2015). "It wasn't about being slim": Understanding eating disorders in the context of abuse. *Violence Against Women*, *21*(12), 1456–1480. https://

doi.org/10.1177/1077801215596243

Murray, S. B. (2014). A case of strategic couples therapy in adult anorexia nervosa: The importance of symptoms in context. *Contemporary Family Therapy*, *36*, 392–397. https://doi.org/10.1007/s10591-014-9301-y

Murray, S. B., Labuschagne, Z., & Le Grange, D. (2014). Family and couples therapy for eating disorders, substance use disorders, and addictions. In T. D. Brewerton & A. B. Dennis (Eds.), *Eating disorders, addictions and substance use disorders: research, clinical and treatment perspectives* (pp. 563–586). Springer-Verlag.

Nagata, J. M., Ganson, K. T., & Austin, S. B. (2020). Emerging trends in eating disorders among sexual and gender minorities. *Current Opinion in Psychiatry*, *33*(6), 562–567. https://doi.org/10.1097/YCO.0000000000000645

O'Connor, P., Daly, L., & Higgins, A. (2019). Partners' experiences of living with a person with an eating disorder: A grounded theory study. *Journal of Advanced Nursing*, *75*(8), 1741–1750. https://doi.org/10.1111/jan.14032

Oral, S., Zeytinoğlu-Saydam, S., Söylemez, Y., Akmehmet-Şekerler, S., & Aponte, H. J. (2022). Developing the person of the therapist when working with couples. *Contemporary Family Therapy: An International Journal, 45*, 228–241. https://doi.org/10.1007/s10591-022-09641-w

Papathomas, A., Smith, B., & Lavallee, D. (2015). Family experiences of living with an eating disorder: A narrative analysis. *Journal of Health Psychology*, *20*(3), 313–325. https://doi.org/10.1177/1359105314566608

Perkins, S., Winn, S., Murray, J., Murphy, R., & Schmidt, U. (2004). A Qualitative Study of the Experience of Caring for a Person with Bulimia Nervosa Part 1: The Emotional Impact of Caring. *International Journal of Eating Disorders*, *36*(3), 256–268. https://doi.org/10.1002/eat.20067

Pinheiro, A. P., Raney, T. J., Thornton, L. M., Fichter, M. M., Berrettini, W. H., Goldman, D., Halmi, K. A., Kaplan, A. S., Strober, M., Treasure, J., Woodside, D. B., Kaye, W. H., & Bulik, C. M. (2010). Sexual functioning in women with eating disorders. *International Journal of Eating Disorders*, *43*(2), 123–129. https://doi.org/10.1002/eat.20671

Powers, T. A., Koestner, R., Denes, A., Cornelius, T., & Gorin, A. A. (2022). Autonomy support in a couples weight loss trial: Helping yourself while helping others. *Families, Systems, & Health*, *40*(1), 70–78. https://doi.org/10.1037/fsh0000663

Quadflieg, N., Strobel, C., Naab, S., Voderholzer, U., & Fichter, M. M. (2019). Mortality in males treated for an eating disorder—A large prospective study. *International Journal of Eating Disorders*, *52*(12), 1365–1369. https://doi.org/10.1002/eat.23135

Reas, D. L., & Stedal, K. (2015). Eating disorders in men aged midlife and beyond. *Maturitas*, *81*(2), 248–255. https://doi.org/10.1016/j.maturitas.2015.03.004

Reid, M., Wilson, W. R., Cartwright, L., & Hammersley, R. (2020). Stuffing down feelings: Bereavement, anxiety and emotional detachment in the life stories of people with eating disorders. *Health & Social Care in the Community*, *28*(3), 979–987. https://doi.org/10.1111/hsc.12930

Reiff, D. W., & Reiff, K. L. (1999). *Eating disorders: Nutrition therapy in the recovery process*. Life Enterprises.

Richards, P. S., Caoili, C. L., Crowton, S. A., Berrett, M. E., Hardman, R. K., Jackson, R. N., & Sanders, P. W. (2018). An exploration of the role of religion and spirituality in the treatment and recovery of patients with eating disorders. *Spirituality in Clinical Practice*, *5*(2), 88–103. https://doi.org/10.1037/scp0000159

Rivera, K. J., Zhang, J. Y., Mohr, D. C., Wescott, A. B., & Pederson, A. B. (2021). A narrative review of mental illness stigma reduction interventions among African Americans in the United States. *Journal of Mental Health & Clinical Psychology*, *5*(2), 20–31. https://doi.org/10.29245/2578-2959/2021/2.1235

Rizkallah, N., & Hudson, E. (2019). Circling the triangle: An EFT approach to working with Christian couples triangulating God. *Contemporary Family Therapy: An International Journal*, *41*(3), 219–226. https://doi.org/10.1007/s10591-019-09496-8

Robinson, K., & Wade, T. D. (2021). *Perfectionism interventions targeting disordered eating: A systematic review and meta-analysis*. International Journal of Eating Disorders, *54*(4), 473–487. https://doi.org/10.1002/eat.23483

Roth, G. (1991). *When food is love*. Penguin.

Runfola, C. D., Kirby, J. S., Baucom, D. H., Fischer, M. S., Baucom, B. R. W., Matherne, C. E., Pentel, K. Z., & Bulik, C. M. (2018). A pilot open trial of UNITE-BED: A couple-based intervention for binge-eating disorder. *International Journal of Eating Disorders*, *51*(9), 1107–1112. https://doi.org/10.1002/eat.22919

Saunders, J. F., Bravo, E. I., & Kassan, A. (2023). "Anorexia doesn't exist when you're Latina": Family, culture, and gendered expectations in eating disorder recovery. *Journal of Latinx Psychology*, *11*(4), 336–350. https://doi.org/10.1037/lat0000236

Schmidt, U., & Treasure, J. (2006). Anorexia nervosa: Valued and visible A cognitive-interpersonal maintenance model and its implications for research and practice. *British Journal of Clinical Psychology*, *45*(3), 343–366. https://doi.org/10.1348/014466505X53902

Schmit, S. E., & Bell, N. J. (2017). Close relationships and disordered eating: Partner perspectives. *Journal of Health Psychology*, *22*(4), 434–445. https://doi.org/10.1177/1359105315603478

Selekman, M. D., & Beyeback, M. (2013). *Changing self-destructive habits*. Routledge.

Seligman, M. E. P., & Csikszentmihalyi, M. (2000). Positive psychology: An introduction. *American Psychologist*, *55*(1), 5–14. https://doi.org/10.1037/0003-066X.55.1.5

Sepulveda, A. R., Kyriacou, O., & Treasure, J. (2009). Development and validation of the Accommodation and Enabling Scale for Eating Disorders

(AESED) for caregivers in eating disorders. *BMC Health Services Research, 9,* 171–184. https://doi.org/10.1186/1472-6963-9-12

Shafran, R., Egan, S., & Wade, T. (2019) *Overcoming Perfectionism 2nd Edition: A self-help guide using scientifically supported cognitive behavioural techniques* (Overcoming Books). Robinson.

Siegel, J. A., & Sawyer, K. B. (2020). "We don't talk about feelings or struggles like that": White men's experiences of eating disorders in the workplace. *Psychology of Men & Masculinities, 21*(4), 533–544. https://doi.org/10.1037/men0000253

Sijercic, I., Liebman, R. E., Ip, J., Whitfield, K. M., Ennis, N., Sumantry, D., Sippel, L. M., Fredman, S. J., & Monson, C. M. (2022). A systematic review and meta-analysis of individual and couple therapies for posttraumatic stress disorder: Clinical and intimate relationship outcomes. *Journal of Anxiety Disorders, 91*, 1–12. https://doi.org/10.1016/j.janxdis.2022.102613

Sim, L. (2019). Our eating disorders blind spot: Sex and ethnic/racial disparities in help-seeking for eating disorders. *Mayo Clinic Proceedings, 94*(8), 1398–1400. https://doi.org/10.1016/j.mayocp.2019.06.006

Skellern, S. K., Sanri, C., Iqbal, S., Ayub, N., Jarukasemthawee, S., Pisitsungkagarn, K., & Halford, W. K. (2021). Assessment of the perceived importance of religion in couple relationships in Christians, Muslims, Buddhists, and the nonreligious. *Family Process, 61*(1), 326–341. https://doi.org/10.1111/famp.12669

Solomon, D. H., Knobloch, L. K., Theiss, J. A., & McLaren, R. M. (2016). Relational turbulence theory: Explaining variation in subjective experiences and communication within romantic relationships. *Human Communication Research, 42*(4), 507–532. https://doi.org/10.1111/hcre.12091

Stierman, B., Ansai, N., Mishra, S., & Hales, C. M. (2020). *Special diets among adults: United States, 2015–2018.* NCHS Data Brief, no 389. Hyattsville, MD: National Center for Health Statistics.

Tantleff-Dunn, S., & Thompson, J. K. (1995). Romantic partners and body image disturbance: Further evidence for the role of perceived-actual disparities. *Sex Roles: A Journal of Research, 33*(9–10), 589–605. https://doi.org/10.1007/BF01547719

Tedeschi, R. G., & Calhoun, L. G. (1996). The Posttraumatic Growth Inventory: Measuring the positive legacy of trauma. *Journal of Traumatic Stress, 9*(3), 455–472. https://doi.org/10.1002/jts.2490090305

Theiss, J. A., Carpenter, A. M., & Leustek, J. (2016). Partner facilitation and partner interference in individuals' weight loss goals. *Qualitative Health Research, 26*(10), 1318–1330. https://doi.org/10.1177/1049732315583980

Treasure, J., Duarte, T. A., & Schmidt, U. (2020, March 14). Eating disorders: Innovation and progress urgently needed. [Editorial]. *The Lancet.* 840. https://doi.org/10.1016/S0140-6736(20)30573-0

Treasure, J., Murphy, T., Szmukler, T., Todd, G., Gavan, K., & Joyce, J. (2001). The experience of caregiving for severe mental illness: a comparison between anorexia nervosa and psychosis. *Social psychiatry and psychiatric epidemiology*, *36*, 343-347.

Tozzi, F., Sullivan, P. F., Fear, J. L., McKenzie, J., & Bulik, C. M. (2003). Causes and recovery in anorexia nervosa: The patient's perspective. *International Journal of Eating Disorders*, *33*(2), 143–154. https://doi.org/10.1002/eat.10120

Tsong, Y., Ward, M. L., Dilley, A., Wang, S. C., & Smart, R. (2023). To seek help or not: Asian American women mental health services utilization for disordered eating and body image concerns. *Asian American Journal of Psychology*, *14*(2), 155–165. https://doi.org/10.1037/aap0000270

van Eeden, Annelies E., van Hoeken, Daphne, & Hoek, Hans W. (2021). Incidence, prevalence and mortality of anorexia nervosa and bulimia nervosa. *Current Opinion in Psychiatry*, *34*(6), 515–524. https://doi.org/10.1097/YCO.0000000000000739

Valente, M., Brenner, R., Cesuroglu, T., Bunders-Aelen, J., & Syurina, E. V. (2020). "And it snowballed from there": the development of orthorexia nervosa from the perspective of people who self-diagnose. *Appetite*, *155*, 104840.

Vendantam, S. (November 4, 2023). *Hidden Brain: Change Your Story, Change Your Life*. [Podcast]. NPR. Retrieved from https://hiddenbrain.org/podcast/healing-2-0-change-your-story-change-your-life/

Villarroel, A. M., Penelo, E., Portell, M., & Raich, R. M. (2012). Childhood sexual and physical abuse in Spanish female undergraduates: Does it affect eating disturbances? *European Eating Disorders Review*, *20*(1), e32–e41. https://doi.org/10.1002/erv.1086

Von Holle, A., Pinheiro, A. P., Thornton, L. M., Klump, K. L., Berrettini, W. H., Brandt, H., Crawford, S., Crow, S., Fichter, M. M., Halmi, K. A., Johnson, C., Kaplan, A. S., Keel, P., LaVia, M., Mitchell, J., Strober, M., Woodside, D. B., Kaye, W. H., & Bulik, C. M. (2008). Temporal patterns of recovery across eating disorder subtypes. *Australian and New Zealand Journal of Psychiatry*, *42*(2), 108–117. https://doi.org/10.1080/00048670701787610

Watson, H. J., & Bulik, C. M. (2013). Update on the treatment of anorexia nervosa: Review of clinical trials, practice guidelines and emerging interventions. *Psychological Medicine*, *43*(12), 2477–2500. https://doi.org/10.1017/S0033291712002620

Weber, D. M., Fischer, M. S., Baucom, D. H., Baucom, B. R. W., Kirby, J. S., Runfola, C. D., Matherne, C. E., & Bulik, C. M. (2019). The association between symptom accommodation and emotional coregulation in couples with binge eating disorder. *Family Process*, *58*(4), 920–935. https://doi.org/10.1111/famp.12391

Whisman, M. A., Dementyeva, A., Baucom, D. H., & Bulik, C. M. (2012). Marital functioning and binge eating disorder in married women. *International Journal of Eating Disorders*, *45*(3), 385–389. https://doi.org/10.1002/eat.20935

Willis, K. L., Miller, R. B., Anderson, S. R., Bradford, A. B., Johnson, L. N., & Yorgason, J. B. (2021). Therapist effects on dropout in couple therapy. *Journal of Marital and Family Therapy*, *47*(1), 104–119.

Winn, S., Perkins, S., Murray, J., Murphy, R., & Schmidt, U. (2004). A Qualitative Study of the Experience of Caring for a Person with Bulimia Nervosa Part 2: Carers' Needs and Experiences of Services and Other Support. *International Journal of Eating Disorders*, *36*(3), 269–279. https://doi.org/10.1002/eat.20068

Winter, R. (2005). *Perfecting ourselves to death: The pursuit of excellence and the perils of perfectionism*. InterVarsity Press. https://doi.org/10.1111/jmft.12473

Wolf, A. W., Goldfried, M. R., & Muran, J. C. (2017). Therapist negative reactions: How to transform toxic experiences. In L. G. Castonguay & C. E. Hill (Eds.), *How and why are some therapists better than others?: Understanding therapist effects* (pp. 175–192). American Psychological Association. https://doi.org/10.1037/0000034-011

Woodside, D. B., Lackstrom, J. B., & Shekter-Wolfson, L. (2000). Marriage in eating disorders: Comparisons between patients and spouses and changes over the course of treatment. *Journal of Psychosomatic Research*, *49*(3), 165–168. https://doi.org/10.1016/S0022-3999(00)00154-9

Woodside, D. B., Shekter-Wolfson, L. F., Brandes, J. S., & Lackstrom, J. B. (1993). *Eating disorders & marriage: The couple in focus*. Brunner/Mazel.

Woodward, K., McIlwain, D., & Mond, J. (2019). Feelings about the self and body in eating disturbances: The role of internalized shame, self-esteem, externalized self-perceptions, and body shame. *Self and Identity*, *18*(2), 159–182. https://doi.org/10.1080/15298868.2017.1403373

Yalom, I. (2003). *The gift of therapy: An open letter to a new generation of therapists and their patients*. Judy Piatkus Publishers.

Zak-Hunter, L., & Johnson, L. N. (2015). Exploring the association between partner behaviors and eating disorder symptomology. *Families, Systems, & Health*, *33*(4), 405–409. https://doi.org/10.1037/fsh0000147

Zamani Sani, S. H., Fathirezaie, Z., Gerber, M., Pühse, U., Bahmani, D. S., Bashiri, M., Pourali, M., & Brand, S. (2021). Self-esteem and symptoms of eating-disordered behavior among female adolescents. *Psychological Reports*, *124*(4), 1515–1538. https://doi.org/10.1177/0033294120948226

Index

emotional stability, 70, 123
emotional storms
  allowing for, 215
  encountering, in relationships, 129
  hardest to weather, 216
  psychoeducation on tolerance of, 204
  sometimes about the listener and
    sometimes not, 216
  TOES intensity scale: 10 levels of, 216
emotional storms (213–218)
  tolerance of, practicing, 216–17
emotion co-regulation, 122–26
emotion-focused therapy (EFT), 50, 51
emotionless countenance, overcontrol
    and, 122
emotion regulation, 118, 120–26, 204
  definition of, 120
  enhancers, 214
  foilers, 214
empathetic engagement: working together
    as a team, 142–52
  empathetic engagement by both
    partners, 143, 145
  nonjudgmental presence of the non-
    eating disorder partner, 143, 144–45
  receptivity of the eating disorder
    partner, 143–44
  see also recovery
empathy, 66, 78, 82, 144, 148, 176
  co-regulation and, 123
  couples therapist and, 157
ending the relationship, circumstances
    behind, 109–10
enduring vulnerabilities, 161, 231
enemas, 6, 7
ethnicity and race
  access to care, stereotypes, and, 31,
    36–37
  binge eating disorder and, 8
  prevalence of eating disorders and, 5
exclusion
  from information, 63, 68–69
  myriad of emotions related to, 68
  from treatment, 63, 66–68
exercise
  compulsive or excessive, 6, 7, 15, 34
  fights and misunderstandings about,
    201, 221
  future planning issues and, 207
  self-care for non-eating disorder
    partner and, 77
Ezra and Abe, 3, 90
  Abe's controlling tactics, 71–72
  Abe's non-eating disorder partner
    experience, 57, 58
  Abe's objective burden, 62
  Abe's subjective burden, 60
  Abe's successful repair attempt, 112

Abe's weight gain, 77
accommodation issues, 107–8
The Aftermath of a Behavior exercise
  introduced to, 228–33
age-related issues and, 32
appreciations shared in session, 220
disclosure during dating, 89
Ezra's anorexia nervosa, 34, 35
Ezra's background, 22
Ezra's discussion dodging, 99
growth in continuing relationship
  between, 251–52
individual choices with relationship
  development, 80
opening the door to therapy for, 34
potential treatment choices for, 53
relationship background, 23–24
secrecy issues, 63
skirting of sensitive topics, 221
social life affected by eating disorder,
  137–38
stories and needs of, when first
  approaching therapist, 155–56
vicarious eating, 98

facilitating behaviors, weight loss goals
  and, 130
Fairburn, C., 4, 95, 96, 147, 148, 205
Faithing Forward: A Search for Shared
  Meaning, 208–9
family, as the people from The Helicopter
  Story, 17–18
Family-Based Treatment (FBT), xvi, xviii–
  xix, 41, 44, 46
family eating disorder history, relevant, 179
family weeks, 42
fasting, 3, 5, 7
favoritism, 156, 167
FBT. see Family-Based Treatment (FBT)
fear, ignorance, and panic stage
  accommodation and, 73
  control and, 71–73
  non-eating disorder partners and, 70–73
feedback
  report, 181
  Session #5, 181
feelings, lack of validation for, 14
feminist-informed emotionally focused
  couples therapy (FI-EFCT), 51–52,
  53
fidelity, 190
FI-EFCT. see feminist-informed
  emotionally focused couples therapy
  (FI-EFCT)
fights or regrettable incidents, repair
  after, 187
financial insecurity, subjective burden
  and, 60

About the Author

Kim Lampson is a clinician in private practice, a professor of psychology, a clinical supervisor, and an author. Currently the clinical director of a training clinic for graduate students, supervising and teaching the next generations of therapists is very gratifying for her. She is passionate about training students to be highly effective clinicians.

Enamored with the Gottman Method of couples therapy, Dr. Lampson became a Certified Gottman Therapist in 2017. She recently became interested in developing Gottman-RED, a new therapy for couples in relationships with eating disorders, in which partners develop empathetic understanding and mutual support with issues regarding food, weight, exercise, or body image. This therapy is intended to minimize maintaining factors and establish a foundation for recovery. She offers training for professionals in Gottman-RED couples therapy as well as online workshops for couples desiring help with eating, food, weight, or body images issues. For more information, please email her at drkimlampson@gmail.com or visit www.relationshipswitheating disorders.com.

In her leisure time, Kim enjoys spending time with her husband and family, playing with their dog, ballet dancing, and swimming.